Persuasion

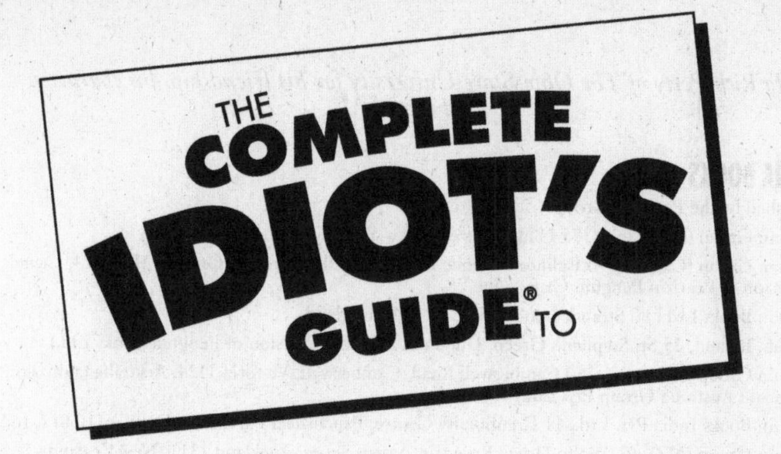

Persuasion

by *Steve Booth-Butterfield, Ed.D.*

A member of Penguin Group (USA) Inc.

To Rich Petty of The Ohio State University for his friendship, his character, and the ELM.

ALPHA BOOKS

Published by the Penguin Group

Penguin Group (USA) Inc., 375 Hudson Street, New York, New York 10014, USA

Penguin Group (Canada), 90 Eglinton Avenue East, Suite 700, Toronto, Ontario M4P 2Y3, Canada (a division of Pearson Penguin Canada Inc.)

Penguin Books Ltd., 80 Strand, London WC2R 0RL, England

Penguin Ireland, 25 St. Stephen's Green, Dublin 2, Ireland (a division of Penguin Books Ltd.)

Penguin Group (Australia), 250 Camberwell Road, Camberwell, Victoria 3124, Australia (a division of Pearson Australia Group Pty. Ltd.)

Penguin Books India Pvt. Ltd., 11 Community Centre, Panchsheel Park, New Delhi—110 017, India

Penguin Group (NZ), 67 Apollo Drive, Rosedale, North Shore, Auckland 1311, New Zealand (a division of Pearson New Zealand Ltd.)

Penguin Books (South Africa) (Pty.) Ltd., 24 Sturdee Avenue, Rosebank, Johannesburg 2196, South Africa

Penguin Books Ltd., Registered Offices: 80 Strand, London WC2R 0RL, England

International Standard Book Number: 978-159257-858-0
Library of Congress Catalog Card Number: 2008937762

11 8 7 6 5

Interpretation of the printing code: The rightmost number of the first series of numbers is the year of the book's printing; the rightmost number of the second series of numbers is the number of the book's printing. For example, a printing code of 09-1 shows that the first printing occurred in 2009.

Printed in the United States of America

Publisher: *Marie Butler-Knight*
Editorial Director: *Mike Sanders*
Senior Managing Editor: *Billy Fields*
Executive Editor: *Randy Ladenheim-Gil*
Development Editor: *Lynn Northrup*
Senior Production Editor: *Janette Lynn*
Copy Editor: *Lisanne V. Jensen*
Cover Designer: *William Thomas*
Book Designer: *Trina Wurst*
Cartoonist: *Steve Barr*
Indexer: *Brad Herriman*
Layout: *Ayanna Lacey*
Proofreader: *Mary Hunt*

Contents at a Glance

Contents

Appendixes

Introduction

If reading this book doesn't start a persuasion fire in you, then your wood's wet. You'll encounter astonishing, useful, surprising, novel, compelling, beguiling, and practical knowledge about how and why people change—simply through words and words alone. You have no idea what awaits you, but it's good.

After reading this book, you will know how to change people with your words, enhance your ability to see persuasion attempts directed at you, and grasp persuasion as a fundamental element of human nature.

All this weaves into one huge advantage: skill. Through this book, you will explore, test, and strengthen your skills as a persuasion communicator in the real world—in real time, with real people. You will acquire the knowledge, desire, and action needed to improve your persuasion skills. While learning about ideas tested from Satan to Aristotle to the Ivory Tower and through Madison Avenue, you will arrive at the state of the art in persuasion.

How This Book Is Organized

The Complete Idiot's Guide to Persuasion is divided into four parts. You can read every word in the order I wrote them if you want to be a good boy or girl, you can skip to specific chapters. I wouldn't want to influence you or anything like that, but you might find this book makes more sense if you read the Part 1 chapters in order first. I'll use common words that have an ordinary dictionary meaning but give them a unique meaning for the world of persuasion. Even the term "persuasion" has a special meaning in this book and if we don't communicate on that word, we're in trouble! Whatever approach you choose, don't worry—I won't test you over this. Of course, you'll be tested during your own life on your persuasion skill.

Part 1, "The Setup," explores the fundamental network of basic persuasion concepts and their links. You'll discover the key definition of persuasion, the advantages of persuasion, and the essential comparisons with power. You then move upriver and upgrade your knowledge of all things communication: the crucial elements, how they relate, then the Communication Cascade, intention, and its three key drivers: easy, fun, and popular. Last but certainly not least, you'll arrive at the rules of persuasion—but not laws. Even if laws of persuasion existed, no one would tell you about them! These rules will complete your setup in the fundamentals of persuasion.

Part 2, "Persuasion Plays for Beginners," propels you into a seemingly familiar world of common sense and common experience persuasion plays. These are the ones everybody knows (or at least thinks they know). You'll initiate your action sequence with respondent conditioning, operant conditioning, and modeling theory. You'll discover new insights into these old persuasion plays as you take a close and unsettling look at obedience and authority. Then, you'll find a remarkable new way to think about persuasion with Thoughtful and UnThoughtful Persuasion and the persuasion light bulb, the two routes, and arguments and cues. Last but not least, you'll dance your way through the Two Step with a foot in the door and a door in the face.

Part 3, "Advanced Persuasion Plays," blows away the mist and mystery surrounding four of the most interesting, compelling, and amazing persuasion plays you'll ever find. You think you know a lot about change, but this section will astonish you. Learn to play the "Why? Because!" game with attribution, then discover the weirdest play of all: dissonance (and how people come to love that for which they suffer. Then, we're onto the play that doesn't change but rather strengthens by attacking receivers with inoculation. Finally, you'll see the man behind the curtain with the most beguiling and troubling persuasion play: subliminals. What you don't see is what you get—or, at least, that's the claim. The science will surprise you.

Part 4, "Payoffs," completes your journey through the world of persuasion. Learn the basic tools of testing all those persuasion claims you see on TV or on bookshelves (or in this book!) with the four forces of science. Next, you'll get fitted with a cool practical concept: the Persuasion Script. Here's a sharp template for building any persuasion play you want. Persuasion Scripts will give you the structure along with easy operation to get the edge you want. Then, we present lessons learned: a quick series of high-level perspectives on persuasion that pull everything together with the persuasion toolbox, practical principles, and finally a revealing look at how persuasion proves our human nature.

Extras

Throughout this book, you'll find four types of boxes filled with definitions, gems, tricks, spells, cautions, rarities, quotes, and other subtleties of persuasion.

The Sizzle

These boxes offer tips, insight, perspective, and contemplation.

def•i•ni•tion

Check these boxes for definitions of key words and terms.

Wise Lines

Here, you'll find quotes from great minds that offer illumination on all things persuasion.

Unintended Consequences

Check these boxes for cautions that may save you from yourself, or at the least, prevent misunderstandings.

Acknowledgements

I wish everyone who publishes a book had the great fortune of working with people such as Jacky Sach, my literary agent; Randy Ladenheim-Gil, executive editor at Alpha Books; Lynn Northrup, development editor; Janette Lynn, senior production editor; and Lisanne V. Jensen, copy editor. Each made me a better writer and made this a better book.

The content of this book flows from my lifelong interest in using words to change the way people think, feel, and act. My understanding of persuasion, however, truly began when I read the ideas of people such as Rich Petty, Shelly Chaiken, and the late Carl Hovland. Many others influenced my thinking, and you can find that long list in Appendix A. On a practical basis, much of my understanding of how to persuade came as a result of the actions of Fred Butcher, then at the Mary Babb Randolph Cancer Center; and Al Munson of the National Institute for Occupational Safety and Health. Both men gave me opportunities to apply my ideas in large, complex, and practical situations. Each also provided friendship, collegiality, and mentoring.

Finally, Melanie Booth-Butterfield has loved me for more than 30 years. It's impossible to imagine this book or my life without her.

Trademarks

All terms mentioned in this book that are known to be or are suspected of being trademarks or service marks have been appropriately capitalized. Alpha Books and Penguin Group (USA) Inc. cannot attest to the accuracy of this information. Use of a term in this book should not be regarded as affecting the validity of any trademark or service mark.

Part 1

The Setup

Every game is the same, and persuasion is no different: you can't play unless you have the right equipment and know the rules. In these chapters, you gear up with all those tools you need to succeed. You learn about the rules of persuasion—but not laws of persuasion, because if there were laws, why would anyone tell you about them? Master these fundamental skills, and you're ready to play. Get your head in the game and start thinking like a persuasion pro.

Chapter 1

Persuasion Basics

In This Chapter

- What is persuasion?
- Changing the way others think, feel, and behave
- Nudging toward change
- The value of internal change
- The difference between power and persuasion
- The limitations of reward and punishment

Welcome to the world of persuasion, where you will find familiar words used in unfamiliar ways. In this book, you'll often find that words everyone uses in common conversation will have unique meaning. Words such as "persuasion," "attitude," and "thoughts, feelings, and behaviors" are part of the ordinary parlance, but here we use them with one particular meaning. In your life, you can continue to use these words the way you always did—but in this book, you use them a little more carefully. And you'll see the payoff very quickly.

Unscrupulous marketers and shady political consultants give persuasion a bad reputation. But you shouldn't allow the bad ethics of some people to blind you to the utility and value of persuasion. In the right hands, persuasion can help people to be safer, healthier, happier, more skillful, better educated, more committed, more involved, and more curious. Furthermore, knowledge of persuasion can help you defend yourself against unscrupulous influence agents. You just have to open your mind and consider the possibilities.

Using Words to Change People

Persuasion is a powerful and amazing type of human communication. Simply through ordinary talk, when you cause other people to alter a belief, change an emotion, or act differently, you have persuaded them. Persuasion involves you, other people, words, and change.

What does this definition of persuasion imply? First, because persuasion uses words, it means that persuasion is a part of communication. Whenever people communicate, they can persuade. And because people communicate to accomplish almost every meaningful goal a human can have, persuasion applies to almost all social situations: sales, politics, leadership and management, marketing, training and education, family and friends, neighborhood associations, religious organizations, relationships, and so on. Persuasion is a fundamental and natural part of human contact and human society.

def•i•ni•tion

Persuasion is the skill of using words to change the way others think, feel, and behave.

Second, persuasion is a skill. While any healthy human can communicate, whether we can communicate *effectively* depends on our experience, training, and insight. The fact that you are reading this book is evidence of your belief that persuasion is a skill. No one reads a book about "breathing in everyday life" or "walking at the grocery store." You seek information in order to enhance your current skills. Persuasion is a skill, just like cooking, quilting, bowling, or typing. It's a behavioral act under thoughtful control aimed at achieving a goal. You can enhance your persuasion skills through reading this book.

Third, implicit here is the idea of intention. We do not accidentally or unconsciously change people with persuasion. Persuasion is a deliberate act where we decide that we desire a specific change with targeted people in the real world. In this book, there is no such thing as unintentional persuasion. Suppose you say something and people change; if you didn't intend the change, it is not persuasion. It's coincidence. Coincidence is not (and never will be) persuasion.

Finally, persuasion is about change. Merely as a result of persuasive communication, people will think, feel, and act differently. "Differently" means that there is a before-and-after picture, such as those you see in weight loss ads. Thus, a change from before to after that is caused by words is persuasion.

Just let that percolate a moment. Persuasion is …

- Words for change
- Intentional and deliberate
- A skill you improve

Categories of Thoughts, Feelings, and Behaviors

I've mentioned that persuasion requires a change in others that involves thoughts, feelings, or behaviors. Let's look at several examples of each category.

Thoughts can be:

- Beliefs
- Facts
- Attitudes
- Values
- Attributions

Feelings can be discrete emotions, such as:

- Sadness
- Anger

- Disgust
- Fear
- Shame
- Happiness

Or feelings can also be enduring moods, such as:

- Disgruntlement
- Optimism

Behaviors include small actions such as:

- Smiling
- Nodding
- Frowning
- Grimacing

Behaviors also can be larger, such as:

- Voting
- Buying
- Volunteering
- Participating

Through persuasion, it's possible to change any of these specific types of thoughts, feelings, and behaviors. In a classic debate or argument, you use persuasion to change the other person's beliefs and facts. But realize that you can change other "thoughts," too, such as values and attitudes, which express evaluation, worth, and esteem. Thus, you don't have to change the "facts" but rather change how people prize things, making them prefer one thing while dismissing another as worthless.

How does that work? Let's say it's a fact that you made $50,000 last year. If I can persuade you to value your time with family and friends even if you make less money, you may feel content about making

$50,000. By contrast, if I persuade you that your family and friends are suffering material hardship and need, you may feel discontent about making $50,000. The same fact of earning $50,000 exists in both examples, but by persuading a different cognitive element—values—I can influence you.

Persuasion also changes emotions and moods. More often, as you'll discover later on in this book, you want to understand the other person's current emotion or mood to help you pick the most effective *persuasion play*. However, sometimes you want to produce specific emotions or moods in people. For example, you might want to persuade people to be angry about a misdeed or injustice and use that emotion to fire up a group that is bored or disinterested.

def•i•ni•tion

A **persuasion play** is a specific, planned act of persuasive communication you design and implement to achieve a goal. It is based upon well-established persuasion art and science.

But most of the time we want persuasion to create behavior change—and the faster the better. However, sometimes the fastest way toward behavior change is an indirect path that starts with changes in thinking or feeling that in turn produce the desired behavior change. For example, if I want you to buy my product instead of my competitor's, I could tell you that while my product costs 20 percent more than a competitor's, it lasts twice as long and requires half the maintenance costs—which means that the useful life of my product costs 40 percent less than my competitor's product.

There are many advantages when you break persuasion down into these categories of thoughts, feelings, and behaviors. All three categories are connected inside us. Our thoughts can change our feelings; for example, if you're feeling slightly down, start thinking "good" thoughts about your past successes and your feelings will change. Our feelings can change our thoughts. For example, you're sitting there calmly in front of your TV when you see a story that outrages and angers you—and soon all those calm and rational thoughts are gone. Our behaviors can change our feelings. If you're feeling down, exercise a bit—even just stretch or walk briskly—and your feelings will improve. Because these three categories are connected, when you change one you can change another, too.

In addition, these three categories broaden your perspective about persuasion. Instead of restricting yourself to the way you usually think about persuasion—debating—you now see persuasion as a more flexible and widely applicable skill. You can use words to change emotions, values, smiles, and nods. You've got a lot more room to maneuver.

The Art of the Nudge

Close your eyes and think about what comes to mind when you hear the word "persuasion." Most folks see an image of two people arguing about something. But for most of us, persuasion is something closer to a debate, such as Lincoln and Douglas and the Civil War or Mom and Dad and whether Tiffany is grounded.

Certainly, each is an accurate example of persuasion. People are using words to try to change each other's views. But I invite you to see a great potential for persuasion and its uses. Remember that persuasion can apply in any communication situation. We communicate in a much wider variety of situations than just arguments. And you can use words in much less-obvious, purple-faced ways that arguing. Words are more than debates or cost-benefit ratios or well-known facts. There are many words (simple and easy) you can use to produce the change you want—and they require no debates or pitched battles!

Actually, the most effective persuasion is what we call the art of the nudge. Rarely does anyone ever collapse all at once in the face of a compelling argument. We know from our own experience that head-on collisions rarely produce any change except for a redoubling of the combatant's original belief that the other guy is completely wrong. In the real world in real time, most change is small, adds up over time, and eventually leads to your desired goal. And often the first change you get is in the way the other guy thinks or feels. It is only later that the behavior change occurs.

Instead of viewing persuasion as just the heavy artillery of communication where you bring out the big guns, you can adjust your perception. Persuasion can be strategic, subtle, and patient. Sure, there are some times where you can go charging in with a direct confrontation; yes, that is persuasion. But don't limit yourself to just that. Open yourself up to a wide set of possibilities, options, and alternatives. The only limit of your persuasion skill is your imagination.

You can achieve not only all the goals you used to achieve with a limited definition of persuasion, but if you open up your definition and see the wider implications, you can achieve those old goals in new ways and also attempt new goals.

Implicit in the definition of persuasion is the sense of having a goal. You don't want to change other people based on a whim or a passing fancy. When you want to go to the trouble of changing other people, you've got a reason, a purpose, and a goal. Consider a laundry list of possible goals. You may want the "other guy" to:

- Buy something
- Study
- Pray
- Drive faster
- Drive slower
- Be more romantic
- Call your father

And that's just the first page of the list that my wife, Melanie, had for me today! Seriously, the most important step in practical persuasion is the goal you pick. The goal of persuasion determines everything else you will do.

What If Words Can Change People?

The benefits to persuasion are obvious. If you're good at it, you accomplish the goals you set for yourself: more sales; more votes; more volunteers; or more shiny, happy, smiling faces. Whatever the goal, if you're good at persuasion, you'll get to the goal faster, better, and more cheaply.

Realize, however, you get more than just hitting or even surpassing that goal. With persuasion, you can save yourself a lot of constant, extra work.

People Internalize Change

Persuasion produces a change in other people that becomes internalized by them. After persuasion, people embrace the change and accept it as a part of themselves. They become the kind of people who now do whatever it is you persuaded them to do. That means, whenever they have the opportunity to perform the desired behavior, you don't have to be there persuading them or even merely watching them. They will produce the new thought, feeling, or behavior all by themselves.

Sure, there will be failures, errors, and misunderstandings. They will not do it exactly the way you want every time, but if you have indeed changed them, they will produce the outcome you want more often. And, you don't have to constantly hang around or double check on them.

You Don't Have to Punish or Reward

Typically, if you want to change people and you're lousy at persuasion, you use rewards and punishments. There's nothing wrong with this approach, and we look carefully at it in Chapter 4. Yet, with rewards and punishments, you have to deliver the rewards and punishments properly and regularly to keep the change going. That's work. Worse still, rewards and punishments have a disappointing way of losing their impact over time. Remember when you could get your kid to do something if you gave him or her a smiley face sticker? Now that your child is a teenager, how's the smiley face reward working? And what happens when somebody else comes along and offers better rewards or worse punishments than you can?

Persuasion produces internal changes that get carried around with the person wherever he or she goes. And the person doesn't walk around with either his or her hands out for the rewards or a wary eye and a flinching back waiting for the punishment. The person does it on his or her own because the change you created has been internalized.

They Do It for You

For several years, I worked as an administrator for the federal government. I ran a communication research unit for the Centers for Disease Control and Prevention (CDC) that focused on worker safety and health. One of the biggest persuasion challenges I faced was trying to get information to everyone who needed it. For example, as part of a Congressionally mandated project on firefighter safety, my agency cooperated with all the stakeholders—everyone who had an interest such as firefighters, fire chiefs, city and state government officials, equipment manufacturers, and insurance companies, for instance—in this problem. Through that cooperation, we developed a series of approved policies and recommendations that would protect firefighters and other first responders from their leading cause of death at the scene: building collapse. Part of my job was to develop a communication plan that both informed and motivated firefighters, fire chiefs, and government agencies to at least consider these cooperative guidelines and at most implement them effectively in their unique circumstances.

At the time of this project, there were more than 36,000 firefighter units in the United States composed of literally hundreds of thousands of paid and volunteer personnel. And they all operated under slightly different laws and regulations. Finally, I had less than $30,000 to develop this communication campaign.

When you face a practical communication problem such as this one, you begin to appreciate the value of persuasion. Through a cascading plan of reaching smaller groups who reached bigger groups who reached larger groups, we were able to get this information to all units and to the overwhelming majority of the people most involved in this problem. It was not simply word of mouth. It was *persuasive* word of mouth. Once you persuade someone, he or she does it for you—not only by performing the desired change but also by doing it for you by persuading others.

Power and Persuasion

When many people think about "persuasion," they also think about *power*. In fact, some folks would use the words interchangeably because

def•i•ni•tion

Power is the ability to deliver punishments and rewards to another person to change his or her behavior.

they both are about changing other people. As I noted at the start of this chapter, we need to use everyday words more precisely—and the persuasion and power concept is a good illustration.

Power is obvious: do it or else. I can make you do something because I have this tasty carrot or this terrible stick.

But just because I have a stick and I say to you, "If you don't do what I want you to do, I'm going to hit you with this stick," does this mean I used persuasion to change you? No. I used power. Sure, I used words in the threat. But if I didn't have a stick and threatened you with mere words and an empty hand, would you change? No.

Power needs only rewards and punishments. It does not require words. People are pretty quick to figure things out with just getting carrots or sticks. Words can speed up the process, but if you get a pay raise in your paycheck when you have a good sales month and you get a pay cut in your paycheck when you have a bad sales month, you don't need a PowerPoint presentation from the boss.

Power is obviously … powerful. It makes things happen. Power is not an inherently bad thing for humans. And sometimes a situation comes down to raw power. People are no longer interested in persuasion and communication. They get locked in a struggle for identity, control, prestige, or tradition. War is the most obvious example, but you still find raw power struggles in business, politics, and even family. Sometimes our differences are greater than our capacity for love, reason, and cooperation. And power is how we resolve many of those differences—even when it produces loss, harm, and destruction. Until we change human nature so that people always shrink from power and the reward or punishment tools, power will always be an important element of the human experience.

While we keep the distinctions between persuasion and power in our minds, an interesting concept emerges—the artful combination of persuasion and power in your life. While they are different tools that have the same goal (change), these tools are mutually supporting and strengthening. In fact, as you read this book, look for ways that you can reduce the need for power through the skillful use of persuasion. That's not to say that you'll never need to use power; rather, persuasion can make your power even stronger.

The Least You Need to Know

- Persuasion is the skill of using words to change the way others think, feel, and behave.
- Persuasion produces internal change in the other person that he or she can use in other situations.
- Persuasion can be applied in any human interaction that involves communication.
- Power is the ability to deliver rewards and punishments to produce behavior change.

Chapter 2

The Communication of Persuasion

In This Chapter

- How process, meaning, and messages work together
- Establishing a communication model
- Producing persuasion through a cascade of stages
- Get TACTful
- Why persuasion sometimes fails

Persuasion happens through your ability to communicate well. You can be an outstanding student of human behavior and a clever observer of human nature, but if you don't know how to communicate effectively, you will do poorly at persuasion. Communication is everything to persuasion!

Messages and Meanings in Process

Communication is the process of creating meaning through verbal and nonverbal messages. Note the three key elements in this definition: process, meaning, and messages.

Process could also be called procedure, development, course of action, method, route, or practice. It's an action verb. Somebody does something. Thus, communication is an activity—something you *do*. And because it's a verb, it exists in time and is something with a past, present, and future. Process is also something than cannot be undone or rewound. Once you do the process, if it isn't what you want, you cannot erase it—but you can try again.

> **Unintended Consequences**
>
> Communication is a lot like sex. Experience makes you think you're pretty good at it—even when you're not!

Meaning could also be referred to as sense, connotation, denotation, import, gist, significance, or experience. It's that internal experience of reactions in your mind, heart, and gut as you respond to the world around you. Meaning is a subjective experience—your private response to the world and how something seems to *you*. Communication starts with meaning, and we want to express or share those meanings with others. But because we're not yet capable of performing the Vulcan mind meld like Mr. Spock on *Star Trek*, we need to find another method. That involves messages.

Messages are codes, letters, notes, and symbols that allow us to express or convey the meanings within us. Messages require rules of syntax, semantics, and pragmatics. Messages can be verbal (such as languages) or nonverbal (such as gestures). A code can be rather simple, such as Morse Code with a set of dots and dashes that can be blinked on a flashlight or tapped on a wall. A code can also be more complicated, such as our DNA, which "communicates" how to build our bodies. The important part here is that messages are conventions, agreements, or practices that we share with each other so that we can communicate our meanings.

For persuasion, we use messages to change the "meaning" in the other person so that the other person changes the way he or she thinks, feels, or acts.

A Model for Communication

The definition of communication requires you, another person, meanings, and messages. These are the fundamental elements, but we need a model that takes our basic definition and theory and turns it into a practical model so that we can actually communicate. To be just a little clever about it, we need to figure out the parts of speech and put them in a working model.

The entire process starts with a source that has meaning. The source encodes that meaning into a message that is then transmitted through a channel to the receiver, who decodes the message into a meaning. The receiver provides feedback during all of this, indicating some kind of responsiveness—"I'm getting it" or "I'm not getting it"—to the source. Throughout this action, noise—either physical noise such as loud music or psychological noise such as boredom—can interfere with the communication process. Finally, this process occurs to achieve goals: people communicate to inform, relate, entertain, and—most interestingly for us—to achieve the goal of change.

Let's put these words into a graphic that shows everything all at once.

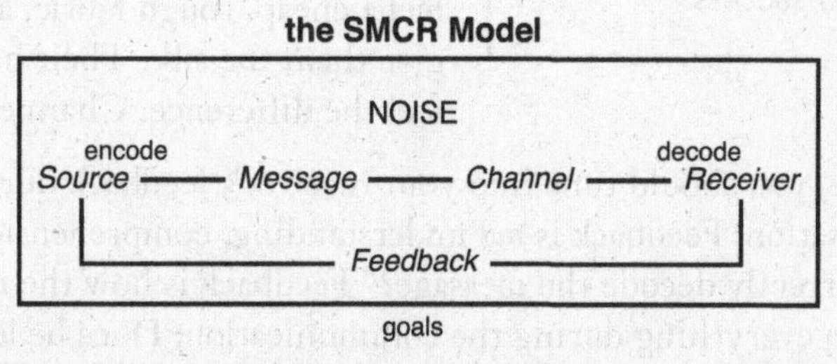

A simple model of communication. SMCR stands for Source Message Channel Receiver, the primary components of the model.

While we know that in the real world, during a conversation, both parties play the source and receiver role, for our examples we'll usually assume that you are the source and the other person is the receiver. As the source, you start the process (you are the initiator) and the receiver is the target (the recipient of the process).

Both of you engage in coding meaning and messages, but coding works in different directions. As a source, the direction moves from meaning to message as you encode—while as receiver, the direction moves from message to meaning as you decode. If you've never thought about the coding part of communication, you need to open your mind to this idea. It reveals a hidden part of communication.

Once we've created a message, it is sent through channels. In human communication, channels correspond to the five senses of sight, sound, taste, smell, and feel. Most communication—and most persuasive communication—relies on sight and sound, but you need to consider how you can use taste, smell, and feel as additional channels. How about cooking a favorite dessert for your persuasion target before you make a request? If you need to scrounge up quick cash, go stand on the street by a bakery and ask for a buck. You'll get it faster than if you're standing beside a trash barrel. Trying to sell a more expensive piece of clothing? First, let your customers feel a cheap, rough fabric, and then give them the silk. Their hands will feel the difference. Channels matter.

The Sizzle

The receiver and decoding are the two crucial elements of communication in persuasion. Understand them both for persuasion success.

As a source, you should tune into your receiver's feedback during the conversation. Feedback is *not* understanding, comprehension, or "Did he correctly decode the message?" Feedback is how the receiver responds to everything during the communication. Does he lean in with interest, or does he pull back with dismay? Is she really smiling because she likes the dinner or is she just being polite on a first date? Is a student really listening intently during a lecture or is he wearing a "fake interested student face" to avoid getting called upon? Is your customer nodding in agreement or just nodding off? You need to observe how your receiver reacts during communication and understand all those feedback indicators.

Despite everyone's best efforts, communication can fail. Noise, as I've mentioned, refers to those factors that interfere with communication. Noise can be a physical barrier, such as a noisy room when you're at a cocktail party and everyone is buzzing. Ever try to make a sale when a construction crew is breaking up concrete outside your store? Noise can also be psychological. Your receiver is hungry, sleepy, bored, or distracted. The mind wanders, and communication fails. As a persuasion agent, you need to understand when you fail because of a bad persuasion effort or because of something simple such as noise. Maybe your receiver really didn't hear your persuasion play, and that's why it failed. Of course, noise can become a convenient excuse, too.

Finally, communication occurs in the service of goals. Communication is a tool used to accomplish practical outcomes. You inform, educate, train, and explain; you entertain, tease, play and joke; you relate, connect, share, and bond; and you persuade, influence, and change. Your communication goal is perhaps the most important element in determining what is effective and what is ineffective.

The Communication Cascade of Persuasion

Now, let's take all we've learned about basic communication and tie it into persuasion. How do we take these fundamental elements such as message, source, and goal and make it work for our persuasion efforts?

Think about a series of waterfalls where water pours over one ridge, drops down in a beautiful waterfall until it hits another plateau, which runs to another ridge, and drops down in another beautiful waterfall until it hits another plateau. I want you to hold this cascading image in your head.

Persuasive communication must pour in a cascade of stages. A message does not have a simple monolithic effect as if all you have to do is say the magic word once—and voilà, you've got immediate, forever, deep, and wide change. Persuasive communication is more complex. You can find books that seem to offer magic words (for example, just say *this* or just say it *this way*, and boom—it happens). Persuasive communication moves instead like that cascading waterfall. You have to take your receivers through a series of communication steps before you get the big boom you seek. Let's call this the *Communication Cascade*. It refers to a series of stages (reception, processing, and response, which I'll discuss in a moment) that communication must achieve in order for any behavior change to occur.

Tipping Points and Dominos

If you read books about change, you'll find metaphors similar to the Cascade. Maybe you've heard of "tipping points" and "blinks" (referring to Malcolm Gladwell's bestselling book *Blink*), or perhaps that infamous "domino theory." Each metaphor explains the process of change the writer is trying to develop. Tipping point suggests a series of minor changes, such as a cargo of weight shifting on a trailer. Early in the process, these minor shifts are no problem—but when the "tipping point" is reached, weight shifts enough to create a major change and the trailer flips over. Blink demonstrates how we can instantly change our knowledge, understanding, or perception of a person or event—moving immediately from one state to another. The metaphor of tumbling dominos suggests a fairly even series of uniform, inevitable, and unavoidable changes as dominos in a line fall one at a time into the next one in line until the last one falls.

The Cascade is another metaphor of change. Like tipping points, blinks, or dominos, the Cascade has a series of steps. It has a sequence, where one thing must happen before another can occur; and it has an end state, where the last change is the one most desired. Please realize that the Cascade is not a criticism of blinks or dominos, nor is the Cascade an ultimate truth. It's a simple, obvious, and useful image for understanding how persuasive communication operates.

The Communication Cascade.

the Cascade

reception
processing
response
behavior

Communication produces behavior change by taking receivers through three cascading stages. First, the receivers must get the message (reception). Second, the receivers must think about the message (process). Third, the receivers must change beliefs and intentions (response). When a message successfully takes receivers through all three stages of the Cascade, behavior change will occur.

You have to take receivers through all three steps if you want any chance of achieving behavior change. If you fail at any stage, then the entire march stops and the tuba players trip over the flute players in a fine heap. The persuasion fails, you fail, the world is not made better from your efforts, you don't reach your monthly sales target, and your boss tries to throw you out the window. Now, let's take a closer look at each stage of the Cascade.

Reception: Did They Get It?

The first stage is the most obvious one. If the person doesn't get it, he or she can't change because he or she didn't hear you. Reception occurs at that point where you realize, "Hey! There's a new picture up on the billboard!" Reception is not about understanding, comprehending, or considering; it's just that first dawn of awareness that there's something new out there and gaining a sense of what it's about. When you look through a stack of mail, you observe some details: who it's from, what's that picture, it's another credit card offer, and so on. You're in reception. Think of a radio tuning dial. You turn the dial until you hit a signal. It may be scratchy at first, but when you fine-tune it, reception comes through strong and clear. Reception equals getting the message.

Now, as obvious as reception is for successful persuasive communication, it's less obvious how to achieve it. Some folks think all you have to do is start talking and the person will begin receiving. Then, these kind, gentle folks have children and realize that they might be talking, but the children aren't close to receiving. How do you improve the odds of gaining reception? Here are three great tools to help you: placement, frequency, and contrast.

Placement means putting the message where your receivers go. TV advertisers air beer ads during sports shows and air cosmetics ads during *Oprah*. That's physical placement. Psychological placement is putting the message out when your receiver is ready for it. Kids demonstrate this when they learn to ask Dad for money when he's in front of the TV.

Frequency means that a message is more likely to be received if it's made available many different times. You could also call this repetition. It also helps if you vary the style of the message so that it looks different even if it's saying the same thing. Let's say as you commute to work you hear an ad on the radio for Nike sneakers while you look out the window and see a Nike billboard with the sneakers. Later that day when you come home, there's a promotional letter in your mailbox from Nike about sneakers. And then after a beer ad on TV, there's a Nike sneaker ad—which you may miss because your kid is trying to get money from you. Nike and other smart persuaders know that a one-shot delivery of a message never reaches everyone.

The Sizzle

Your life is a nonstop message machine. Your message is competing against thousands of words and images we're exposed to every day. In such a busy message environment, you cannot expect one statement from you to be the one message everyone gets, remembers, considers, and acts upon. Thus, frequency with variation is necessary to generate reception.

Finally, *contrast* means that message is more likely to be received if it sticks out in the environment. One of the earliest scientific studies of contrast comes from the field of Gestalt psychology. You've probably seen some famous visual examples, such as these. Notice the simplicity of this example. Black dots on a white field, yet merely through shifting one line of dots to the left makes them stand out and grab your attention. It is through that visual offset we can make one line of identical dots seem unique, special, and interesting compared to the others. Advertisers are always looking for contrast to make their message stick out in the noisy and crowded information marketplace.

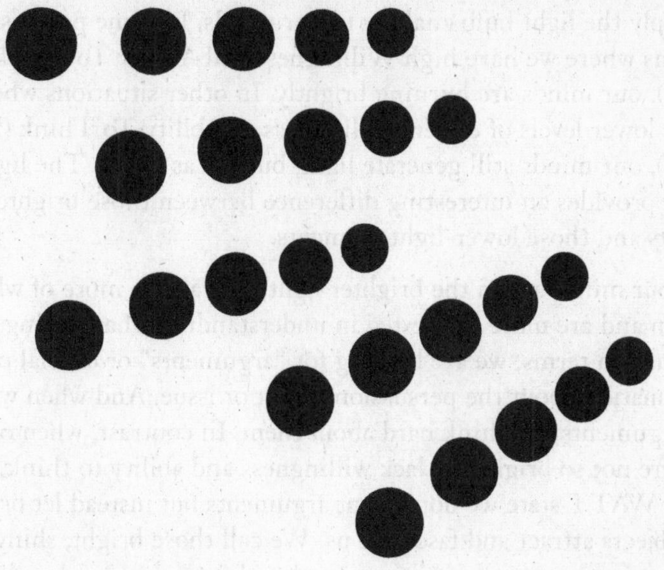

Gestalt contrast example.

People respond to contrast in a way that grabs them and makes them receive the message. You must make a message stand out in the message environment, as this nice black-and-white illustration demonstrates.

Processing: Did You Think About It?

After a person receives the message, what does he or she do with it? Do people toss that glossy print advertisement for a new car into the garbage bin? Do they change the channel? Or do they engage in the cognitive work needed to understand and consider the meaning of the message? Processing is all the effort needed to interpret a received message. Processing may be shallow, where we think only as hard as we have to, or it may be deep, where we consider with effort all the implications and ramifications a message holds. One image is most important to understanding processing: the light bulb.

Imagine that your mind is a light bulb on a dimmer switch. When you are highly thoughtful, the bulb burns brightly. When you are completely thoughtless (drugged, injured, or asleep), the bulb doesn't burn. Because we're on a dimmer switch, the bulb brightness can range between these two extremes.

Let's apply the light bulb analogy to our minds. In some persuasive situations where we have high Willingness and Ability To Think (high WATT), our minds are burning brightly. In other situations where we have lower levels of either Willingness or Ability To Think (low WATT), our minds still generate light, but not as much. The light bulb analogy provides an interesting difference between those brighter-light moments and those lower-light moments.

When our minds are in the brighter light, we can see more of what's going on and are more interested in understanding what's going on. In persuasion terms, we are looking for "arguments" or crucial pieces of information about the persuasion object or issue. And when we find these arguments, we think hard about them. In contrast, when our minds are not so bright, we lack willingness and ability to think, and in our low WATT state we don't want arguments but instead let bright, shiny objects attract and fascinate us. We call those bright, shiny things *cues.* A persuasion cue is easy to see and understand in our low-lit minds, and a cue requires little WATTage to process. (You'll read more about cues such as Authority, Liking, and Comparison in Chapter 7.) Thus, in persuasion terms, we can persuade people under both bright, high-WATT conditions and dim, low-WATT conditions—but they are very different things. However, the key insight here is that the high-WATT bulb is a lot more interesting and useful for persuasion.

The persuasion light bulb is a key concept that applies in all persuasion efforts. You have to understand that light bulb in your receiver(s) and learn to move the dimmer switch to obtain the processing needed.

Response: Did It Change Them Internally?

Okay—we got reception and processing. We are two thirds of the way through the Cascade. Now, we have to get our receivers out of the eternal cycle of thought and translate all that mental work into action. What appeals do you make to activate action in your receivers? Here are two:

It's easy, fun, and popular! When your message demonstrates to receivers that their lives will be easier, they will have more fun, or they will become more popular, then it's more likely that you will get the desired response from the receiver. In persuasion geek speak, "easy" is called "self-efficacy"; "fun" is called "attitude"; and popular is called "norms." But, like a rose, regardless of the name it's still the same thing. Messages that create beliefs concerning "easy, fun, and popular" are much more likely to produce that internal response change that will drive the final step of behavior change.

Of course, the message is rarely as simple as, "Gee, honey … why don't you go clean the basement? It's *fun!*" Or, "Gee, my dear, why don't you do your math homework? It's *easy!*" Such approaches seem like the most direct route through the Cascade, but we're adults here. You know that "easy, fun, and popular" requires a little more work than just blurting out those words. But these words should guide your planning. If you want your spouse to clean the basement, what could you say that would make him or her believe, "Yes, it would be easy, fun, or popular?"

Make it intentional. An intention is a belief concerning the likelihood of a future action. A positive intention is a belief that I *will* do it. A negative intention is a belief that I *will not* do it. Messages that create strong intentions are more likely to generate resulting behavior.

One way to generate the desired intention is to use those "easy, fun, and popular" messages. When we think something is more "fun," we also have a stronger intention to act. Thus, intention tends to follow those simple but fundamental elements of easy, fun, and popular.

A second way to use intention is to focus solely upon it in the message. In many persuasion situations, our receivers already may have a pretty favorable sense of "easy, fun, and popular." What we want to do is merely make the intention stronger or more active.

Become More TACTful

Behavior is something you can observe another person doing. It may be small, such as a smile, or it may be large, such as running a mile every day—but behavior is a concrete, observable performance that anyone can see. I want to take this common-sense definition of behavior and give you another way to understand it. You need to get TACTful.

Behavior should be defined as Target, Action, Context, and Time (TACT), or "who does what, when and where." A TACTful behavior is a more suitable candidate for persuasion than just a one- or two-word descriptor such as "clean up," "be nice," or "do homework." If this sounds confusing, hang on. It will become clear shortly.

Target (who), Action (what), Context (where), and Time (when) provide the necessary screws to tighten down the definition of behavior. Let's look at an example: exercise!

To say that we seek the behavior change of "exercise" sounds concrete enough, but from a TACTful perspective, we should realize that "exercise" doesn't say who is doing the exercise, how often, to what degree or intensity, or where and when. Is there "enough" exercise? Is there a "right kind" of exercise? Do we want all people to exercise or just a particular group? And, really, what is exercise, anyway? The goal of "more exercise" is really quite fuzzy and needs a more TACTful view. How about …

- We want all adults over the age of 50 to walk for 20 minutes a day, most days of the week.
- We want everyone who walks during the week to add 20 minutes of vigorous exercise (running or weight lifting, for example) once a week.
- We want all sedentary adults who drive to the donut shop to walk to the donut shop every time!

Each of these TACTs are explicit on who does what when and where. All people over 50. Everyone who is already walking. Any adult who is sedentary. Walking for 20 minutes. Vigorously running or lifting. Walking instead of driving to the donut shop. Most days of the week or once a week or every trip for donuts.

Do you see the difference between the persuasion goal of "more exercise" and each of the TACT examples? Note the specificity of the Target (who), Action, (what), Context (where), and Time (when). When you get TACTful you focus all of your persuasion effort more efficiently. Every persuasion tactic in this book works more effectively when you start with a TACTful behavior. If, instead, you begin with a well-intentioned but vague statement like "I want my children to be nicer" or "I want my employees to have better morale" or "I want my customers to buy more stuff," you put yourself behind the persuasion eight ball and handicap your efforts even before you start talking.

If you take a moment, you begin to realize how important the behavior step is. This definition determines virtually every next step you take with the Cascade and your persuasion plays. It tells you the kind of people you will target, the resources you will need to reach them, the kind of research you need to do to understand them, and how you can measure the progress and outcome of your efforts.

Once you have a TACTful behavior, you can work the Cascade stages of reception, processing, and response backward! That's right. Backward. Let's go back to our exercise behavior example. I worked on a persuasive campaign to encourage adults over the age of 50 to walk 20 minutes a day, most days of the week (the TACT). Here's how we used the TACT with the Cascade.

We analyzed arguments and evidence that said walking 20 minutes a day was "easy, fun, and popular." After a lot of research we found that most older adults don't like to exercise because it's "hard" in the sense that it's hard to find time in a busy schedule and stay on that schedule. People already knew that walking was good for them ("fun") and everyone approved of it ("popular"), but that time factor ("hard") made regular exercise difficult to start or maintain. This filled in the Response part of the Cascade. We knew that if we wanted to persuade our target audience to walk, we had to overcome the schedule and time barrier.

With this research, we then developed messages for the Processing stage that made powerful arguments for "walking is easy." We created several print, radio, and TV ads that showed older adults making time in their schedules and finding ways to make walking easier. We tested these ads to make sure they really did provide strong arguments for high-WATT thinkers and convinced them that, "Hey, you know what? Walking 20 minutes a day most days of the week is easy!"

We then bought an enormous amount of advertising time in our experimental communities and ran hundreds of ads on TV, radio, and print. We created fun events to encourage walking that attracted free media attention from local news sources. We did fairs, school projects, and church meetings. And we ran this persuasion campaign for several weeks. In other words, we developed a huge Reception plan to make sure everyone got our messages.

Here's the Cascade:

1. Reception (long campaign saturates community with messages)
2. Processing (messages provide strong arguments that walking is easy to schedule and maintain)
3. Response (high-WATT processors changed their beliefs about the difficult of walking)
4. Behavior (more adults over 50 walked 20 minutes a day most days compared to control communities)

Do you see how the Communication Cascade produces change?

A good behavior definition explicitly identifies the person (Target-who), the activity you want to change (Action-what), and the situation where all this occurs (Context-where and Time-when).

If You Don't Flow All the Way, You Fail

One of the nice features of the Cascade is that it provides a simple but realistic model of how persuasive communication operates. And it highlights how persuasion can fail due to communication failures. If we don't flow our persuasion receivers through all stages of the Cascade, then persuasion fails.

The Cascade and the communication model combined clue you into why persuasion is so difficult most of the time. Many people think that persuasion is simply a matter of coming up with the best arguments, but with this chapter you realize that it's more complicated. Even if you have the best arguments, you can still fail if you don't communicate effectively (noise interferes as well as improper decoding by the receiver) or if you don't Cascade (they "get" it, but they don't "process" it). There are many moving parts in a persuasion engine, and you have to be firing on all cylinders to get where you want to go.

The Least You Need to Know

- Communication is the process of stimulating meaning with messages.
- To achieve persuasion success, Cascade receivers go through three stages.
- Reception, processing, and response lead to behavior change.
- Failure at any stage in the Cascade dooms persuasion efforts.
- TACTful behavior definitions sharpen your persuasion focus.

Chapter 3

The 10 Rules of Effective Persuasion

In This Chapter

- Following the rules to develop strategy and execute tactics
- Introducing the 10 rules of persuasion
- Enhancing persuasion skills
- Developing a guiding philosophy of persuasion

Most of this book is concerned with specific persuasion plays people can use in the real world, in real time. It shows you the how-to's of doing different types of persuasion, such as a the Two Step or Thoughtful Persuasion (covered in later chapters). But, which play do you use? How do you size up the situation? What do you look for in the people you wish to change? The answers to questions such as these don't require skill in delivery of persuasive communication but rather need wisdom, principles, or—as I'll call them here—rules. These rules provide the overall structure you need as you make persuasion plays.

Wise Guidelines for Action

When I was a 12-year-old on my first real job as a newspaper carrier, I learned both skill and rules. The skill part was obvious basic operations—stuffing inserts, rolling the papers, delivering in a box or a door, and collecting monthly payments. The rules part came more slowly—learning to be nice to the guy who dropped off the papers so he'd throw them on my doorstep rather than on the lawn, handling little kids and dogs who liked to follow newspaper carriers, and most important, dealing with people who had cavalier attitudes about paying newspaper carriers.

You can view this book as supplying these same two kinds of knowledge: skill and rules. In this chapter, we're going to acquire persuasion wisdom—the guidelines for doing persuasion well. In the following parts of the book, we'll work hard on the skills—but a little wisdom will help a lot. We'll look at rules that will make the application of your persuasion skill easier, stronger, or happier. With each rule, we'll start with a headline, then develop it.

Rule No. 1: There Are No "Laws" of Persuasion, Only Rules

Imagine the Queen of Tomorrow who knows the laws of persuasion the way Albert Einstein knew the laws of physics. With merely a well-chosen word or gesture, she could change the way everyone thinks, feels, and behaves in any situation. She'd be one dangerous person.

Now, why would she tell anyone about these laws?

Once you, me, or that guy behind the tree knows the laws of persuasion, the Queen of Tomorrow loses her monopoly and all that goes with it. If we knew the laws, we could immediately and easily counter-persuade anyone the Queen of Tomorrow had changed. It goes against simple human interest to tell anyone the laws (assuming that they exist). Consider two implications of that.

First, be wary of hawkers armed with exclamation points, percentages, and smiling faces who claim to know anything even remotely approaching a law of persuasion. Why should they sell you this killer application at any price? Sure, you want to listen to experts, but you need to keep your head on a swivel and your hand on your wallet when the pitch sounds like the Queen of Tomorrow.

Second, realize that because the Queen of Tomorrow is hiding the laws, what we do know about persuasion is flawed, limited, and tentative—similar to what we know about most things in this world. I claim that there are no laws of persuasion in that sense of an absolute, always-works, and can't-miss application. However, there may be rules that are frequently, but not always, useful. Thus, you cannot expect 100 percent effectiveness with any persuasion knowledge the same way you cannot expect 100 percent effectiveness with any stock market knowledge, parenting knowledge, or any kind of human knowledge. I'm as close to a persuasion wizard as you're going to find at the price of a book—and I'm telling you, I'm not even the sorcerer's apprentice. I know some interesting stuff that works reliably under particular conditions, and if you correctly apply this knowledge to your situation, you'll be more persuasive. However, if you do not correctly apply the knowledge, it won't work. You need to accept the limitations of human knowledge and realize there is no magic here.

This rule makes you realize that persuasion is always difficult, unpredictable, and changeable. You can never get into a simple routine, a winning habit, or an automatic system that always works. You've got to be on your toes, looking for unique variations, unusual angles, and surprising turns.

Wise Lines

Genius is 1 percent inspiration and 99 percent perspiration.

—Thomas Alva Edison, American inventor

Now, I've done the due diligence and pointed out all the potential problems. Realize that there are still rules of persuasion. There are guiding principles, proven proverbs, and hard-earned nuggets of experience that tend to work in many situations when properly applied. You can be more effective than you are right now.

Rule No. 2: It's About the Other Guy

This statement is as close as we get to a persuasion law. Persuasion is almost always about the other guy (and I'm using "guy" to mean either a man or a woman). In persuasion, no one cares what *you* think or want or do. We care about the other guys and how they think, feel, or behave. If the other guys are doing what you want them to do, then keep going. You're persuading. By contrast, if you're giving them SureShotTactic 22 with an O'Malley nod, a BarBuster smile, and the Take 'Em to Philly close and they still don't do what you want, you weren't persuasive.

Are you having a bad hair day? Are you putting on weight and your clothes don't fit right? Were your kids up all night seeing the Boogie Man under the bed? Did the boss's nephew delete all the price lists? I don't care. Is the other guy having a bad hair day, putting on weight, or dealing with scared kids or foolish nephews in the corner office? That's want I to understand. I can use that information to identify my persuasion play and make smart adjustments along the way.

Effective persuasion requires relentless attention to the other guy. What's he like (apart from obvious stuff like race, sex, and age)? Does the other guy seem happy or sad? Is he paying attention? Have you seen him before, or is this a one-shot encounter? In other words, you focus on the psychological state of the other guy. I want to know what's in his head and heart. I want to understand him, body and soul. You want to look at the other guy and see him as a human stumbling through life just like you. You have to look past obvious, surface appearances and dig more deeply.

Unintended Consequences

Always consider the possibility that when you're trying to persuade the other guy, the other guy is actually trying to persuade you.

As you read this book, realize that it's a manual on human nature—on why people do what they do. You can't provide the words of persuasion unless you understand the correct words to use for that other guy right there in front of you in this time and place.

Sometimes there is no difference between persuasion and deception. Are you trying to persuade your kid, or do you just want him or her to leave you alone? Are you trying to persuade a coworker, or are you hiding an error you made? You need to understand your values and ethics and realize that if you're not careful, you can cross lines that violate your principles. Simply because you *can* persuade the other guy doesn't mean that you *should*.

Rule No. 3: People Tend to Resist Change

I don't need a dossier on you to know that you could make serious changes in your diet and exercise. You probably eat too many calories and eat too much of the wrong kind of calories—and there's a 50 percent chance you are a current or former smoker. And I haven't even gotten to the alcohol cabinet yet.

We know from both Mom and science that good diet and exercise are two actions anyone can take that will give them the best chance at good health and a longer life. And you don't need anything from anybody else to eat right and exercise regularly. It's all under your control. Yet, most of us don't come close to good diet and exercise habits—even though we know it's good for us. Why? Because change is hard, and we tend to resist it.

> **Wise Lines**
>
> Nothing has an uglier look to us than reason when it is not on our side.
> —George Savile, seventeenth-century English leader

Why? If change occurred frequently, we'd all be crazy and our civilization would be chaotic. So much of how we live depends on consistency across time. A large part of our survival and success stems from doing the same thing every day. Every time you get a demand for change, you always ask yourself, "Hey, if this change is so important and I should have been doing it, how come I'm not dead or in jail or starving or whatever the dread outcome may be? And, hey, this routine is working—if we change it, things might get worse!

Change is a risky thing, and most people naturally resist it. Change can be good, but a lot of times it isn't. How'd it go on the job interview when they noticed that tattoo on your wrist? Wow, those sure were some funny pictures of you on MySpace—think how voters will react when they see them in a few years when you're running for State Assembly!

More seriously, this rule schools us to be careful with persuasion. You are messing around with the other guy when you try to persuade, so you'd better be sure. Is this change really a good thing? Will it really work? It's going to take a lot of effort on your part to move folks, so shouldn't you make sure it's a good thing? The rule also informs us to be patient, long suffering, and persistent. People resist, so this will take some time and effort on your part.

Rule No. 4: All Persuasion Is Local

"Local" means everything that is going on in your persuasive situation. Exactly how anyone should go about persuasion will vary widely—because everyone's situation is always a little different. You need to develop a persuasion situational awareness to see all the local elements, then select the ones you need.

Local depends on at least four big factors:

- You and your goals at that moment
- The other guy and his or her goals at that moment
- The nature of the relationship between you and the other guy
- Other stuff that's going on in the situation

Let's get scientific here and make an equation:

> The correct persuasion play = you + your goals + the other guy + his or her goals + your relationship + other stuff in the situation

When you correctly figure out the key variables in this swirling mess of human interaction, then you can pick a persuasion play with poise. So go back to algebra class and fill in the variables. Here's the quick list of choices within each variable.

What are "you" and the "other guy"? Variables could be mood (happy, sad, or indifferent), mental state (alert, bored, or distracted), physical condition (strong, tired, or sick), skill (inexperienced, trained, or old fashioned), or motivation (internally directed, externally directed, or strong or weak).

What are "your goals" or "the other guy's goals"? Goals are the things you want to accomplish, right now with this person but also in the long term (the kind of person you want to be and how you want to live your life). Do you want to sell this widget right now or forge a long-term contract? Do you want to develop a contact into a relationship or just make a one-time deal? Do you want to make the deal at all costs or do nothing without any cost?

What's "your relationship"? It could be duration, intensity, likelihood of future contact, affection, need, benefit, or type. The variable could also be friends or lovers; colleagues, competitors, a supervisor, or a subordinate; teacher or student; strangers on a plane; or spouses celebrating their fiftieth wedding anniversary.

And what's "the situation"? It's everything going on in life around you and around the other guy—the time of day; the day of the week; public or private; work or play; or religious, political, or educational.

With just this quick sketch, you realize how complicated persuasion can be and why all persuasion is local. And you know that this unique combination can change in a flash as something new enters the equation. Another person may burst into the room. It may start or stop raining. Life happens—and when it does, the circumstances of persuasion change.

The upshot of this rule is that you cannot read this guide like a cookbook and follow a recipe. Persuasion is more like playing basketball, where the best play varies from moment to moment. Should you pass, dribble, or shoot? It depends and varies. To play a fluid, dynamic, and variable game such as basketball, you cannot approach it like a cookbook and hope to bake a victory. You have to learn principles of the game, work on recognition and reaction skills, acquire a sense of flow, and get your head in the game—and even then, you still may lose many games.

All persuasion is local means that you have to pay attention to life as it's happening right now, in all its glory, confusion, and complexity. Everything can matter, and just one thing can matter. It depends on a unique combination of factors. You have to develop a persuasion situational awareness.

Rule No. 5: If You Can't Succeed, Don't Try

Is that bear dead or sleeping? Dunno. Let's give it a poke and find out.

I'd argue that it's better to let bears lying on the ground lie on the ground than it is to poke 'em with a stick. If you're not sure, don't try. It's the same thing with persuasion. If you're not sure you can deliver the words to produce the desired change, just shut up. Give 'em a smile. Try a line such as, "I'm just happy to be here and hope I can help the team."

When you try to persuade somebody, you're in essence poking a bear. Now, you're hoping that you poke the bear the proper way and that things work out positively for you—but if you're wrong, you don't have the status quo anymore. Things don't remain the same as they were before you poked the bear. You've stirred things up and changed things.

Persuasion pokes the other guy. It makes that person move in the direction of change. We've already established that people naturally tend to resist change. And everyone knows that usually when you change one thing, you also change other things—things you forgot about or didn't realize were connected. If you attempt the change but fail, you have really failed twice. First, you failed in your immediate persuasion goal. Second, you have just made the other guy even harder to persuade in the future, because your failure has made him or her stronger and more resistant.

Rule No. 6: Effective Persuasion Takes Planning

Effective persuasion is seldom a spontaneous, natural reaction. Effective persuasion is more likely to occur when you plan in advance, knowing that you'll be walking along the road today and that you'll find plenty of targets of opportunity.

After you read Parts 2 and 3, you'll also appreciate the need for strategy and planning. The persuasion plays will make clear that you need to know your persuasion goal and have a plan to reach that goal before you get anywhere near saying a word to anyone about anything. Effective persuasion is rarely like sitting on a sofa with a remote control, where all you have to do is press a button to get what you want from the television. Typically, each persuasion situation is slightly different and requires a unique plan. Sure, you can reuse certain ideas and messages—but you have to make enough modification each time.

The Sizzle

How much planning is enough? Here's a simple guide: if you get the desired outcome, you have planned enough. If you didn't get the desired outcome, you need to plan more.

Rule No. 7: All Bad Persuasion Is Sincere

Sincere communicators are lousy persuaders. They wear their hearts on their sleeves, run their true colors up the tallest flagpole, and call things exactly how they see them. They keep it real, which means we understand everything about them and nothing about the people who they're trying to persuade. They tell you what most moves them, not what moves the receiver. Now, this might work if you are trying to persuade your identical twin—but past that, it's not so good. Effective persuaders must set aside (if only briefly) their feelings, values, and motivations if they want to achieve "good" persuasion (the other guy actually changes) rather than "bad" persuasion (the other guy doesn't change, but you feel good about yourself precisely because you were so sincere).

Community websites aimed at politics are great illustrations of this rule. Just for fun, go online and find two popular websites from different political philosophies and read the entries. Although the writers from both websites take opposite sides on an issue, their arguments are both the same: intense, raw, dense, and over-detailed. And when you read them, do you often find yourself shaking your head? You certainly know what the writer believes, but is it persuasive?

Does this rule mean that good persuasion is dishonest, manipulative, deceitful, or not authentic? Of course not. Good persuasion may start with your sincere, authentic, and natural feelings and desires—but your persuading needs to be calm, controlled, and flexible with that persuasion situational awareness.

Unintended Consequences

Sincerity rarely works as a persuasion play. I've spent most of the past 20 years working with persuasion applications in health and safety and from that experience I've learned that the biggest problem is not diet, exercise, recklessness, stupidity, fear, or greed, but rather the abiding sincerity of many health advocates. For example, a British professor of Metabolic Medicine at the University of Glasgow proposed this earnest solution for the obesity epidemic: "Oversize clothes should have obesity helpline numbers sewn on them to try and reduce Britain's fat crisis." This from a December 15, 2006 article in the *Daily Mail* newspaper quoting Dr. Naveed Sattar. (Why not just blow a horn and have a prerecorded voice shout, "You're fat!" whenever a customer takes a plus size item off the rack, too?) This persuasion play exudes sincerity, and now, two years after the suggestion, you notice the public reception of the good doctor's plan: nothing. It's a bad idea that has no reasonable basis in persuasion science.

Rule No. 8: Remember the Persuasion KISS: Keep It Simple, Sweetie

Do you ever watch Road Runner and Wile E. Coyote cartoons? Road Runner is a tasty but very fast prey while Wile E. Coyote is a hungry but slower predator. To close the speed gap, Wile E. must devise ever more complex schemes to catch up with the Road Runner. He uses rocket-powered skates, anvils tied to large balloons, and gigantic springs attached to granite canyon walls. And of course, none of these devious, complex, and exquisite plans ever work.

Many people who try persuasion are like Wile E. Coyote. They are motivated. They are resourceful. And then, they make things complicated. They keep thinking they need just one more step, one more trick, or one more persuasion play, and bang—they'll catch the Road Runner. But of course, just like Wile E. Coyote, their reach never quite equals their grasp—and they are left hungry.

Effective persuasion is more like judo. You want to let the other guy do as much of the work as possible, then you figure out the one move you can make to change his or her direction. To acquire that kind of skill in action, you must become smarter and wiser about persuasion. Again, the judo metaphor is helpful here. You might have seen the classic movie, *The Karate Kid*, which shows the relationship between a teenage boy coming of age and his relationship with an older man who is a karate expert. The boy initially displays his fighting skills as a wild combination of wild energy, music video choreography, and scary shouts, which the old man effortlessly parries with one quick, simple move, dropping the boy to the floor. The old man then teaches the boy not only the complexities of the fighting moves but, more importantly the intelligence needed to understand and control the fighting situation.

If the fighting metaphor bothers you, let me share an example from my theater days. I got cast in a chorus line part for the musical, "George M," in high school. It was an old-fashioned musical based on the song and dance of George M. Cohan. Now, my dancing skills are modest at best, but I looked like the winner of *Dancing with the Stars* because my partner was great. She was a large girl, heavier than me and almost as tall. Many of our dance routines required the male to "throw" the female around the floor in a series of lifts, dips, spins, and tosses. At first, I actually tried to make these moves happen with my physical strength, but my partner quickly schooled me. She actually dominated the dance moves and executed all the lifts, dips, spins, and tosses herself. I just lightly kept my hands on her waist or shoulder or arms and acted as if I'd "moved" her. My family, friends, and the rest of the audience thought I was a great dancer when really all I was doing was keeping my hands on the great dancer and showing a big smile now and then. She was dancing and I was acting.

Most effective persuasion plays require simple moves or combinations of simple moves: a Persuasion KISS. The deeper skill, however, is that persuasion situational awareness, of being able to size up the moment, expertly identify the correct play, then deftly execute it, like a karate master.

Rule No. 9: Walk Softly and Carry a Big Stick

Let's take Teddy Roosevelt's admonition and make it work for us. The "big stick" in our terms is "power," the capacity a source has to deliver rewards and punishments; while the "walk softly" is "persuasion," using words to change thoughts, feelings, or actions. While this book focuses on persuasion, don't overlook that other common tactic, power. You always have both tools in your possession. The point of this rule is that if you use persuasion and power in combination, you will obtain more success than if you primarily or exclusively use just one.

As illustrations of this rule, consider former president George W. Bush and his predecessor, former president Bill Clinton. I think that Mr. Bush was primarily a power president while Mr. Clinton was primarily a persuasion president. (That's not to say that each man always and only used just one approach; they clearly used both, but seemed to prefer or excel at one over the other.) Some observers would assert that Mr. Bush would have been more effective at foreign policy if he'd been more persuasive, while others would assert that Mr. Clinton would have been more effective at foreign policy if he'd been more powerful. Now, contrast them with men who are perceived by many as "great" presidents: Abraham Lincoln, Franklin Roosevelt, and more contemporaneously, Ronald Reagan. These more highly esteemed leaders showed a stronger balance between persuasion and power.

> **Wise Lines**
>
> Nearly all men can stand adversity, but if you want to test a man's character, give him power.
> —Abraham Lincoln

Most people look for power as the means to change rather than persuasion because power is fast and simple. Get it, use it, and move on. Persuasion, by contrast, always seems trickier, unpredictable, and uncontrollable. Power is beguiling in that regard, but you can easily overrate the value of power compared to persuasion and miss the value that arises from skillfully combined power and persuasion.

Certainly, one of the biggest advantages to combined power and persuasion is that you don't have to use power as often. If you've ever had any power at all, you probably learned that the more you use it, the less effective it becomes. People begin to recognize your limitations and learn to work around your power. Further, as you'll see in Chapter 4, rewards and punishments tend to wear out over time. Thus, if you're a one-trick pony, your overuse of power will isolate and weaken you.

Thus learn to use persuasion. Understand the principles. Master the plays. It will enhance your power and make you more effective in everything you do. Walk softly and carry a big stick: you'll go farther with both than with either alone.

Rule No. 10: Power Corrupts Persuasion

You may recall Lord Acton's famous quote that "power tends to corrupt and that absolute power corrupts absolutely." Consider now how overreliance on power weakens or "corrupts" persuasion skill. In Rule No. 9, we noted that persuasion and power combined will produce more effectiveness than either alone. What happens when you always go to a power play and ignore persuasion possibilities?

Most obviously, you get worse at persuasion because you don't practice it. Persuasion is a skill, which means that it's something that is learned and can be improved with training, experience, and practice. Did you take piano lessons as a kid? You probably remember quite a bit from that training, but if you haven't been practicing your scales, even "Chopsticks" is a challenge for you today. The same thing occurs with persuasion. If you do not work on it regularly, whatever skill you have with it will diminish. Again, this is an obvious inference from Rule 10.

Less obvious, however, is the fact that over-reliance on power changes how receivers look at you and what they expect from you. If you are always or almost always a power player, in those rare times you try persuasion, receivers will immediately spot the difference and most probably become suspicious. Why would someone who always uses the carrot-and-stick approach suddenly try to convince someone to do something? Receivers may start looking for the "catch" or the "trick" behind your words, trying to determine the angle you're playing. Worse still, some receivers might perceive your sudden, uncharacteristic, and unexpected persuasion attempt at a sign of power weakness. If you stop using power is it because you've lost power?

Further, if you almost always use power plays, you will tend to elicit the same tactics from your receivers. Everyone quickly learns how you play and they will respond in a like manner. They will meet your power plays with power plays of their own. Thus, receivers may take the example of your power plays, copy them for themselves, and use it to the exclusion of persuasion.

The Least You Need to Know

- In order to successfully persuade, you need persuasion wisdom.
- While there are no laws of persuasion, there are valid and useful rules to guide you.
- Persuasion rules focus on the big picture—planning, opportunity, goals—but not on specific persuasion plays.
- If you remember only one rule, remember this one: It's about the other guy!

Part 2

Persuasion Plays for Beginners

Let the games begin. Start with these basic, standard plays—the ones everyone knows (or at least thinks they know). Hone your skills and maybe even pick up a new trick or two. Compare the state of your art to the art of proven winners. Every persuasion pro knows if you can't handle the fundamentals, you don't really know the game.

Chapter 4

Conditioning and Modeling

In This Chapter

- Common sense and basic persuasion plays
- Conditioning works with animals as well as with humans
- Persuasion plays for behavior change
- Reinforcing or modeling for behavior rather than thoughts or feelings

The fundamentals of persuasion are conditioning and modeling. Classical conditioning, reinforcement, and modeling demonstrate essential and eternal elements of our human nature. All people at all times can change through conditioning and modeling, and this will always be so.

Most of us begin and end our persuasion efforts with conditioning, reinforcement, and modeling because they are simple to understand. However, we often fail to change others with these plays because we misunderstand key points about their operation. They are the common-sense approaches to change, and virtually all humans figure out how to employ them—even when we can't see other people using them on us!

Common Sense Persuasion Theories

Most people approach the world with common sense as their guide to understanding and action. You watch the world, then figure things out. Small children who lack the skill to get what they want watch their parents very closely and learn how to get more food or attention. We discover the methods of change because we want things from the world we cannot get ourselves—and the only way to acquire those things is through manipulating other people. Classical conditioning, reinforcement, and modeling are the most obvious and apparent methods of change.

Now, simply because these persuasion plays are simple and common sense does not mean that they are unsophisticated, foolish, or weak. Most change in everyday life occurs through these plays, and for that reason alone they are worth understanding. Furthermore, realize that these methods are the most common ways that other people change *you*. (Think about that for a minute.)

Yet, because we grasp these persuasion plays so easily with our common sense, we often overlook subtle elements that moderate the effectiveness of the play. With each play there is a trick, a finesse, and a fine point that often eludes common sense and requires more training, thinking, and learning.

Classical Conditioning

What do you do when you hear a bell ring? I've taught public school teachers about persuasion theory, and one teacher told this funny story. He was at home, sitting in his favorite chair reading the newspaper, when somebody rang the doorbell. He stood up with his newspaper and walked into the nearest hallway of his house and began to monitor the hallway while reading the paper. The call of that bell was so strong that this teacher produced the right behavior (monitoring a hallway) in the wrong place (his home). Ding-dong!

A similar event occurred with one of my colleagues during a federal government meeting. She was nodding off during the discussion when a bell sound chimed in a PowerPoint presentation. She popped up from her seat moving to a door, saying, "I'll get it!" She took the ribbing in good nature, but the rest of us nearly choked to death laughing.

And of course, it's not just bells. If you're a parent, somebody else's crying child can elicit an automatic response from you. Simple ding-dongs pop up in our lives all the time.

Pavlov Goes to the Dogs

How does this happen? You might recall the name Pavlov. He was a Russian physiologist who won the Nobel Prize for his work in medicine. As part of his work in the early 1900s, he discovered the physiological basis of conditioning. The easiest place to start is with an example from his research. Consider a hungry dog who sees a bowl of food. Something like the following might happen:

food → salivation

The dog is hungry, the dog sees the food, and the dog salivates. This is a natural sequence of events—an unconscious, uncontrolled, and unlearned relationship.

Now, because we are humans who have an insatiable curiosity, we experiment. When we present the food to the hungry dog (and before the dog salivates), we ring a bell. Thus …

bell
↓
food → salivation

We repeat this action (food and bell presented simultaneously) at several meals. Every time the dog sees the food, the dog also hears the bell. Ding-dong, Alpo. Now, because we are humans who like to play tricks on our pets, we do another experiment. We ring the bell, but we don't show any food. What does the dog do?

bell → salivation

The bell elicits the same response that the sight of the food gets. Over repeated trials, the dog has learned to associate the bell with the food, and now the bell has the power to produce the same response as the food. This is *classical conditioning*. You start with two things that are already connected with each other (food and salivation). Then, you add a third thing (the bell, in this example) for several trials. Eventually, this third thing may become so strongly associated that it has the power to produce the old behavior. (In persuasion geek speak, this is "respondent conditioning.")

def•i•ni•tion

Classical conditioning (in other words, "respondent conditioning") takes an existing connection between a stimulus and a response and adds a new stimulus over repeated trials so that the new stimulus can produce the old response.

Ordinary Life Examples

Classical conditioning doesn't just happen with animals, of course. People can be classically conditioned as well. Let's look at a few real-life examples of this conditioning in action, with both animals of the four-legged and two-legged variety.

If you've ever had a cat or a dog and an electric can opener, this situation will be familiar to you. You take the canned food out of the cabinet, ready to feed Fluffy or Fido their supper. In fact, if you have a dog, he's probably already at your side at the opening of the cabinet door. But what happens when you hit the can opener or make that popping sound when you break the seal? The pets come running! This will happen even if you are opening a can of green beans. It's classical conditioning!

Classical conditioning works with people, too. Remember K-Mart and the blue-light specials? K-Mart would fill a table with a special item at a special price, then turn on a rotating blue light much like a police car. Cost-conscious shoppers would make a beeline to that table because they associate a good sale with the blue light. Beer ads often feature attractive young women wearing sexy clothes. The young women naturally elicit a favorable, mildly aroused feeling in most men. The beer is simply associated with this effect. The same thing applies with the jingles and music that accompany many advertisements. The music may be patriotic or take us back to the days of our youth when we were wild and free and the future was an open book. Then, they connect the product or service with the feeling elicited by the music.

We can see applications of this theory if we look at rules and discipline in schools and similar organizations. Teachers will flip the lights off and on to signal the class to be quiet. Now, flashing lights clearly will not naturally cause children to be quiet. This is an association the teacher taught the students. The same reasoning applies with our use of bells and whistles and other signals in work environments. We use classical conditioning to train and warn.

Perhaps the strongest application of classical conditioning involves emotion. Common experience and careful research both confirm that human emotions condition very rapidly and easily. When the emotion is intensely felt or negative in direction, it will condition particularly quickly.

When I was in college, I was robbed at gunpoint. This happened at dusk, and for a long time thereafter I often experienced dread in the late afternoons. Although I was quite safe, the lengthening shadows of the day were so strongly associated with the fear I experienced in the robbery that I could not help feeling the emotion all over.

The same process can occur with students, employees, or customers. Threatening tests or aggressive teachers create fearful students who hate school and learning. Surly, rude, and obnoxious supervisors generate dread and anxiety in their workers who then hate the job, the boss, the work, maybe even the customers, too.

Because classical conditioning is so obvious, simple, and transparent, it is sometimes hard to see it in operation—but clearly, it is a fundamental path of persuasion and influence. Look around in your life and consider how it affects you. And now consider how you use it to affect others.

Reinforcement

This is the one theory of influence almost everyone knows. It works in a variety of situations, can be simply applied, and has just a few basic def•i•ni•tion

Reinforcement (in other words, "operant conditioning") changes behavior through the consequences that follow the behavior.

ideas. In fact, *reinforcement* boils down to a main point: consequences influence behavior. To understand this theory, go back in time to the fourth grade. Think about school, teachers, and rows of desks. Remember the smells. Think about your teachers. Yeah, that one, too, the mean one.

The Three Consequences

There are three principles of this theory—the rules of consequences that describe the logical outcomes that typically occur after consequences:

1. Consequences that give rewards increase a behavior.
2. Consequences that give punishments decrease a behavior.
3. Consequences that give neither rewards nor punishments extinguish a behavior.

If you want to increase a behavior (more frequent, more intense, or more likely), then when the behavior is shown, provide a consequence of reward. If you want to decrease a behavior (less frequent, less intense, or less likely), then when the behavior is shown, provide a consequence of punishment. Finally, if you want a behavior to extinguish (disappear, delete, or forget), then when the behavior is shown, provide no consequence (ignore the behavior).

Rewards and Punishers

Now, the big question becomes, "What is a reward or a punisher?" The answer is easy. A reward is anything that increases the behavior. A punisher is anything that decreases the behavior.

Is this circular reasoning or what? Reinforcement is a functional theory. That means all of its components are defined by their function (how they work) rather than by their structure (how they look). Thus, there is no "consequences cookbook" where a teacher can look in the chapter, "Rewards for Fifth-Grade Boys," and find a long list of things to use as rewarding consequences.

Many kids find candy to be rewarding. If they sit quietly in their chairs for five minutes and you give them each a sweet, those kids will learn to sit quietly. The candy (a consequence of reward) is used to increase the behavior of sitting quietly. So, we have discovered a reward and can put it in the consequences cookbook, right? And then the next time your spouse spends the afternoon cleaning up some grubby corner of the basement, all you have to do is give him or her a candy bar—and next week you'll find him or her in the bathroom scrubbing out the tub, right? Of course not. The same consequence (candy) moves different people in different ways because it functions differently for each. For a little kid candy is dandy, but for adults it rarely works. Instead, remember: liquor is quicker!

The functional nature of reinforcement is important to understand. It explains why the theory sometimes appears to be incorrect. Here's an example: when Sally Goodchild interrupts the class, Mrs. Reinforcer stops the class, tells Sally she's a naughty girl who broke Rule 24, and now tells her she must leave the classroom and go to the principal's office. Ouch! That really hurt Sally Goodchild. And Mrs. Reinforcer knows that when Sally returns, she will not interrupt again. Mrs. Reinforcer then goes to the teacher's lounge and sings the praises of this really great theory.

Well, don't you know that the other kids in the class watched this event with great interest? And when Bad Bill interrupts the class, Mrs. Reinforcer stops the class, tells Bad Bill he's a naughty boy who broke Rule 24, and now tells him that he must leave the classroom and go to the principal's office. Ouch! That really hurt Bad Bill. And Mrs. Reinforcer knows when Bad Bill comes back to class, he will not interrupt again because he will want to avoid that wicked punishment. Well, we all know what happens next. Bad Bill keeps on interrupting so he gets out of class. Mrs. Reinforcer is totally confused at this point and goes back to the teacher's lounge complaining about this stupid reinforcement.

To understand whether you have a reward, you must observe its effect. If the consequence increases the behavior you want to increase, voilà—you have a reward. If the consequence decreases the behavior you want to decrease, then you have a punishment. Most people have had the unfortunate experience of Mrs. Reinforcer. They have persisted in giving a consequence of punishment, and lo and behold, the "other guy" keeps doing the bad thing. If the behavior does not increase or decrease the way you want it to, then you need to rethink your rewards and punishments.

Wise Lines

If I am not in front of my building at 6:15 when my parents get there, they are going to put me on an aggravation installment plan that will compound with interest for decades.

—The character George Costanza on his parents use of reinforcement from the TV comedy *Seinfeld*

The Process of Reinforcement

The rules of consequence are used in a three-step sequence that defines the process of reinforcement. We call these steps the When-Do-Get:

1. When in some situation …
2. Do some behavior …
3. Get some consequence.

According to reinforcement, people learn several things during the process of reinforcement. First, they learn that certain behaviors (Step 2: Do) lead to consequences (Step 3: Get). This is the most obvious application of the rules of consequence. A student realizes that if she does well on an assignment (Do), then she will get a rewarding consequence of a pretty sticker (Get). Another student discovers that if she speaks out inappropriately (Do), then she will receive the punishing consequence of reduced recess time (Get).

But second (and just as important), people learn that the Do-Get only works in certain situations (Step 1: When). For example, a child may discover that when he is with his parents (When) and he throws a temper tantrum (Do), he embarrasses them and they give him rewards such as attention, toys, or candy (Get) to calm him down. Now when this child goes to school and tries this trick, he is cruelly disappointed when the teacher provides a punishing consequence rather than a rewarding consequence. He soon learns that being rewarded for a tantrum only works when he is with Mom and Dad.

So the equation goes like this: When in some situation-Do some behavior-Get a consequence. And there are only three consequences: rewarding, punishing, and ignoring. Let's look at some examples in action.

Practical Applications

One of the best examples of reinforcement I've ever heard came from an assistant football coach at a college. A little background: some football players have trouble getting to team meetings. When this happens, the coaches want to punish the players so they will be on time. What to do?

The standard answer is extra exercise. When the team is in a workout, at the end of the session the coaches identify the tardy players and make them run extra laps or do more pushups, right?

Well, this coach had a better idea. At the end of the workout, he called everyone together and identified the tardy players who missed the team meeting. Then, he made the rest of the team run extra laps while the tardy ones sat and watched. The coach claimed that this application had to be given only once a year. And I believe him. Imagine what happened in the locker room when everyone who got the extra work closed the door with all the "tardy" guys. Do you think the team delivered a wide range of consequences to the tardy boys?

And a wife told this story about her lazy husband of 50 years. He'd become cavalier about cleaning up after himself, in particular leaving his favorite cereal bowl lying around anywhere in the house after he

Unintended Consequences

Whenever you try to reinforce someone, consider the possibility that they are reinforcing you. Dogs are surprisingly good at this.

was done eating. After several weeks of arguments, she hit upon an effective reinforcement play. She put the offending cereal bowl on top of his computer keyboard. Worse still, his computer was a very long way from the kitchen sink and he had to walk that trip with a cane because he had bad knees.

What's Wrong with Reinforcement?

While reinforcement is a powerful tool, it does have several serious limitations. To use it effectively, you must be aware of these difficulties in application:

- **It's difficult to identify rewards and punishments.** As noted earlier in this chapter, reinforcers are identified by their functions. Thus, there is no cookbook list of rewards and punishments. Further, they can diminish in effect over time.
- **You must control all sources of reinforcement.** You are never the only source of reinforcement in somebody's life. This is most obvious from our school experiences, where the call of the peer group can be much stronger than any authority source. Those other sources can destroy your efforts. If you cannot control those competing sources, you need to realize your limitations. Every parent has seen this happen at some point in the life of their children. One day you simply do not have the consequences and you must find other tactics for persuasion with your kids.
- **Internal changes can be difficult to create.** The ultimate goal of reinforcement is habit formation. You want them to do "it" all the time, even when you are not around to supply rewards or punishments. Creating habits from reinforcements is a subtle, tricky, and difficult art and science.
- **Punishing is difficult to do well.** Compelling research shows that effective punishment must be immediate (right now), intense (the biggest possible stick), unavoidable (there is no escape), and

consistent (every time). If you cannot deliver punishment under these conditions, then the punishment is likely to fail.

- **People may come to hate sources who use punishment.** Punishment is, by definition, an aversive, painful consequence. People experience very negative emotional states when they get punished. And as we learned with classical conditioning, it is easy to condition emotions. Thus, when a source uses punishment, the targets will probably feel angry, fearful, or hopeless and will then connect or associate these negative feelings with the source of the punishment.

Skillful Reinforcement

If you want to become more skillful at reinforcement, do it less often. It is used too often by everyone (and typically under the wrong conditions). Please understand that reinforcement will work marvelously when it is properly employed. Under the correct conditions, monkeys and pigeons, boys and girls, and men and women will be strongly influenced through the skillful use of reinforcement principles.

What are those correct conditions? Here's the list:

- The source is well-trained in the theory and practice of reinforcement.
- The source has complete control of all significant reinforcers for all receivers.
- The source has complete control of each receiver (in other words, what the receiver does, when the receiver does it, and what other receivers are in the situation).
- The source has a detailed and consistent plan of reinforcement.
- The reinforcers are always delivered under the same conditions to each different receiver.

To the extent that you deviate from these general rules, the application of reinforcement will be ineffective. It is also important to realize that these inefficiencies do not make the theory a failure; rather, these inefficiencies simply show it is difficult to implement the theory in the real world.

Modeling

I travel a lot to big cities and typically use the subway when available. Each is different, although they all have the same goal of mass transit. I always feel like I'm an anthropologist on a strange island trying to figure out the natives, because each subway island has a different way to pay for a ticket, determine a route, and enter a line or subway car. And of course, while I'm standing there, everyone else is pushing around me and muttering something ugly about anthropologists. So, what do I do? I *model*. I observe others, see what happens to them, and then model their actions. (Sometimes social science is real simple.)

def•i•ni•tion

Modeling is change through observing another person's behavior.

Monkey See, Monkey Do

We model like this all the time in our lives. So, what's the big deal with modeling theory? First, it's surprising that people can be influenced so easily. Just by watching what other people do, we can acquire new ideas and behaviors. Second, modeling seems to be a dominant way that people get new behaviors. Whenever we are in a new situation, we almost always look around to see what others are doing. Third, the entire process requires very little thinking on the part of the observer. Indeed, modeling is faster if you simply copy the model rather than try to figure out everything that's going on.

How Modeling Works

Modeling theory operates in three simple steps:

1. You observe a model's behavior.
2. You imitate the model's actions.
3. You get a consequence.

The marvel of this theory is that people are influenced simply as a result of observing other people (monkey see, monkey do). From the observation of others, we learn what to do, what not to do, when to do it, and what to expect when we do it.

After we observe the model, we imitate. That is, when we get into a similar situation that we observed earlier, we now produce the same behaviors we saw the model produce. We observe someone put money in a machine, press some buttons, get a ticket, then walk over to the turnstile and slide the ticket into a slot. So we walk over to the machine, look for a place to put our money, look for some directions for those buttons, press a few—and we receive the ticket and head for the turnstile.

Now, our imitation should lead to the desired consequence. We saw the model get the money, right? If our imitation produces money for us, too, we got the desired consequence—and now we have truly been influenced. (I watch you do it, and when I do it, I get what I want.) If our imitation fails, then we will drop the model.

Modeling Case Studies

The catch phrase "monkey see, monkey do" has more than a common sense basis. Just before the start of World War I, a German researcher named Wolfgang Kohler did experiments with a colony of chimps. He arranged a special cage with several boxes and sticks lying around. He would then hang bananas high in the cage so that they were inaccessible to the chimps. Kohler made a film that showed various chimps having that "ah-ha!" experience of insight learning where first they stood there stupidly surveying the scene, then "getting it" and putting together the various objects to build a scaffold, and then retrieving the bananas. Now, what has insight learning got to do with modeling? Other chimps would observe the first chimp in the cage, see the failure, and then see the solution. When these chimps got in the cage, they got to the solution a lot faster due to monkey see, monkey do.

This same kind of process is apparent in many advertising campaigns. Those before-and-after pictures of a boy or girl who looks a lot like you (or who you'd like to be) depict what good thing happened to them when they started using a new toothpaste, a certain weight-loss program, or a little blue pill. You observe the model "before," then see the model use the product and achieve a desired consequence ("after"). All you have to do is buy the product and imitate the model. This modeling process is also a key element in those hot trends that suddenly appear and then die, such as pegged pants, peasant blouses, miniskirts, cosmetic tans, Hula hoops, slinkys, paisley shirts, and bell bottoms.

How Modeling Is Used

Among the many uses of modeling, consider the following practical implications:

- **You have to know what is being modeled.** Do you remember Mrs. Reinforcer and her student, Bad Bill? Bad Bill broke a rule, and Mrs. Reinforcer used punishment to influence Bill's behavior. (Except Bad Bill really *wanted* the punishment to escape the classroom, so he kept doing the bad thing—which confused Mrs. Reinforcer.) Something else was also going on in Mrs. Reinforcer's classroom. Every other kid was watching the event, and because of the principles of modeling, every kid was being influenced. Each one of them learned, simply through observation, several important lessons.

  Many students learned that misbehaving kids do get punished. That's good. When you enforce a rule, everybody in the room—not just the target—is influenced because of modeling. But bad things are learned, too. Some of the kids learned that if they act like Bad Bill, they can escape Mrs. Reinforcer's room. Others learned (by seeing what happened before Bill got thrown out) all the things they can do and still not get in trouble. Finally, some learned how to pull Mrs. Reinforcer's chain.

  The point of this example is direct. When things happen, people may be modeling. Look for it.

- **Use modeling to change simple, automatic behavior.** Modeling theory is designed primarily to explain behavioral influence. It is less useful in creating or understanding changes in thinking or feeling. Therefore, whenever you want to influence behaviors, consider modeling. For other types of changes, use other persuasion tools.

- **Show (don't tell) modeling.** As noted earlier, modeling theory works well at influencing behavior. The best way to implement modeling is to do it rather than to say it.

  Here's a good example. Organizational rules are important, and many such rules deal with behavior (for example, how to take sick leave or vacation time, who answers the phone and how, norms for group conduct, and unacceptable actions). Rather than write out these rules and only discuss them verbally, modeling theory would suggest we could be more effective. Show the behaviors! With new employees, for example, a training session with modeling would be more useful than just handing them the rule book.

The Least You Need to Know

- We are already well on our way toward becoming master persuaders when we tap into our own innate common-sense abilities.
- Conditioning begins with a relationship between a stimulus (see food) and response (salivate) and connects a new stimulus (bell) to the old response over time.
- Reinforcement uses consequences to change behavior in the When-Do-Get.
- Modeling operates through imitation to get a desired outcome.
- We learn these methods through common sense but improve them with training and practice.

Chapter 5

Obedience and Authority

In This Chapter

- The relationship between authority and obedience
- Obedience as compliance
- The Milgram Study on pain and learning
- Understanding shallow and deep obedience

One of the most powerful change methods is through authority. Human nature appears to have a built-in element whereby all of us are easily drawn to authority, credibility, and power. And like most things in life, this human nature is both a benefit and a harm. Our ability to organize into groups with a hierarchy, structure, and roles enhances our chances of survival and success—yet a thoughtless obedience response can lead to disaster for us as individuals or in groups.

We need to understand the nature of our obedience response, what makes it more and less likely, and how we can use it to our advantage—both as a means leading others toward positive goals and as a way of protecting ourselves against blind obedience.

Jim Jones and the Jonestown Massacre

Do you remember the Jonestown Massacre in 1978? Among the many details of that horrible event, these are the most bewildering. More than 900 people willingly committed suicide at the urging of their leader, the Rev. Jim Jones. Individuals killed themselves. Husbands and wives killed themselves. Parents and their children killed themselves. And they did this because they were told to do so.

Our first response to such an event is to assume that these people must have been seriously crazy. It is more frightening to consider the possibility that these acts were not driven by madness but rather by normal human reactions. Why do events such as these occur? Our perspective is based on the concept of *obedience*.

def•i•ni•tion

Obedience is the receiver's compliance to source authority.

Obedience, Hierarchy, and Power

A classic example of obedience is an officer giving orders to a soldier who obeys them. The soldier complies with the officer because the officer has legitimate, organizational power. The compliance does not occur because the soldier likes the officer or necessarily respects the officer's judgment and expertise. Rather, the officer simply has legitimate power from the hierarchy—and the soldier must obey.

Now, while this example is rather straightforward, it appears to have nothing to do with events such as the Jonestown Massacre. No one has the power to order another person's suicide. As strange as it might seem, the research strongly suggests that obedience is a powerful influence tool that has far-reaching implications.

The Milgram Study

We now turn to perhaps the most controversial social science study ever done: the obedience studies of Yale University psychologist Stanley Milgram. In a series of studies completed in New Haven, Connecticut, during the 1960s, Milgram tested human obedience in an ordinary social situation—a psychology experiment. Milgram's research is very simple and easy to understand, but its implications were astonishing when they were first reported—and they remain troubling to many to this day. Here's what Milgram did.

Pain and Learning

First, he recruited volunteers for a study on learning and memory with ads in local newspapers. He got regular folks this way—ordinary adults. He also did some studies with college students, but it was important to note that he did this research with older people, too.

When a volunteer showed up for the experiment (which was done in a storefront office in downtown New Haven, Connecticut), he or she was met by an experimenter and another waiting research subject (we'll call him George). The experimenter was dressed in a lab coat and carried a clipboard as he explained the experiment to the volunteer and to George.

"See," the experimenter said, "many people believe that punishment helps people learn better. The classic example is a parent who spanks a child for running into the street. We hurt the child because we believe it will prevent the kid from doing a dangerous thing."

"Well," the experimenter confessed, "social scientists really do not know whether punishment works the way we think. That is, we have no scientific information to claim that punishment does any good or any bad for that matter. The purpose of this experiment is to determine whether punishment helps or hinders how well people learn new things."

The Apparatus

At this point, the experimenter explained how the experiment worked and what equipment would be involved. The task was easy. Either the volunteer or George would be randomly assigned to be the "teacher." The other person would then automatically be the "learner." The teacher would supply the learner with a list that contained pairs of words. For example, the first pair might be "tree—up," and the next pair would be "box—gone," and so on for 20 or so pairs. The teacher would train the learner in acquiring the pair, such that on a later trial, the teacher would only supply the first word and the learner would respond with the matching word for that pair.

Now, here's where the punishment part comes in. Every time the learner made a mistake, the teacher punished him or her. And the punishment came from a machine. Here, the experimenter revealed a piece of equipment that was about the size of a large boom box stereo. On the box was a row of toggle switches, and above the switches was a description of the voltage and danger level for each switch. There were 20 switches, and the labels above the switches started at "low" and went up to "dangerous."

Every time a mistake was made, the teacher would give the learner a shock, then set the toggle for the next-highest level of voltage. Thus, the more mistakes the learner made, the larger the shocks would become.

To demonstrate the power of the shocks, the experimenter attached the lead wire from the shock box to the volunteer's hand and gave the volunteer a shock from the toggle marked "mild."

It hurt.

The Script

Now it was time to pick who would be the teacher and who would be the learner. The volunteer and George looked at each other nervously as the experimenter had them choose straws from his hand. The volunteer gulped as he compared his straw to George's. The volunteer had the long straw and was the teacher. George, an older man with thinning hair and a thickening waist, sighed.

The volunteer and the experimenter strapped George into his chair and attached the lead wire from the shock box. The volunteer sat down beside George and began training him in the word pairs. The experimenter watched carefully, making notes on his clipboard.

After the training, the important part of the experiment was ready to start. All the volunteer-teacher had to do was provide the first word of the pair, then George was to respond with the correct second word.

"And every time George makes a mistake," the volunteer asked, "he gets a shock, right?"

"Correct," replied the experimenter.

"Well, how far do we go with the shocks?" the volunteer asked as he noted the highest levels that said "dangerous" beside them.

"All the way, of course," said the experimenter, without even looking up from his clipboard.

Okay, let's take a break in the action here for a minute. You understand how this experiment works and what is going on. Two people who've never met are playing teacher and learner in a study of learning and punishment. An escalating series of painful shocks is supposed to be administered with every error. The teacher knows that even MILD shocks hurt and can only imagine how bad the DANGEROUS ones must be.

I'll ask you the question that Milgram asked of psychiatrists and random samples of college students and working adults: "How far with the shocks will the "teacher" go?"

Most people predicted that all "teachers" would quit the experiment after one or two shocks and certainly no higher than the demonstration shock each teacher received. Furthermore, most people predicted that most teachers would refuse to give any shocks at all. What do you think?

Milgram ran this basic experiment with some interesting variations. Sometimes he separated the teacher from the learner. Thus, George would be strapped to the shock box in the next room and the volunteer would communicate via an intercom. Sometimes the teacher and the learner were in the same room but at different desks many feet apart.

And sometimes, the volunteer had to sit right next to George and hold his arm down on a "shock plate" to make sure the shock was administered correctly. (Think about having to hold someone down like that.)

Unintended Consequences

"Well, when he first began to cry out in pain, I realized this was hurting him. This got worse when he just blocked and refused to answer. There was I. I'm a nice person, I think, hurting somebody, and caught up in what seemed a mad situation ... and in the interest of science, one goes through with it." "Mr. Braverman," a participant in the study, from home.swbell.net/revscat/perilsOfObedience.html.

Sometimes as the experiment progressed and the shocks became more intense, George would start complaining about chest pains and his weak heart. He was under a doctor's care, and these shocks were really hurting. Once, when George was in a different room, he started pounding on the wall and hollering for the teacher to stop, to stop, to please stop.

What do you think happened? How many people quit the experiment? How soon did they quit?

Results: They Did What?

First, no matter how close or how far apart George and the volunteer were, at least 10 percent of the teachers would go all the way and deliver the highest, most dangerous shocks. When George was in the other room, more than 60 percent of the teachers went all the way and complied fully with the demands of the study. And of the hundreds of people who participated in this study, fewer than 10 refused to participate at all. In other words, a significant number of people were compliant to the demands of the authority figure—even if it meant hurting another person.

To summarize, most people demonstrated a surprisingly high degree of compliance. Few "teachers" refused to participate. Most went much farther than predicted, and many teachers went all the way.

The Big Secret: A Confederate

Here's an important postscript: in case you are worrying about George … it was all a setup. George was a confederate who was in on the experiment from the beginning. George simply acted out a script and was always selected as the learner every time. Now, to make the story work, the volunteer was given a real shock from that shock box, but there was a catch. The shock box was really an empty shell and did not control any voltage. The real shock came from a small battery hidden in the shock box. Also at the end of the experiment, all this deception was explained to the volunteer. Interestingly, no one who participated in any of Milgram's experiments reported any serious upset during the debriefing after the experiment. Most people were relieved and pleased that George was okay. No one complained to Milgram or Yale University or even wrote an angry letter to the newspaper.

Unintended Consequences

The Milgram study worked because people perceived "science" as a profound authority. Given the results, this evaluation was clearly misplaced.

Obedience and Thoughtfulness

There are two general reasons for obedience. The first one I call the "shallow" reason, and the second one is "deep." These are not the only explanations for obedience, but they are a good beginning for more discussion.

The Path of Least Resistance

The shallow reason for obedience is simple: people often do not think about what they're doing. As I discuss in Chapter 6, our mental state varies wildly. Sometimes we are very engaged and highly thoughtful, considering all the implications in the persuasive situation. Other times we are just coasting along, giving just enough thought to keep from looking foolish.

From this perspective, obedience is the path of least thinking and least resistance. Obedience is mentally easy. It's easier to assume that the authority knows what is best and to just do what you are told to do. Milgram's research and the violent human record all stand as evidence of how far this lazy thinking can go. If we assume that people can be peripheral processors with issues of life and death, it is simple to assume that people will be even lazier thinkers in the normal comings and goings of everyday living.

A Matter of Survival

The deep reason for obedience is survival. Humans are not biologically well-equipped for survival in the cold, cruel world. We are not the strongest, the biggest, the fastest, or the meanest creatures on the planet. We cannot handle the large variations in climate and weather that many other animals have little problem with. Thus, as individuals, most people have very little chance of surviving alone.

Therefore, one of the primary reasons humans have survived is their ability to form groups. By banding together, we can pool our resources and translate our individual abilities into powerful tools and weapons. It becomes imperative, then, that we do what it takes to make groups survive.

The next step in this logic is obvious. One of the ways we make groups function effectively is through obedience to the hierarchy of the group. If obedience stops, then the group will slow down and eventually fall apart.

Seen from this perspective, negative examples of obedience are not necessarily failures of the receivers but more often failures of the sources. Deep obedience is a reasoned and rational action. It translates to survival and success at the most basic level. Only when unethical or incompetent sources corrupt the proper use of obedience does it become dangerous.

To summarize, both of the shallow and the deep reasons for obedience can be operating in the same situation. They are not exclusive or even antagonistic forces.

Practical Implications

Obedience is a powerful human response. Under many conditions, it is easy to elicit—even when it leads to dangerous or painful consequences. And if you think about it, when a source gets obedience from a group of receivers, that source can be a wildly effective influence agent. (Imagine trying to directly talk somebody into shocking another person. It would be next to impossible to produce a set of arguments and evidence that would directly persuade people to do this. However, set up a hierarchy and give people instructions …)

> **Wise Lines**
>
> The social psychology of this century reveals a major lesson: often it is not so much the kind of person a man is as the kind of situation in which he finds himself that determines how he will act.
>
> —Stanley Milgram from *Obedience to Authority* (1974)

Four Points of Obedience

There are at least four points you should consider about obedience:

1. **Encourage people to think and act independently.** Recall the shallow reason for obedience. It's merely the path of least resistance. It requires no central thinking—just a simple acceptance of what a source tells you to do. If people think more carefully about a situation, it's less likely that they will be swept along by authority, peer pressure, or mere convention. The key idea here is thinking, not defiance. We should teach and encourage each other to think about authority and compliance. There is a fine line between questioning authority and defying authority. If you have authority, you should permit people to focus much more on the former than the latter.

2. **Be careful when you assign authority to those in your command.** Do you think that most of the volunteers in Milgram's study typically used shocks and punishments in their daily lives? I doubt it. Most people (most of the time) do not deliberately use

pain to control or influence others. Yet, many of the volunteers went to the highest levels of shocks when given the authority to do so. Now, if adults can be this way, imagine how children and adolescents react when they have authority. Imagine how new, young employees would react?

3. **Question your own use of authority.** Many of us achieve some level of authority, especially by mere length of service. Do you use it properly? Many of us have deliberately harmed people under our authority. We may have embarrassed, humiliated, or shamed them. We may have denied them rewards or given them punishments. And we did it for a reason—to make them grow up, to teach them a lesson about life, or perhaps to make a big point. We had the authority to do these things, and we used it to accomplish some goal. My question is this: would you have done these hurtful things if you did not have the authority to do so? Another question: could you have accomplished these goals without merely using authority?

4. **Understand how your own obedience may reduce your effectiveness.** Authority responses move in both directions. Some people are obedient to you, and you are obedient to others. And to the extent that you demand obedience from others, you in turn may give the same measure of obedience to others. Thus, while we may worry about our children or employees becoming the helpless volunteer in Milgram's study, we must not lose sight of our own risks.

The Sizzle

How do you defend yourself if you ever get caught in the real world as the learner receiving shocks from a teacher/authority figure? Milgram found that many participants in the teacher role would stop complying with orders to continue with the shocks the first time the learner began to complain. It didn't work all the time, but it was the only thing Milgram found that stopped the punishment. So, if you think that authority is punishing you unfairly, complain about it to the person in the authority role. It won't work all the time, but for some people your complaint will cause them to think about the ethics of the situation and stop.

Making Choices

Every time a supervisor gives us an order, we have the choice to be merely obedient or to be something else. For example, after a teacher's strike, one teacher related to me an interesting example of teacher obedience. This teacher was part of a legal picket line that was gathered in a legal place in front of the school. The teachers had parked their cars in front of the school and were now picketing in a quiet and peaceful manner. The principal of these teachers waved one of them into the building and then told her that the teachers must move their cars (from their legal parking spots). This teacher then went back out to the picket line, instructed her colleagues of this event, and then everybody moved their cars.

From this common and rather simple example, we can easily move into more serious concerns. Each of us knows of examples where someone has "followed orders" and done things that were personally repugnant to them. For example, teachers will be ordered to suspend students unfairly or to unfairly lift a student suspension. Middle-level managers will be ordered to terminate some employees improperly in order to hit the bottom line. You might have succumbed to that kind of pressure in your own life.

This is not meant to raise a revolution here. It is meant to raise awareness. Each of us must make our own choices and defend those choices to ourselves and to others. You should, however, see how the powerful and very human motivation to obey can make things happen in ways you do not intend.

The Least You Need to Know

- Obedience is the receiver response to a source's legitimate authority.
- Obedience and authority are basic elements of our human nature.
- Questioning authority can reduce automatic compliance.
- Our compliance to authority can have surprising consequences.
- Physical and psychological distance between the authority source and the receiver increases obedience.

Chapter 6

Thoughtful Persuasion

In This Chapter

- Understanding how people think
- Deploying the four principles of Thoughtful Persuasion
- Objective, biased, and cue-based thinking
- The keys to Thoughtful Persuasion

The eager persuasion beginner often jumps into persuasion like it's a debate—where the person with the best reasons wins and the other guy must change. It doesn't matter whether the debate concerns voting for the president, selling shoes, the 1927 Yankees baseball team, country music, or who's going to take the kids to soccer practice: the tactic is always the same. This approach is in the right church but the wrong pew. You most surely can move people with thoughtful, active, and complex persuasion, but you have to understand the moving parts. Most particularly, you have to understand the "persuasion light bulb."

Are They Thinking? The Persuasion Light Bulb

If you want to change people through *Thoughtful Persuasion*, you need to understand how people think and in particular how they think in persuasive situations—in other words, how brightly their persuasion light bulb burns. Most people cannot observe themselves to gain the needed insight. It's like trying to observe your form while you're swinging a golf club, a tennis racquet, or a ball bat. If you watch yourself while you're actually trying to swing, you'll fail. It's the same thing with thinking. It's really hard to think about thinking while you're thinking! That's why most of us are so bad at Thoughtful Persuasion.

> **def•i•ni•tion**
>
> **Thoughtful Persuasion** is the central route to change that requires a high-WATT processor, strong arguments, and that "long conversation" in our heads.

From ancient Aristotle to modern scientists, we've accumulated good evidence of Thoughtful Persuasion. It's more complicated than just having the "best" reasons. And it is easy to fail at it. But, armed with 2,000 years of studies and a desire to make the world a better place, you can improve your skill.

The Four Principles of Thoughtful Persuasion

Thoughtful Persuasion has a checklist of four key principles you must understand and deploy correctly. If you fail at any one principle, your Thoughtful Persuasion attempt will fail. Consider the list as a whole:

1. A person uses two routes of thinking: central or peripheral.
2. Situational and personality variables influence which route a person uses.
3. Persuasion plays have different effects depending on the route used.

4. Change achieved through the central route is more persistent over time, more resistant to counter-arguments, and more predictive of future behavior than change from the peripheral route.

Mull these over and open a mental landscape for them. Two routes of thinking … situation and personality determine which route … different tools have different effects depending on the route … outcomes vary with the route. This "route of thinking" idea gets repeated a lot, doesn't it?

Two Paths of Persuasion

The central route refers to someone who thinks carefully and with much effort. The thought process is active, creative, and alert. The peripheral route, in contrast, is at the other extreme. Here, people are not thinking carefully and instead skim along the surface of ideas. They think enough to be aware of the situation, but they do not think carefully enough to catch flaws, errors, and inconsistencies in persuasive messages.

Now we'll apply this concept to Thoughtful Persuasion. The choice between the two routes depends on a person's Willingness and Ability To Think (WATT). High-WATT thinkers have a ton of motivation and skill. They are locked and loaded on the topic. In contrast, low-WATT thinkers conserve their mental resources for more important things and instead travel the peripheral route. Imagine that your mind is a light bulb on a dimmer switch. When you are high WATT, the bulb is burning brightly. When you are thoughtless, the bulb is dim. Because we're on a dimmer switch, the bulb brightness can range between these two extremes. Think about this common example.

Peripheral shopper (PS) is looking for a can of spaghetti sauce in the grocery store. PS finds a shelf filled with many different brands, prices, and sizes. Reaching up, PS grabs one, thinking, "Gee, that's a pretty red label. I'll bet it tastes good."

Central shopper (CS), waiting impatiently behind PS, scans the shelf of sauce cans with the cold, calculating eye of a poker champion. As PS ambles down the aisle, CS strides forward with great concentration, thinking, "Yes, but the sodium content is probably off the chart, so what about the percentage of tomato—all that lycopene, a natural antioxidant. But look at the price! Good grief, you could buy a peck of tomatoes for that price. But then you'd have to clean the tomatoes yourself, then cut them and lose a finger—plus, who knows what kind of pesticides they used on the tomatoes. And I don't even what to think about those greedy corporate farms that pay slave wages …"

We all have an ongoing conversation running in our heads. On any given topic, sometimes the conversation is short, and sometimes it's long. Sometimes the content of the conversation is relevant, sharp, focused, balanced, analytic, articulated, and thorough. Sometimes the content of the conversation is just plain simple.

When these thoughts are about the persuasive situation, the conversation is called central-route processing. In the shopping example, CS has a focused, long conversation with considerations of health, price, and effort. PS also thinks about the situation, but with fewer thoughts and thoughts that were not exactly crucial (sauce in a can with a "pretty red label" will taste better?).

Let's make two sharp points of exception right now:

1. Just because the conversation is short doesn't mean it's always peripheral. "They all taste the same to me, so give me the cheapest" is a short conversation, but it's central. Sometimes central-route thinking is shorter because it cuts right to the chase and finds the key element that determines the change.
2. Just because the conversation is long doesn't mean it's central. If the thoughts are irrelevant to the situation, it doesn't matter how many of them you generate. For example, if our shopper is having a great and involved conversation that includes humming along to the music and remembering that time back in high school (classical conditioning with music and old memories) and wondering what happened to that fabulous blonde and that one date—wow—then, "Oops, I just walked past the spaghetti sauce. Isn't that on the list? Hey, that red label looks good. I'll bet that tastes great." You've got a long conversation, and it's peripheral.

Realize that when we are on the central route, we have a longer conversation in our heads that contains topical, relevant thoughts. In contrast, when we're on the peripheral route, we have shorter conversations with more irrelevant thoughts.

Unintended Consequences

Thoughtful Persuasion does not require red-faced arguing. You want the "other guy" to do all the work. Your part in this play is simple: make sure the other guy is high WATT, make sure he finds good arguments, and give him time to have the long conversation in his head. None of this requires a lot of talking, yelling, or arguing from you. In fact, you'll make things worse if you make Thoughtful Persuasion a debate.

Different People in Different Situations

People can move back and forth between the two routes. Sometimes we are central; other times we are peripheral. The route we use depends on situational and personality factors. For example, if the situation has strong relevance for us (imagine you see an editorial titled, *People Should Be Executed for Reading Practical Persuasion Books)*, chances are we will use the central route of thinking. Now if the situation has little relevance to us (you see an editorial titled, *People Should Be Executed for Dressing Like Penguins)*, chances are we will use the peripheral route of thinking. Situational factors affect our WATTage and shift the route.

People also have strong personality preferences for routes of thinking. Some people have a high need for cognition and typically think carefully about things most of the time. In contrast, some people have a low need for cognition and typically think as little as possible about a situation. In between are most people who are sensitive to situational factors.

Here's a short quiz to determine your need for cognition. For each statement, pick one of the following responses, then add your points.

Strongly agree	1
Disagree	2
Neutral	3
Agree	4
Strongly agree	5

1. I prefer complex to simple problems.
2. I like to have the responsibility of handling a situation that requires a lot of thinking.
3. I would rather do something that is sure to challenge my thinking than something that requires little thinking.
4. I look for situations where there is a likely chance I will have to think.
5. I like tasks that require lots of thought.

Your possible score can range from a low of 5 to a high of 25. Most people score between 10 and 20, with the average being 15. If you score more than 20, you're got the burning desire for thinking—while if you score less than 10, you run away from thinking like your hair's on fire. Remember, this is your general preference, but you can shift depending on the circumstances.

There's a tendency to equate this individual difference with intelligence. Yes, people who are smarter also tend to think about everything (including spaghetti sauce). But simply because you think a lot doesn't mean you are smarter. Hey … increase your intelligence quotient (IQ) score by thinking more thoughts as you take an IQ test! Notice the color or tone of the paper, the typeface, the spacing format … count the number of words in the question, compare the proportion of vowels and consonants … yeah, a scholarship to MIT awaits!

Thus our route can be driven by the situation or our personality predispositions. Even people who prefer to be peripheral thinkers can still shift into the central route when the situation calls for it. And people who are normally high-WATT thinkers can be situationally distracted and go down the peripheral route.

Arguments and Cues

When people take the central route, certain elements are important. While reading that editorial on executing persuasion readers, the central thinker looks for facts, evidence, examples, reasoning, and logic. We call these things "arguments." In contrast, when people take the peripheral route, other things are important. Because arguments (facts, evidence, reasoning, and so on) require cognitive effort and energy, the peripheral thinker won't use them very much. They will use easier-to-process information instead. Things such as the attractiveness, friendliness, or expertise of the source are more influential for the peripheral thinker. We call these things "cues."

Knowing nothing more about arguments and cues than what you've just read, it should be obvious that each tool works differently. Arguments work through that long, focused internal conversation in our heads. In essence, an argument is a chunk of meat that we run through the sausage grinder of central-route processing. In goes the chunk, it gets ground up, and out comes strings of thoughts.

Cues, in contrast, are simple and direct. We respond quickly in either a positive or a negative way, then make a change. If an attractive person hands us a can of spaghetti sauce and says, "You'll like this. Buy it.", that cue will generate a warm feeling and we'll probably buy the product. If someone dressed like a physician says, "You'll like this. Take it.", that cue will generate a trusting feeling and we'll probably take the pill.

The Sizzle

Arguments and cues are like rewards and punishments of reinforcement in that you find them by the way the operate, rather than by how they look. Just as there is no cookbook for reinforcers, there is no cookbook for arguments and cues.

Each persuasion tool is effective in its own different way. Arguments require serious processing time and work. Cues require immediate reactions.

Different Outcomes

Change achieved through the central route is more persistent over time, more resistant to change, and more predictive of behavior than influence from the peripheral route. When people are thinking centrally, if they do change, it's more likely to stick precisely because they thought about it more carefully, fully, and deeply. For peripheral thinkers, however, any influence is likely to be rather short lived—simply because they did not really think that much.

Now, these assumptions say nothing about magnitude differences. There is no claim made that the central path leads to more change in the short term compared to the peripheral path (or vice-versa). This means that regardless of path, we can get the same amount of immediate change in a receiver. Thus, in the short term—whether the receiver is central or peripheral and whether we provide arguments or cues—we can still get the same amount of change. This is very important to remember. Both paths can lead to the same amount of change. Persistence, resistance, and prediction, however, favor the central route.

What Kind of Thinker Are You?

Researchers make a split in the central route. Several studies and common-sense thinking reveal that central-route thinkers may be on two different sub-routes, either objective or biased. In both cases, the person is high WATT, but he or she can direct that thinking in two different directions. Objective central thinkers focus clearly on the arguments and follow the arguments to a conclusion. Biased central thinkers, on the other hand, let their existing beliefs distort those arguments. They make arguments fit existing beliefs. Let's look at an example.

Which candidate should you vote for in the next election? While the answer to that question is not as simple and unambiguous as "What does 2 + 2 equal?", it's possible to make voting selection a highly rational and empirical process. An objective thinker does his or her best to find all of the relevant information under these uncertain conditions—and if he or she can't find the "true" answer, at least he or she can find the "best" answer.

In contrast, the biased thinker will not follow the data wherever it leads but rather will tend to select arguments and generate internal conversations that are congenial to an existing bias. In our election example, if you are a political conservative, chances are pretty good that you hold favorable beliefs and attitudes toward candidates with a conservative orientation. When you think about the candidates, you will unconsciously tend to pick arguments that bias toward the conservative. For example, you'll look for candidate voting records only on the conservative positions (foreign policy and free markets, for example) and ignore more liberal positions (such as human rights and international cooperation). And although the biased thinker is elaborating on arguments carefully and with much effort, the deck is stacked in favor of an existing position.

We can contrast both objective and biased central processing with the simpler peripheral processing that relies on cues. Here, the receiver does the minimum amount of thinking needed for the situation. Instead of searching for arguments, the cue-based processor finds the obvious cues, reacts to them, and then changes based on the cue. We take a detailed look at cues in Chapter 7.

The Sizzle

Prejudice and stereotyping can be understood as biased processing, where people use an existing template or belief to select and interpret arguments. Prejudiced people are often highly thoughtful but biased by their existing beliefs.

What Thoughtful Persuasion Requires

After reading this chapter, you should understand why Thoughtful Persuasion is so difficult. It *is* complicated, but it can be done. You need to focus on four key points.

Control the Light Bulb

The main point for Thoughtful Persuasion is the receiver's mental state. If you misunderstand that, everything else you do is just plain luck. For any persuasive situation, you must determine your target's current WATTage and then figure out how to move it to the desired brightness.

To determine the current WATTage state, do two things: first, watch your target; second, ask him or her questions. There is a huge behavioral difference between high-WATT and low-WATT thinkers. Just observe your targets and ask yourself whether they're alert, attentive, active, focused, and aware. Then, ask questions of your targets. When you do this, do they hear the questions, respond quickly, and stay on topic? To the extent that you answer "yes" to both questions, you can assume your target is high WATT and ready for arguments.

If you plan on Thoughtful Persuasion but your target is low WATT, you have two choices: wait until your target naturally brightens or else turn the dimmer switch yourself. There's nothing wrong with waiting for a better moment (remember Rule No. 5 from Chapter 3: If You Can't Succeed, Don't Try). Everyone's light bulb brightness varies, and you can wait. But you can also turn the dimmer switch.

You'll recall from Chapter 2 that WATT stands for Willingness and Ability To Think. You can turn the dimmer switch by increasing your target's willingness or ability to think right now.

The best way to increase willingness is to make your information personally relevant to the target. When people believe the situation is personally important to them, they are much more likely to think centrally about it. If the situation holds little relevance, they will stay in the peripheral route. So you must demonstrate how the issue is meaningful and relevant to your targets if you want them to be central thinkers.

The second factor you need to consider is ability. When people have the ability to work harder, they are more likely to do so. What makes people better able to think harder? If you're selling your product to a mass audience that includes Hispanics, you might consider writing some of your ads in Spanish. If you're selling a high-tech product to a group of low-tech buyers, you might translate your PowerPoint presentation from jargon into plain language. Basically, what we're talking about here is comprehension. Can your target understand what you're talking about? Don't blame your customers, clients, suppliers, friends, or family for their lack of understanding. You are trying to persuade them. If they don't change, you did something wrong. Remember Rule No. 2 from Chapter 3: It's About the Other Guy!

Finding Strong Arguments

Once we've established the route, we have to provide the correct persuasion tool. Central thinkers want arguments. It should be easy to produce lists of arguments—and away we go. But hold on a minute and think about this.

Your teenage son needs a new pair of sneakers. Assume that both you and your son are going to be central thinkers as you decide which sneakers to buy. You both want arguments. Consider yours first: cost, durability, convenience of purchase. Now, consider your son's arguments: who endorses them, do the other guys wear them, would that great-looking blonde go out with me if I had them?

You see the problem. Arguments depend on the target. Everything listed for you is an argument, and most parents would probably have the same list of cost, durability, and convenience near the top. But of course, everything listed for the teenager would show up on every other teenager's list of arguments, too.

Who's right? From a Thoughtful Persuasion perspective, it depends on the target. If you're working at a shoe store and you see a parent and teen walk through the door, you've got a problem to solve. Who controls the purchase? If you think the parent is in charge of the purchase, then you run the first list of arguments. If you think the teen is in charge, you run the second list. Best of all, run both lists and persuade them both!

Developing a list of arguments for any given persuasion situation requires some careful thought on your part. You must ask, "What is of central importance to the receiver?" If you can figure out the answers to this question and the receiver is in the central route, then you will be effective as a persuader.

This is an important point, and I want to give you an example to illustrate the "relative" meaning of arguments. The example concerns teenagers and smoking. In the past, persuasion sources (parents, teachers, and the federal government) have tried to prevent teenage smoking with arguments based on health ("Smoking causes cancer"). And despite the best efforts of all concerned, teens continued to smoke. Why? The health argument lacks central importance to a teenager. Teenagers still embrace the myth of immortality, and they believe they will live forever—maybe even to 40. Threats about cancer and death are empty.

New approaches use different arguments and have shown better results. The new arguments are based on social factors ("You smell bad if you smoke" and "No one wants to kiss somebody with cigarette breath") and more lately on control factors ("Greedy tobacco companies are manipulating you"). Peer acceptance and independence are of central importance to teens. These arguments appear to be more powerful to teenagers and therefore produce the kind of change we prefer.

There is no cookbook list of arguments because argument quality depends upon the receiver. To produce good arguments, you must understand your receivers and be able to think the way they do. However, Thoughtful Persuasion provides two excellent standards for your planning. First, the argument must pass inspection with people who are alert, active, and involved. You cannot run a weak argument in front of a high-WATT processor. Second, the argument must affect that conversation in our heads. A "good" argument should make the other guy engage in that nice, long conversation.

Remember: It's About the Other Guy

Everything about Thoughtful Persuasion cuts back to the other guy. You must determine the current mental state of the other guy. If it's low-WATT and you want to go the central route, you must figure out how to motivate and enable the other guy right now. You must develop arguments that make the other guy engage in the long conversation. Even the outcomes of change depend on the specific characteristics of the other guy.

What's great about Thoughtful Persuasion is that it provides a blueprint for looking at your target. It trains you to become a more consistent and careful observer of people. How do they look and act when they are high WATT versus low WATT? What causes the dimmer switch to move for them? Do they reveal information that might be an "argument" to be used later? What kind of cues appeal to them most?

The principles of Thoughtful Persuasion give us insight into human nature and how we respond to the world. And, just as these principles help us understand others, they also tell us something hidden about ourselves. Do you understand your own dimmer switch? Can you distinguish between information that is a strong argument for you but not for your spouse or best friend?

Think Like They Think

During the mid-1980s, Burger King spent millions of dollars on a major advertising campaign. The purpose of this campaign was not merely selling a few more burgers but to challenge McDonald's for leadership in the competitive fast-food market. Burger King did careful planning and quiet pretesting, then unleashed its ad attack.

The campaign revolved around a character named Herb, a balding, thin fellow who wore glasses, too-short black pants, and white socks. Herb represented a whimsical sort of "every man" with whom everyone could identify.

But … it didn't work. No one identified with Herb, and instead everyone made a lot of Herb jokes. The ad campaign backfired, and Burger King actually sold fewer burgers. The campaign, scheduled to run for more than a year, died within a month. Somehow, Burger King terribly misunderstood the market and produced messages that no one found to be compelling, influential, or even enjoyable.

And these guys were professionals! Money, training, research, experience—and kaboom, it all went up in smoke. What hope is there for you?

First, remember Rule No. 3 from Chapter 3: People Tend to Resist Change. Persuading isn't easy, even when you're a pro. Recall Rule No. 1: There Are No "Laws" of Persuasion, Only Rules. There are no living geniuses, wizards, or sorcerers. As a result, no one has yet devised a sure-fire, systematic method for inventing strong arguments *before* you use them.

Usually, the worst arguments are precisely the ones we prefer. We offer arguments that are compelling and powerful to us. We tend to assume that other people will respond the same way. That's a bad assumption.

The best way to develop good arguments is through a combination of art and science. The art element is accurately observing your targets. For example, if I wanted to open a chain of fast-food restaurants for monkeys, I'd hire Jane Goodall as my argument consultant. She spent most of her life living in the jungles with monkeys and knows them better than I do. Her advice on the monkey light bulb dimmer switch and monkey arguments would probably be very good because of her incredible personal knowledge of and experience with my target customers. Thus, the art part of arguments is simply living with the monkeys and all that implies.

The science part is planning, preparing, and pretesting. Here, you're wearing the white lab coat, testing your latest potion on many handy volunteers, then carefully observing the effects. If you're using persuasion on the job where you have a lot of contacts with many different people (customers, students, subordinates, supervisors, and volunteers), you can pick a couple of likely suspects and see how it goes. Think about it. What could have worked better? Try it again with the new wrinkles. You're like a comedian trying new material on friends and family, then in real small clubs before you go big time with your act. But, through the entire process, you should carefully monitor your success and failure—thinking more like a scientist.

The Least You Need to Know

- Thoughtful Persuasion requires a high-WATT processor, strong arguments, and opportunity to think.
- Monitor and/or manipulate the persuasion light bulb—look for signs of interest, awareness, and alertness
- Objective processors want arguments, and peripheral processors want cues Make sure you match the right play to the proper WATTage.
- It's a good argument if your receiver thinks it's a good argument, not if you think it's a good argument. It's About the Other Guy!
- Survey the monkeys and pretest on volunteers: use art and science to invent arguments.

Chapter 7

UnThoughtful Persuasion: Cues

In This Chapter

- Working with dimmer bulbs
- Comparison, Liking, Authority, Reciprocity, Commitment/Consistency, and Scarcity (CLARCCS) cues
- Using a variety of low-WATT tactics
- Choosing a route of persuasion

Ever look in your closet and wonder why you bought *that?* Maybe it's a pair of slacks, a blouse, a tie, or a pair of sneakers. You only vaguely remember purchasing it—did you get it at a store, or did you order it online? And as you look at it while dressing for the day, you recoil in disgust. Look at those colors! A pirate wouldn't wear that! And it looks like it would fit a penguin. What were you thinking?

That question answers itself. There was nothing in your head when you bought that, so you made a choice that sure seemed good at the time. But now, with just a little thought, you realize your error. In this chapter, we travel down the peripheral route with careful attention to persuasion cues. Don't be surprised when you see how somebody else used these cues on you to get you to buy *that*.

The Persuasion Light Bulb: Low-WATT Version

A cue is a persuasion tool that persuades the low-WATT thinker. Thus, a cue is anything you say or do that requires little or no thinking from the receiver yet still persuades a change. We can contrast this *UnThoughtful Persuasion* with Chapter 6 on Thoughtful Persuasion. You'll recall the central route requires a high-WATT thinker and the opportunity for that long conversation on strong arguments. With the peripheral route, no one wants to work that hard and instead is more easily and UnThoughtfully influenced with cues.

def•i•ni•tion

UnThoughtful Persuasion is the peripheral-route change that occurs with a low-WATT processor using cues.

Beginning persuaders often find the notion of cues unbelievable. They want to start a debate and run a raging discussion filled with facts, evidence, examples, and careful reasoning. Cues? How ridiculous. Yet, if you read most popular press books on persuasion and influence—especially with a sales or marketing emphasis—you'll find that the majority of them deal with cues.

Now, these other books will not always use the term "cue" to describe their topic. Popular press books sometimes call them "heuristics," "mental shortcuts," "choice architecture," or "click, whir." A researcher named Daniel Kahneman even won a Nobel Prize in economics for his work about 30 years ago on these persuasion plays. He called them "heuristics" and meant that label as "a rule of thumb." Another researcher, Robert Cialdini, described the process as "click, whir" to mimic the sound of a fixed action pattern turning on, then whirring as it runs. More recently, Cass Sunstein and Richard Thaler have applied cues to public policy and called their approach "choice architecture," which means deliberately presenting options in different ways to produce a more likely decision.

Whatever the label, realize that these tactics operate on the peripheral route. You start with a low-WATT processor, then add a persuasive tactic that requires little thinking to understand (and in fact, a tactic that works better the less thinking the receiver uses)—and we're all on the same journey. But the key element is the light bulb in our minds. People don't stop "thinking" just because they are low WATT, but the nature and quality of that "thinking" is very different compared to the high-WATT state. Even if you have trouble grasping the nature of low-WATT processing, just observing that you can change people with cues should be enough to make you realize we're dealing with a horse of a very different persuasion color.

CLARCCS Cues

In this chapter, I focus on an approach made popular by Professor Robert Cialdini. As Cialdini describes in his book, *Influence* (see Appendix A), he learned about real-life persuasion by living with professionals. He took part-time jobs with sales groups that pushed vacuum cleaners, aluminum siding, or dance lessons. He hung out with cops who worked the Bunco squad. He worked with fund-raising groups and advertisers. And he did this as a trainee, not as a scientist, so that the people felt comfortable with him. Now, being a good professor, Cialdini saw immediate connections between these real-world jobs and the theories he taught in the ivory tower. (It happens sometimes.)

From his experiences, he derived six general CLARCCS cues of influence. CLARCCS cues appear to transcend occupation, region, personality, gender, religion, ethnicity, and education. In other words, they work in many different situations. These six cues also share another important similarity: they work.

The six CLARCCS cues are:

- **C**omparison
- **L**iking
- **A**uthority
- **R**eciprocity
- **C**ommitment/**C**onsistency
- **S**carcity

Take a minute and look over that list, considering each term. Ask yourself a question such as these: "If my target was low WATT, could I persuade them with Liking or Authority?" "How could reciprocity make a low-WATT thinker more persuadable?" Although these cues work when the "other guy" isn't thinking, they work better when you're thinking about both the cue and the "other guy!"

Comparison: When Others Are Doing It, You Should, Too

You're walking down the street and notice ahead of you three or four people just standing there looking straight up in the air. As you move closer to them, what do you do? You look straight up in the air, too.

Is it a bird? Is it a plane?

No, it's the comparison cue. When others are doing it, you should, too.

When we aren't thinking very carefully, we use the behavior of other people as a guide to what we should think or do. We essentially compare our behavior against the standard of what everybody else is doing. If there is a discrepancy between our actions and what we observe in others, we change. Here are more examples of the comparison cue.

The Sizzle

In the great novel *War and Peace,* Leo Tolstoy presents a princess who understands the uses of comparison for social effect during the grand party that opens the book. "From time to time Princess Helene smoothed the folds of her dress, and whenever the story produced an effect she glanced at Anna Pavlovna, at once adopted just the expression she saw on Anna's face, and again released her radiant smile." Here we see comparison employed in a subtle way. A woman who wanted to impress people used the expression on other people's faces to guide her own actions.

TV producers will add a laugh track to even the most witless situation comedy as a way of inducing our laughter. And it works. If there are two audiences watching the same comedy, but one comedy has a laugh track added to it and the other doesn't, guess which audience will laugh more? Right. The one with the laugh track.

I suspect TV producers learned this trick from the theater. In the past (and it may still go on today), theatrical producers hired professional audience members. These highly skilled people would show up to a new play, musical, or opera and provide the "proper" response at the right time. They would start applauding when the star entered, begin crying when the heroine died, or erupt into gales of laughter when the clowns appeared. This would elicit the desired response from the audience, who would automatically start clapping, sobbing, or giggling on cue.

Even religious groups are aware of and use the comparison rule. There is a practice known as "salting the collection plate." Before the collection plates are handed out to the faithful, ushers will throw several different bills or checks onto the plate. Thus, no one ever gets an empty plate. This makes a considerable difference in contributions. People are slow to fill up an empty collection plate, and a little "salt" gets things going. Also, the heavier the salt, the stronger the contribution. That is, you get more contributions if you salt the plate with tens and twenties than if you salt it with ones and fives.

The Sizzle

"Upward" comparisons (more positive) motivate action; "downward" comparisons (more negative) discourage action.

Liking: When You Like the Source, You'll Do What Is Requested

Joe Girard sells cars and trucks. He sells a lot of them. As a matter of fact, some consider him to be the greatest car salesman in the world. What's his secret?

Every month, Joe Girard sends a handwritten card to every customer he has ever had and signs it, "I like you, Joe Girard." That's all.

Now, he does send out a lot of cards every month (13,000, he estimates), but he swears by the tactic. Is such a simple thing as, "I like you" sufficient for influence?

Here's another example. At a Tupperware party, a group of people who know each other come over to the house of a mutual friend. Everybody eats a little. Everybody chats a bit. Everybody has a little fun. Then, the mutual friend steps up and introduces a new person. And the new person breaks out the product: Tupperware.

Gee, isn't that new person friendly? Isn't that Tupperware grand? Everybody smiles, everybody laughs, and everybody buys something.

Of course, Tupperware is not the only product sold in this way. Mary Kay cosmetics has pushed a lot of makeup with these kind of parties. The important point is this: the basis of the sale is liking. The receiver likes somebody involved in the transaction. Maybe you like the sales person. Maybe you like the friend throwing the party. Exactly who you like is less relevant than the fact that you like somebody. (I'll also bet some comparison is operating here, too. You see other people buying things, so you buy, too.)

The Sizzle

Generate liking with smiles, appropriate laughter, and easy eye contact.

Here's the last example. Physically attractive people are very influential in our society, but the primary reason appears to be because we like attractive people. (If you do an experiment where you have one source who is attractive and likable and another source who is attractive and dislikable, only the likable source will be influential. So, it appears that attractiveness operates through liking.)

A researcher trained courtroom employees to rate the attractiveness (and indirectly, the likeability) of people accused of crimes as they came before a judge for the first time. The people were accused of a wide variety of misdemeanor charges. The meeting with the judge was to determine the amount of fines for the misdemeanors. The courtroom employees were not involved in the arrest and were only escorting the person.

What happened? Less-attractive people received fines two to three times larger than more attractive people. (Sometimes it's better to look good than to be good, right?)

Authority: When the Source Is an Authority, You Can Believe It

Like me, maybe you're old enough to remember the TV series *Marcus Welby, M.D.* The actor, Robert Young, portrayed a friendly, wise, and incredibly available physician who never lost a patient (except when it would increase the show's Nielsen ratings).

Most interesting was the fact that Robert Young parlayed his fame as Dr. Marcus Welby into a very productive sideline. He sold aspirin on TV ads—*as Dr. Marcus Welby.*

There were enough lazy thinkers out there who didn't realize that the guy in the ad selling aspirin was merely an actor and not the real thing. It didn't matter. Robert Young looked and acted like an authority. And sales of his brand of aspirin increased.

Eventually, the federal authorities got wise to this gimmick and cracked down on it. It's now illegal to use an actor in this way. So what have advertisers done? Their response and its impact is so amazing to me that it stands as the best example of how lazy we can be.

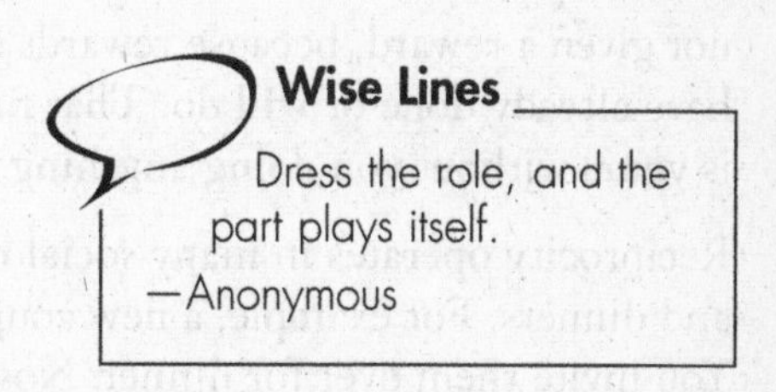

Here's the new trick. The advertisers will still use a popular actor to sell their aspirin and stay legal with their ads. Here's what happens. The famous TV doctor looks at the camera and says, "I'm no doctor, but I play one on TV—and here's the aspirin I recommend." And sales of that aspirin increase.

The authority rule is quite powerful and useful. Just recall Chapter 5!

Reciprocity: When Someone Gives You Something, You Should Give Something Back

You're walking down the street, minding your own business, as a stranger approaches in your direction. The stranger makes eye contact with you, then smiles. If you are like most people, you will automatically and thoughtlessly respond with a smile of your own as you continue down the street.

The stranger gives us something, and we give back something in return. It's a nice rule for meeting people, but how does it relate to influence? Ever get free gifts in the mail along with a request for a magazine subscription? "Here, keep this valuable prize," the letter goes, "as a token of our esteem. And by the way, if you like magazines, how about this one?" *Time* magazine used to send a free pencil with their subscription offers. The pencils were very small, very thin, and very red. And you got to keep it even if you didn't subscribe to the magazine. But, what the heck? *Time* is a pretty good magazine … and before you know it, you have a year's subscription.

The rule is very simple. First, the source gives you something. Once you accept it, you are now obligated to give something back. You are not given a reward, because rewards are given for something that you have already done or will do. That first something given by the source is yours without you doing anything to earn it.

Reciprocity operates in many social relationships—especially with visits and dinners. For example, a new couple moves into the neighborhood. You invite them over for dinner. Now, the new couple is obligated to invite you to dinner in return—even though you said nothing about it. And if the new couple fails to reciprocate (they don't invite you over) or fails to reciprocate in kind (you serve steak; they serve hot dogs), you may be angry. The compelling advantage to reciprocity stems from the unequal exchange between the source and the target. Typically, the persuasion source provides a gift but then receives a larger resource in return from the persuasion target. Take those gifts that accompany informational mailings from charitable groups for abandoned animals, disabled veterans, and ravaged rainforests. The gift is typically a cheap but useful item, such as personalized return address stickers that costs perhaps a penny per item and is probably a donation from a printing company that earns a tax write-off. The gift essentially costs the persuasion agent nothing, yet the agent will acquire a higher charitable return in both the number of targets who respond and the amount they give compared to a mailing without the free gift. The goal of reciprocity is to acquire that unequal exchange based on the natural human response to meet a favor sent with a favor returned.

Commitment/Consistency: When You Take a Stand, You Should Be Consistent

Earnest Salesperson: "Excuse me, but do you think that a good education is important for your kids?"

You: "Yes, of course."

Earnest Salesperson: "And do you think that kids who do their homework will get better grades?"

You: "Yes, I'm sure of that."

Earnest Salesperson: "And reference books would help kids do better on their homework, don't you think?"

You: "I'd have to say yes to that."

Earnest Salesperson: "Well, I sell reference books. May I come in and help improve your child's education?"

You: "Ahh, wait a minute ..."

This is the famous "four walls" sales technique. The salesperson asks four questions that in essence wall in the receiver—literally forcing the conclusion that those reference books must be purchased. The logical force comes from the commitment/consistency rule. When you take a stand on something, you must be consistent with it. This can be a very powerful tactic, and the business world is filled with variations on it.

Here's another one, called "bait and switch," and it's illegal in most states. It works in two steps. First, some attractive offer is presented as bait. The customer rises to the bait, demonstrating his or her interest in the product. Second, the bait is taken away and a new product (of lower value or higher cost) is presented. Many people will ruefully take the second offer.

For example, you need a new stove and you notice an ad for a really high-quality stove at a very good price. You think to yourself, "I'm going to buy a new stove." So, you pack up the kids and zoom over to the mall.

When you get there, a friendly salesperson greets you with a smile. "Ahh, you saw the ad … I guess you really want a new stove, don't you? Let's see if I can help you get what you need. I'll go back and check on it for you."

You, of course, are out of your mind at the prospect of getting this great stove at such a great price. You even let the kids act wilder than usual because you are so excited yourself. But wait.

The salesperson returns with some bad news and some good news. The bad news is that they just ran out of those advertised specials. The good news is that they just happen to have a similar stove right here that's yours for the taking, and it only costs $100 more. Not surprisingly, many people will buy the more expensive product—never catching on to the game.

The driving force is consistency. In these business games, the customer commits to some initial position ("I want to spend money in this store" or "I want to buy a new plasma screen TV"), and the salesperson simply forces the customer to maintain consistency with that initial position. This is an extremely powerful and popular persuasion tactic, and we will see more applications in Chapter 10.

Scarcity: When It's Rare, It's Good

I admit it: I am a closet fan of home shopping networks. If you have never seen these stations, it could be that you don't have cable TV. All the stations do is sell retail merchandise over the television. They will feature some product for 10 or 15 minutes. If you like it, you call its 800 number and place an order, which is mailed to you the same day.

There are several different home shopping stations, and they are extremely successful. The reason is because these people really understand the principles of influence and use them well. In particular, they use the rule of scarcity. They know that rare things are highly valued in our society.

What are some of their scarcity tricks?

They always have a little clock running in the corner of the screen. You only have 10 minutes to buy this precious beauty, and the clock lets you know how little time you have to make the buy of a lifetime. They make time the scarce resource.

They often have a counter on the screen, too. Sometimes the counter runs down with every sale. "We only have a limited number of these fabulous quilted party skirts, and when they're all gone, we will never sell them again." So, that counter starts with 100—and every time somebody calls, the counter decreases. They make the product scarce.

Scarcity is a time-honored tactic. How many times have you seen the phrases, "Limited Time Only," "Weekend Special," and "Sale Ends at Midnight"?

Here's a great one from photographer Olan Mills. They will take a zillion pictures of your child. They then send you one copy of each photo and ask you to choose the shots you like and the number of copies you want. Then (here's the scarcity trick), they say that you had better order plenty of pictures because they will destroy all the images after a certain date. How many parents can face the prospect of losing forever all those darling shots?

Control That Light Bulb

CLARCCS cues work because they are mental shortcuts for lazy thinkers. Receivers easily apply these cues to guide their thinking or action with a minimum of mental effort and activity. (And a lot of the time, the cues really are helpful and correct.) As soon as the receivers change routes of thinking from peripheral to central, these cues typically become useless.

Thus, if you want to apply any of the cues in your own situation, you must learn to use them with peripheral processors. To the extent that people are systematically thinking in the situation, these cues will not work and indeed can make the user look rather foolish.

Now please don't lose your head here and believe that CLARCCS cues only function as cues. Generally speaking, these persuasion plays function more effectively when you present them to a low-WATT processor ambling down the peripheral route. However, these variables can function differently under different conditions.

Take physical attractiveness, for example. Look at that pretty girl in the bikini or that cute guy in the swim trunks. Hubba-hubba! Scantily clad, attractive women and men do have an effect. But is it the swimwear that's a cue?

Let's say I'm running a new chain of physical fitness businesses. Join my training plan for six months, and I guarantee you'll like what you see. You'll look like that pretty blonde in the skimpy bathing suit or that hot guy in the tight jeans. Is a picture of a good-looking body a cue for a physical fitness business? I don't think so. In fact, I think it's an argument—and a strong argument, at that. Yeah, we know that we won't look exactly like the person in the picture, but if your fitness plan will help me drop 30 pounds of fat and tone my muscles, I will look more physically attractive.

Now, think about scarcity. It has to be a cue and only a cue, right? So, you mean that if something is only available for a short period of time or is running out that there's no argument there—no reason to get all high WATT? Of course, in a situation like this there's good reason to go high WATT. Suppose, we're talking about commodities such as oil, where there's a rising demand curve against a falling supply curve. So, if the price rises, it's because investors and consumers are cue-based processors? No way. Sometimes the operation of scarcity is not a cue, but rather a stark fact that demands high-WATT processing.

All of the variables in CLARCCS function persuasively when they hit as a cue. That, however, does not mean they cannot also function as an argument or a dimmer switch that affects the light bulb. You've always got to keep the functional nature of persuasion in the front of your mind. How any persuasion variable operates depends on what else is going on in the situation.

Unintended Consequences

Consider what happens when you misjudge the WATTage of a receiver. If you throw a cue at high-WATT processors, you'll be seen as a low-credibility source. They want arguments, crucial information they can think about, and here you are prancing around in your bathing suit or white lab coat or playing the commitment/consistency game. Not only are you likely to fail at persuasion, but you'll also appear incompetent and untrustworthy. Always monitor or manipulate WATTage before you make a persuasion play.

Comparing High WATT and Low WATT

Draw together the two ideas on thoughtful and UnThoughtful Persuasion. You clearly see the two routes to persuasion and realize that the light bulb controls the route people take. You also see the huge difference in the persuasion play between a high-WATT play (a bright bulb and lots of strong arguments with that long, involved mental conversation) and a low-WATT play (a dim bulb and pretty, shiny cues requiring little conversation). And you now have more respect and understanding for the big outcome differences between the two routes. Isn't it obvious why the central route leads to change that is more persistent, resistant, and predictive? Hey, just look in your closet, right?

You also now have a strong sense of how all of us shift back and forth between the routes in our daily lives. Even on the same topic or issue, we're not always central route or always peripheral route—but instead, we're like persuasion Rule No. 4 from Chapter 3 claims: All Persuasion Is Local. It depends, because everyone's situation is always a little different.

There is lots of practical and scientific evidence that demonstrates the usefulness of CLARCCS cues. Just start thinking like a salesperson. Create your own applications.

The Sizzle

How do you defend yourself against a persuasion source who is skillful with cues? You've got to know your WATTage. Cues will almost always fail with a high-WATT processor. Learn to recognize when you are low WATT. You might also consider leaving your credit card in the car when you go shopping in a low-WATT state of mind.

The Least You Need to Know

- Cues operate best in low-WATT conditions.
- Cues are also called heuristics, mental shortcuts, choice architecture, or click, whir.

- Remember the acronym CLARCCS for easy reference: Comparison, Liking, Authority, Reciprocity, Commitment/Consistency, and Scarcity.
- Make sure you have correctly assessed the receiver's WATTage before you pitch a cue—you'll look foolish if you throw a cue to a high-WATT hitter.
- Cues don't work with stupid people—they work with low-WATT people; remember the difference!

Chapter 8

The Two Step

In This Chapter

- Creating a setup with either "No!" or "Yes!"
- Real-world examples of doing the Two Step
- Effectiveness and limitations
- Why does it work?

Let's dance. We'll do a Two-Step number. Guess how many steps you need for this one? That's right: two! See how simple persuasion is? Feel the rhythm. Just two steps and you'll be persuading like a pro in no time.

There are two versions of the Two Step. The first one begins with the "No!" step, and the second begins with … what did you say? Good for you. That's right. The second one starts with "Yes!"

Ah-One, Ah-Two … Doing the Two Step

A stranger approaches you at the shopping mall one day and politely asks whether she can have a minute of your time. You stop and say, "Yes."

The stranger goes on to describe the importance of the local blood bank to the well-being of your community. (You nod your head in polite agreement, but you know there's a pitch coming.) Then, the stranger gets to the point: "Would you be willing to be a blood bank volunteer? You'd have to give 10 hours a week for the next year and solicit blood donations from the people of our community by contacting them over the phone or face-to-face. Will you give us your time for this worthy cause?"

Your mind races, "Ten hours a week? For a year? That's crazy. Volunteering is important, yes, but this is ..."

And so, you politely tell the stranger, "No, thanks."

The stranger looks disappointed and replies, "Well, if you can't give your time, could you at least give a unit of blood right now? We have a station set up right down this hall."

Now, this is a more reasonable request. And although you've never given blood, before you find yourself walking down that hallway with this stranger.

Something happened here.

A stranger stops a person. The stranger makes an extreme request. The person says, "No, thanks." The stranger makes a second, less-extreme request. The person says, "I'll do it."

Amazing as it may sound, this persuasive strategy is a reliable means of influencing people. It is also effective at getting behavior change, which can be the toughest kind of change to get. It doesn't work in every situation, and it's very important to know its limitations—but the *Two Step* (or sequential requests, as we scientists call it) is simple to implement and effective in outcome.

def•i•ni•tion

The **Two Step** is a sequential request message strategy that makes the receiver say either "Yes" or "No" to a first request to increase compliance to a second request (the real goal).

Take a Dance Lesson and Learn a New Move

From our example, you can see that this tactic has two steps. The first step is a setup. It's not the true target; rather, it's used to get the receiver in the right frame of mind. The second step is the real target. It's the action the requester really wants you to perform.

Now, if you think about it, you can do this Two Step two different ways. The first way is called the door in the face (DITF). The second way is called the foot in the door (FITD). Both dances require two steps, and both do a setup on the first step. Both have the real target on the second step. The difference is how the first step hits the receiver.

Our example illustrated the first tactic, the DITF. Here, the first request was aimed solely at getting the receiver to say, "No" very quickly. The second, less-extreme request then followed and is more likely to be accepted.

The other tactic, FITD, pushes the first request in the opposite direction. Instead of starting with an extreme request, FITD starts with a little request that almost no one would refuse. After getting a "Yes!" response to this little request, the receiver is hit with the second, larger request.

Take our blood donation example. Our real target is to get people to give a unit of blood right now. To do the FITD, the first request has to be small and acceptable. Then, after we get affirmative action at step one, we hit them with step two: giving blood. Think of a smaller request we could make of a person that would elicit a "Yes" response before we ask for the blood donation.

We could ask the person whether he or she would sign a petition that offers public support for the local blood bank. That would work. It's a small request and takes hardly any time to sign a petition. It's for a worthy cause; everybody supports it. Almost everyone would sign that petition, wouldn't they?

Then, as soon as the ink dries on the signature, the requester follows up with, "Well, since you obviously support the blood bank and are willing to say so on this public petition, maybe you'd like to show a little more support and give a unit of blood right now. We have a station set up …"

If you've been carefully following along, you realize that both versions of the Two Step can lead to the same target. With the DITF, we get to the target by starting with a "large" request. With the FITD, we get to the same target by starting with a "small" request.

Two-Stepping Research

Researchers have completed dozens of Two-Step experiments over the last 40 years. Because they are rather simple to execute, many of them have been done in real-world settings—which vastly increases their utility for us. Consider these for your edification!

Call Me a Taxi!

Drinking and driving is a serious problem, and as a society we're getting better at reducing the prevalence. But it requires constant attention and reminding, especially with younger people just beginning their adult lives with freedom, cars, and alcohol. When I was a university professor in a college town, it was an annual rite to read about the deaths of students at my school from drinking and driving accidents. As a result, in many of my classes I'd work with students to develop persuasion-based projects aimed at reducing this dangerous behavior. Here's one small project that Ted Taylor, a student of mine, developed, tested, and published.

Wise Lines

Give them an inch, and they'll take a mile.
—Common lament of parents, teachers, and supervisors on the receiving end of FITD

Ted was a part-time bartender at a local bar. He developed a simple FITD intervention and tested it one semester. His ultimate goal was to get impaired drinkers to call a taxi at his request. Thus, the key message request at step two was: "Can I call a taxi for you?"

He randomly selected patrons over the age of 21 who came into the bar. He then randomly assigned each person he selected to be either in his treatment or control group. Ted then began tracking each customer through the semester, waiting until the customer became impaired from drinking. (Ted had received specific training as part of his employment and used the same rules for the study that he was taught by his employer.) When and if the customer became impaired, Ted would offer that key request: "May I call a taxi for you?"

Now, with the control customers, Ted did nothing beyond provide his normal service. He just observed them, then when they became impaired, he made the key request. With the treatment customers, Ted did a simple FITD intervention. He asked each treatment customer to read some material from the local state police office on drinking and driving, then sign a pétition against drunk driving (all treatment participants did sign).

Of the 15 people in the control group, 10 reached the drinking "danger zone" during the 6-week study. Of these 10, only 1 complied with the request to call a taxi. Of the 15 people in the treatment group, 12 reached the "danger zone" during the study. Of these 12, 7 complied with the request to call a taxi. Thus, 10 percent of the control group complied while 58 percent of the treatment group said, "Call me a taxi!" Even without knowing anything about statistics, this is an obvious, positive effect for FITD. (For you gearheads out there, the kappa effect size was .47 which is "large," but you already know because you're a gearhead. Oh, it was also statistically significant, but you figured that, too, right? I can't get anything by you.)

Unintended Consequences

"Lowballing" or "bait and switch" is another form of FITD. This sales tactic—illegal in some cases—first allows a customer to receive a product or service at an impossibly good price. Before the customer can close the deal, however, a supervisor or manager intervenes, cancels the sale, then offers the sale again—but at a significantly worse price. Some people will stay consistent with the first commitment although they know the deal is worse. As illogical as this sounds, some of us will commit to the stand we first made because consistency is worth more than money.

Mammogram, Ma'am?

Medical tests are often great tools for reducing mortality rates, because when you catch some problems earlier, they are usually easier to treat. But who wants to go to the doctor's office and get poked, probed, or squeezed? Best of all, who wants to do these things in the pursuit of potentially scary news? It's a wonder anyone ever gets a test. So, how do you motivate people against all these barriers?

A graduate student of mine, Danielle Dolin, developed another simple FITD intervention for her research thesis. She targeted women and gynecological exams (including breast exams). Nowadays, mammography test rates are approaching 90 percent with many American women, but when Danielle did this test in 1991, rates in West Virginia were around 50 percent.

Danielle devised a smart, simple, and clever FITD intervention. Ever been to one of those health fairs in a mall? All the local health and safety providers run booths and displays in the open areas of the mall and give free information, tests, counseling, and advice to anyone who wanders in. Usually these events generate a large crowd in a noisy, almost festive atmosphere with little kids hopping around with free balloons. Danielle partnered with the local county public health department and did a piggyback intervention.

The public health department gave free vision tests. People really wanted these tests, because they'd line up in a fairly long queue to wait their turn. One at a time they'd take the test, then get in another line awaiting the results of the free test. Then, they'd sit down and talk with a health expert about the test results. Danielle thought about all these people standing in line with nothing to do but wait and knew she had a great setup.

Over the weekend of the fair, Danielle randomly assigned women standing in line to either control or treatment by 2-hour time periods with a 15-minute break between sessions. During the two hours, all women in control were simply observed, then received a key request in that results interview. The key request was: "May I schedule a gynecological exam for you now?"

For women in the treatment time period, Danielle approached them standing in line, held out a plastic shower card, and asked them, "Would you like this free shower card that explains how to do a breast self exam? You just hang it from the shower head in your bath as a reminder. It shows how to do this yourself. Would you like it?" All of the treatment women accepted the card, then proceeded in line to the free vision test, then that results interview where they got the critical request: "May I schedule a gynecological exam for you now?" There was no mention of the shower card in the results interview.

In the control group, 25 percent of the women said "Yes" to the critical request, while in the treatment group, 41 percent of the women said "Yes." This is a small to moderate effect and was statistically significant. Now, first realize that the shower card was *not* a reward. It can't be. It was given before the request, so it cannot be a reward because rewards follow an action, right? While the shower card is more functional than a brochure, it contains the same information you'd find in one of those public health pamphlets. The crucial point here is that Danielle asked women whether they wanted information, not a gift.

The Sizzle

The foot in the door is a great team tactic. One person can do the setup while another person can deliver the target request. Consider a large electronics store that is running promotions on a couple of items. "First" salespeople could greet incoming customers with a commitment request: "Hi. Would you like a free information sheet on new wireless technology?" Then, a bit later, a "second" salesperson would intercept that wandering customer with, "Would you like to look at cell phones? We've got a great sales promotion running right now; they're right over there on aisle 3." Get creative here with the applications. Think about team Two Stepping.

The Effectiveness of the Two Step

Researchers have published dozens of Two-Step studies since 1966. If you read all of them and draw conclusions, here's what we know about effectiveness. Assume that you make only the second request to a group of people (for example, would you give a unit of blood right now?).

Let's say for the sake of argument that 30 percent of the group would volunteer right on the spot if you just ask them. The question becomes, "How many more volunteers could we have gotten if we had used a Two Step?"

The research is in strong agreement that on average, you would increase your volunteer rate about 10 percentage points. Thus, in our running example, a Two Step would produce a total of 40 percent of volunteers versus the simple request. If the simple request had gotten, say, 60 percent of volunteers, the Two Step would produce a 70 percent rate.

A 10-point improvement may not sound like much, but consider this. The requester only has to say a couple extra sentences to get those 10 points. Merely through a careful and thoughtful consideration of how to get a "No!" or a "Yes! response at step one can get (on average) 10 points more impact.

Beating the Average Two Step

With just a few well-chosen words you can gain a 10-percentage-point advantage over a simple request. Now, can you improve this average? The research clearly proves you can enhance each Two Step and gain more change in more people. The enhancements are a bit different for DITF compared to FITD, so we'll consider them separately.

Improving DITF

Two factors improve the success rate of DITF: prosocial requests and no delay between requests.

A prosocial topic is anything that provides a general social benefit. For example, topics like neighborhood safety, blood drives, recycling, and pollution control are considered prosocial because they involve large groups of people in neighborhoods, communities, and states. Of course, the receiver derives some benefit here, too, but the key point is that others will benefit. The first example in this chapter on giving blood is an excellent illustration of a prosocial request. Sure, someday, you might get a blood transfusion, but when you give blood, the odds are good that someone else will actually receive your donation.

Any delay between requests kills DITF. The research strongly illustrates that DITF needs to be executed rapidly with quick combinations of the two messages. You need to do the setup, get that "No!" response, then immediately follow with the second target request. Delays of just a few seconds kill DITF. It appears that receivers quickly forget they said, "No!" to that first request if the delay is too long. (Again, remember we're talking about interactions between strangers. Generally speaking, as a norm of conversation, we don't talk with someone, delay, then talk again. As a general guideline we'll make one request, strike up a conversation, or remain quiet.)

If you use DITF on a prosocial topic with no delays, you will gain an additional 10-percentage-point improvement over the average. A properly planned and executed DITF should produce a 20-point improvement over the simple request. Thus, if the control condition (for example, just making a simple request for a donation) produces a 20 percent compliance rate, an enhanced DITF (prosocial topic with no delay) will lead to a 40 percent rate. And if the control rate was 50 percent, the enhanced DITF would produce a 70 percent rate.

Improving FITD

Two factors also improve the success rate of FITD: prosocial requests (again) and no incentives. As with DITF, FITD works better on prosocial topics. Thus, the same ideas I just discussed on DITF apply here, too.

FITD tends to fail when you offer incentives to the receiver for complying with the request. If you provide payments, coupons, gifts—anything of value to the receiver—the Two Step will tend to fail.

If you do an enhanced FITD (prosocial topic with no incentives) the research indicates you will improve your rate to 20 percent, just like with the enhanced DITF. Thus, again, if the control condition produced a 30 percent compliance rate, an enhanced FITD would produce a 50 percent rate.

Unintended Consequences

DITF is somewhat like a comedy routine, except that it's aimed not at humor but instead at the second request. In any standup routine, there's a setup, then a well-timed punch line. Usually there is very little delay between the setup and the punch line, and the same is true of DITF. Delays are fatal..

Why Does the Two Step Work?

Surprisingly, there is no widespread agreement on why either the DITF or the FITD work. Some explanations have received partial support. But at present, much more theoretical work needs to be done. Here is the best current thinking.

Why "No!" Leads to More "Yes!"

The strongest explanation of DITF is called "reciprocal concessions." It simply means this: I give a little, you give a little. This connects directly to Chapter 7 and the reciprocity cue. As the requester, I make an "offer." As the receiver, you counter and say, "No!" I come back with another offer—this time, a smaller one. I have made a concession, right? I am no longer asking for that big thing but rather for this little thing. In the rules of polite society, you should respond with a concession of your own. In this case, you should accept my lower offer. I give a little, and you give a little.

A second explanation of the DITF that has been given is called "perceptual contrast." Briefly, this explanation holds that the first, large request sets up a "perceptual contrast" that makes the request seem too large. When the request is reduced, the contrast level shrinks and seems more acceptable. For example, imagine if you had to judge the "heaviness" of a 20-pound weight. If you first lifted a 50-pound weight, then the 20-pound weight wouldn't feel so heavy, right? It's the same thing with DITF. There is an intuitive appeal to the perceptual contrast explanation, but not much research support.

Clearly, more theoretical work needs to be done with DITF. We know that it works, but we're not sure why. The reciprocal concessions explanation has good appeal. It demonstrates that the receiver is not a helpless pawn but rather part of a communication interaction commonly called negotiation. The DITF, however, is a negotiation that strongly favors the requester.

Why "Yes!" Leads to More "Yes!"

The preferred explanation of FITD is self-perception theory. This theory says that we learn about our internal states (attitudes, beliefs, preferences, and so on) by observing our own behavior. If we observe ourselves doing something (for example, signing a petition in support of the local blood bank), then we reason that we must like whatever it is. Do you see the application of this to FITD?

With FITD, the first step is to get a "Yes!" response to a small request. According to self-perception theory, what happens here? Right, the person observes his behavior. "Ahh, here I am signing this petition. If I'm doing this, it must mean that I have a favorable opinion about it."

Now, the second step comes along, right in line with the first one—and what happens? The person knows he should accept the second request because he is "that" kind of person. He has already seen himself do other behaviors in support of it. He obviously supports that kind of thing, he is that kind of person. So, he complies with the second request.

Another interesting explanation again comes from Chapter 7 and the commitment/consistency cue: when you take a stand, you must stay consistent with it. The basic principle of this cue is that people need to maintain psychological consistency in their thoughts, actions, and feelings. Inconsistency is painful and causes us to restore a sense of balance.

FITD fits in nicely with the commitment/consistency cue. Step one gets the receiver to take a stand. "Yes! I'll sign that petition." Step two comes along and literally forces the person to maintain consistency. "Well, Sir, since you've signed this petition in support of the local blood bank, I'm sure you're the kind of person who also wants to give blood, and because we have a station set up just down the hallway …" The receiver is in a difficult psychological position. Saying "No!" to the second request would demonstrate an obvious inconsistency. The pressure to maintain consistency, therefore, leads to compliance.

You may be wondering why someone doesn't just say "I'd like to, but I don't have the time right now." In fact, some folks say exactly this. However, the Two Step reduces the likelihood of the person saying it. We're talking about average effects across a large population consistently applied. You'll never get 100 percent persuasion; you're just trying to improve your odds.

Unintended Consequences

If you're thinking closely about the explanations for DITF and FITD, you might spot contradictions in this theorizing. For example, why doesn't the commitment/consistency cue apply to both FITD and DITF? With FITD, you take a stand and must remain consistent with it.

At present, there is no reason to prefer the self-perception theory over the commitment/consistency cue or vice-versa. It's an interesting area of research and one that clearly requires more research. Yet, even with our lack of thorough understanding for why the Two Step works, we know that it does.

The Two Step in Action

Applying the Two Step is simple and straightforward, but it does require careful advance planning. You must clearly define your target request, then figure out how to get either the desired "No!" or "Yes!" response to the first request. If you don't plan correctly, you will be doing the Two Step by yourself.

Mom announces at the dinner table one day: "I've been reading this really interesting magazine article about diet and health. It says that a vegetarian diet is all that anyone needs to be healthy and strong."

Dad and the kids exchange panicked looks across the table. "Is Mom reading too much?" everyone thinks.

Mom continues with barely contained excitement.

"I think that we should go on a vegetarian diet starting tonight. How about it, everyone? Will you go on a vegetarian diet?"

The family now gives voice to their panic.

"Well, honey, I don't know about all that and so soon," Dad hedges.

"That's gross, Mom!" the daughter offers defiantly.

"Vegetarians are dumb!" the son opines.

Mom stares with dumbstruck amazement. "You don't want to become vegetarians?" She pauses for effect and looks hurt. Then, her face brightens.

"Well, if you won't do that, can we at least eat a serving of fruits and vegetables at every meal?" Mom asks with a smile.

Parental involvement in student learning is critical. The more support and effort parents give to their child's education, the higher the achievement for the child. Some parents, however, need to show a little more support than they do. It may not be reasonable to hit parents with a long list of activities they should be doing for their kid and expect them to follow all the items on the list. You need to bring them along slowly, one step at a time.

Get your foot in the door with a phone call.

"Hi, Mrs. Jones? This is Mrs. Watson, your son's teacher. Oh, no, he's not in trouble. I just need a little help from you. We send some work home with all the students every Tuesday and Thursday, and I'm asking my parents if they would just put a little checkmark on the homework to show that the children are doing these projects at home. On Tuesday and Thursday, your Jimmy will bring home an assignment—and all you or Mr. Jones need to do is just put your initials on the front or some other little mark. It would really help us a lot. Will you do this?"

Assuming you get the "Yes!" response (and if you don't, you have definitely learned a lot about the Joneses), you have your foot in the door. What do you do next?

That's right. The next time you see or speak with the Joneses, you remind them about their helpfulness, then bump them up to the next level.

"… and thank you for doing those little checkmarks. I know it seems minor, but it does help. Tell me, when you look over the homework before you initial it, have you noticed if Jimmy seems to do better on some projects than others? I mean, does he seem to need some help with spelling or sounding things out? He does? Well, of course, you could help him a little bit if you think he needs it …"

The Sizzle

The Two Step works best with prosocial topics. So, should charitable organizations use it to increase donations? Or should counselors and psychotherapists use it on their clients? The Two Step is clearly a persuasion play that works, but consider the ethical limits.

The FITD can be a continuing chain that links a series of desired behaviors together. You start with actions that almost anyone will do, then build on them. Make sure they appear consistent with each other. Make sure the receivers "see" themselves performing the action.

The Least You Need to Know

- Sequences of two requests can work better than just a simple request.
- DITF goes from "No" to "Yes" while FITD goes from "Yes" to "Yes."
- Gain a 10 percent advantage with either and improve to 20 percent when well done.
- The Two Step works best with prosocial topics and less so with profit motives.
- DITF requires quick timing with no delay between requests.

Part 3

Advanced Persuasion Plays

You're moving up in class now. These plays are the big leagues for the big kids. It took persuasion wizards more than 2,500 years to figure these out, but now you've got them right in your hands. These are the moves that blast you into another standard of excellence. You're going to stretch yourself here and push yourself hard, but if you want to move to the next level, it's what you have to do.

Chapter 9

"Why? Because!": The Explanation Game

In This Chapter

- Explanations drive behavior
- Attributing causality to internal or external forces
- Persuading positive internal attributions
- Why less is really more

People can explain anything. Kids listen in slack-jawed amazement as dads explain the principles of internal combustion engines and moms explain why you should always take your car to a trained mechanic after taking Dad to the emergency room. Much of our lives are spent either asking "Why?" or else declaring "Because." And once we have our explanation, we know what to do. If believe our dads, we get the toolbox. If we believe our moms, we get the first-aid kit. So if we can persuade the explanation, we can drive action.

I Explain, Therefore I Am

You can persuade by influencing how people explain why things happen the way they do. People try to explain events with one of two types of *attributions:* external or internal. External attributions assign causality to outside forces ("He made me do it") while internal attributions assign causality to inside forces ("It's all my fault.").

We respond differently after assigning each type. When we make external attributions, we tend to feel less responsible and less in control. We tend to wait for somebody else to do something, and then we might respond. In contrast, when we make internal attributions, we believe that we have obligations or duties that compel our attention and action. We tend to take charge for ourselves even if we'd rather be somewhere else.

> **def•i•ni•tion**
>
> An **attribution** is how people explain why things happen. They can be internal (inside the person) or external (outside in the situation). Attribution theory explains how people explain things. When you see the term "attribution," you should think of the term "explanation" as a synonym.

It's pretty easy to influence attributions. Using just a few well-chosen and well-timed words, you can move people to see the world in a way that you prefer. The persuasion skill comes from deciding what is the "right" attribution for your persuasion goals.

Attributions at Work

Consider this example. Imagine that your boss picks three people in your work group to get identical pay raises. Why did these three people get the pay raise? Because …

- Betty is the boss's niece, and she's on the fast track to a corner office—and the sooner we get her out of here, the better.
- Larry has no life outside of work, lives and breathes for Acme Widgets and Software, and outsells everyone every month. But who wants to live a life like that?

- Sheila is the best you've ever seen, and you want to work on her team every chance you get so you can learn from her.

Your boss has one simple explanation for the pay raises: they each earned it with their performance.

Regardless of the "truth," realize how differently you'd think, feel, and act following each of those explanations. With Betty, you might chalk it up to nepotism, shrug your shoulders, and maintain a cordial relationship because she's leaving the department anyway. With Larry, you might feel a bit envious, but then you'd realize you live a fuller life. And with Sheila, you'd be pleased for her and for yourself.

Explanation Drives Change

In these examples, it's the "same event" in each case, but our explanation of it is absolutely, positively, and unmistakably crucial to our following response. The explanation drives the change. Therefore, if we make people follow the explanation *we* prefer, we have persuaded them. To accomplish this goal, we need to understand how the game operates.

Imagine that after you read this chapter, you have to take a test on it. When you get the test results back, you've received a 65 percent. You think about these disappointing results for a minute and realize what a lousy teacher you had and how badly written the book was and how unfair the test was and … you make a lot of external attributions. What caused you to get a 65 percent? Events outside you (the teacher stinks)—external things.

But what if you got the test results back and earned a 95 percent? When you're hot, you're hot. Some people are born great. Where's the causality? Inside you, right? You assign causality to factors within the person and make internal attributions (you are sooo smart!).

When the world asks us, "Why?", we provide either an internal attribution or an external attribution. Now, how do we make a persuasion play on this?

Here's the basic outline:

1. You make the receivers wonder, "Why?"
2. You provide an attribution (the "because") that you prefer.
3. Their future behavior depends on the type and content of attribution.

Attribution in Action

The basic play with attribution is simple to execute. But exactly how do you do it? What kinds of words do you use? And when do you use them? Let's look at several examples to illustrate the process.

Litterbug Kids

A constant battle with younger children is getting them to clean up after themselves. Especially in the classroom, where there are 20 or 30 kids, neatness really makes a difference. How can you get kids to be neater?

Our first example makes kids neater with attribution theory. The researchers got the kids to perform a desired behavior, then provoked the kids to think about why they did it. And of course, the situation was set up so that the children would make an internal attribution ("I did it because I'm that kind of kid"). Here's how.

First, the researchers established a baseline for littering. They visited the fifth-grade class just before recess and handed out little candies wrapped in plastic. After the kids went to the playground, the researchers counted the number of candy wrappers that were on the floor or in the waste can. And there were many more wrappers on the floor than in the can, of course.

Over the next two weeks, people visited this classroom. For example, the principal stopped in for a little chat, and on her way out she said, "My, this is a neat classroom. You must be very neat students who care about how their room looks."

And one morning the class arrived to find a note on the blackboard from the custodian, which said, "This is the neatest class in school. You must be very neat and clean students."

Finally, the teacher would make similar kinds of comments throughout the two-week training period ("Neat room, neat kids"). That's all the researchers did.

Then, they came back for a second visit just before recess. Again, they handed out little wrapped candies. This time when they counted whether the wrappers went on the floor or in the waste can, they found a lot more wrappers where they belonged: in the can. There was a very large change in the littering and cleaning up behavior of the kids.

Let's review this simple study and make sure we understand what happened. First, we used candy wrappers before and after as an objective measure of littering. Second, we had a variety of sources observing the classroom and offering explanations ("neat room, neat kids").

The Sizzle

In this experiment, researchers tried another persuasion tactic that involved those typical lectures about cleanliness and neatness adults deliver, with all the appeals to virtue and character, delivered with finger wags and stern faces. It had no effect on the candy wrapper test. Kids, huh?

The analysis the researchers made is this. When the kids heard, "neat room, neat kids," they had to think about what had happened. In essence, they had to answer the question, "Explain why the room is neat." And their answer was simple: "The room is neat because we don't litter. We're the kind of kids who pick up after ourselves."

In other words, the children made internal attributions. And if you believe that you are the kind of person who is neat and doesn't litter, what happens when you have a candy wrapper? That's right—you throw it away.

Math Makes Me Feel Pretty!

Our next study goes much deeper in illustrating the impact of attribution. Littering is a simple behavior that doesn't depend on many factors. So it should be easier to change. But what about something like math achievement or enhancing a child's self-esteem? These things are complex. They are related to other factors (ability, persistence, training with math and family, life experience, and peer support with esteem). Can we change a child's math performance or self-esteem with attribution?

Here are the details on the second study. First, the researchers used before-and-after measures of math achievement and self-esteem with second-grade students. Second, the researchers developed simple little scripts for each student. All the teacher had to do was read the folder provided for each student, then say or write the appropriate statement. Thus, this study was highly automated. Each teacher simply followed the instructions in a preplanned, scripted way. Third, the researchers had three different kinds of treatments. Kids either got the attribution training, the "persuasion" training, or the "reinforcement" training. The study lasted eight days.

Here's the attribution training. The teachers would say or write to the student: "You seem to know your arithmetic assignments very well," "You really work hard in math," or "You're trying more—keep at it!"

Here's the persuasion training. The teachers would say or write to the student: "You should be good at math," "You should be getting better grades in math," or "You should be doing well in math."

Here's the reinforcement training. The teachers would say or write to the student: "I'm proud of your work," "I'm pleased with your progress," or "Excellent progress."

Unintended Consequences

Some teachers in this study had trouble sticking with the script. They felt dishonest when they provided positive comments if the child was not actually doing well. Remember Rule No. 7 from Chapter 3: All Bad Persuasion Is Sincere. Yet, some of us have trouble being actors with a script. It's your choice, and you need to know your limits and what you're comfortable with.

First, consider the self-esteem results. After all the training was over, all the kids had higher self-esteem (on a self-report scale). But interestingly, children in the attribution groups had the greatest increase in self-esteem.

Next, what about those math scores? That is the really important and interesting part of this second study. The children took two tests after training. One occurred immediately after the eight training days. The second was given two weeks later. Each test was composed of 20 math problems.

Kids with attribution training averaged 17.5 on the first test and 17.8 on the second test. (The baseline for everyone was 15). Kids with persuasion training averaged 15.5 and 15. The kids with reinforcement training averaged 16 and 16. Thus, the students with attribution training scored one to two points higher than other groups and maintained that advantage during the two weeks following the training. (The standard deviation was approximately 1.0, so these mean differences are quite large.)

The training here was simple. Each teacher followed a script of written or spoken statements. All the teacher did was provide the statement to each kid. So the teacher would mosey over during seatwork and say to a child, "You really work hard at math." Or the teacher would write on a homework assignment, "You are good at math." That's it.

How I Learned to Stop Worrying and Love My Mammogram

The preceding examples demonstrate what attribution is and how simple it is to implement. Simply ask, "Why?", then try to elicit an internal attribution. We've seen it work with children, but what about adults and their health? I have a great research illustration that involves just three words: "you" and "your doctor."

Mammograms are great for early detection of breast cancer. Earlier detection makes cancer easier to treat and the odds of survival and higher quality of life greater. So how can we motivate more women to regularly get them?

Alex Rothman, currently a psychologist at the University of Minnesota, and colleagues did a simple attribution study. They presented an information session about breast cancer and mammography to working women older than 40 at their job site. The 250 women who participated were randomly assigned to one of three information groups.

In the control group, women got the bare bones information with no attribution manipulation. For example, the information might have a line such as, "A mammogram can reveal very small masses that aren't detectable by a self-exam."

In the external attribution group, women got the bare bones presentation, but the words "your doctor" were added to the information. Thus, a line would be changed as follows: "*Your doctor* will look at the mammogram for very small masses that aren't detectable by a self-exam."

Finally, in the internal attribution group, women got the same information, but "your doctor" was dropped and "you" was inserted, changing to: "*You* will ask whether the mammogram revealed very small masses that aren't detectable by self-exam."

Everyone got the same fundamental facts about breast cancer and mammograms. What varied was the type of attribution in the explanation. The "your doctor" phrase put the responsibility for action on an external agent (the physician). In contrast, the "you" phrase put responsibility in the internal agent (the woman). And of course, there was no explicit assignment of responsibility in the bare bones control condition—just the scientific data.

The outcome variable in this study was the percentage of women from each group who got a mammogram in the following 12 months. Consider the percentages:

66 percent	Internal attribution group ("you")
57 percent	External attribution group ("your doctor")
55 percent	Information-only group
48 percent	Rate for all women in 1992 in Connecticut (location of the study)

Now, while the information-only (55 percent) and external attribution (57 percent) groups had higher rates than the control group (48 percent), after careful mathematical analysis, the researchers concluded these were not meaningful differences. However, the 66 percent rate in the internal attribution group was considered significant. Also consider how easy it was to produce this meaningful improvement: saying "you" rather than "your doctor" to persuade an internal attribution.

What's going on here is subtle. When people get information that describes an active role for themselves ("You will ..."), they believe that they have responsibilities for action and involvement that motivates them. In contrast, when people get information that explains what "your physician" will do, they expect to play a more passive role. They will be expecting someone else to handle the details and move the process along. This is a classic difference between an internal attribution and an external attribution. With internal attributions, you are motivated to handle things for yourself. With external attributions, you look to other people to act for you.

The Sizzle

Attribution can persuade with pronouns. "You" messages set up internal attributions while "they" messages set up external attributions.

Music Man, Love, and Money

By now, you see how to play the game and understand how simple it is. Through the skillful timing and wording of a message, you can get people to see themselves in a different way and therefore, behave differently. Now, if we can use attribution to make people look at themselves differently, can we also use attribution to make people see us differently?

In this example, we're going to manipulate a classic contrast: love or money. We want to influence our receivers as seeing a source's behavior as coming from either an internal attribution ("I do it for love") or external attribution ("I do it for money").

In this study, the researchers recruited adult volunteers to take music lessons from a piano teacher. The teacher was always the same person, a real piano teacher, and he gave the same lesson every time. The participants were told that the study aimed at understanding instructional methods and that they were testing different ways of teaching to see what worked best.

The basic setup was simple. Participants showed up for the study and went to a room with a couple of pianos and music stands. The piano teacher waited on one side of the room wearing headphones, practicing on his piano while the experimenter explained the study. All participants got an introduction to the teacher, took a lesson, completed rating scales on the experience, and were then left alone in the room for several minutes before the experimenter returned. (This was done to allow for "free play" to see whether participants just waited quietly or perhaps continued to play on the piano without the teacher.)

Now here's the special part. Before the lesson started, the experimenter told the participants one of two different stories about the teacher (and the teacher didn't know which one because he was wearing headphones and turned away). Half of the students were told the teacher was hired—doing this to make money. The other half were told that the teacher was a volunteer doing this because he loved music and teaching it. Thus, the only thing that's moving here is the attribution: love or money. Here's the $64,000 question: what difference does that attribution make?

When the participants got the volunteer explanation, they rated the teacher as more skilled, reported higher interest and motivation to learn, and when left alone tried more new music compared to the hired gun introduction. Furthermore, the participants rated the volunteer as more enthusiastic, as enjoying the lesson more, and as more innovative and creative than the hired gun.

The teacher did the same lesson every time (and the researchers also recorded each lesson, then listened to them to confirm that the lesson was the same each time.) As far as the teacher was concerned, this was just standard operating procedure, the routine, the habit, the job—what music teachers do. He delivered the same behaviors each time. Yet, the participants reacted very differently depending on that introduction.

Therefore, other people can perceive us in very different ways depending not on what we're actually doing but instead based on why they think we're doing it. And I can persuade them to have this different perception of you with just a message about love or money.

Wise Lines

They were willing to pay me more money than I could believe. But it's more than money, I've never been about money. I made one decision based on money in my life—when I signed with the Mets rather than go to Stanford—and I promised I'd never do it again.

—Billy Beane, general manager of the Oakland Athletics baseball team, on an offer from the Boston Red Sox

Not only does the presence of money affect how we see others, but it also affects how we see ourselves. Do you do the job because you love it (internal attribution) or because it pays well (external attribution)? How you answer that question makes a huge difference in your approach.

The Dark Side of Attribution

As we have seen, when people make an internal attribution for their actions, it appears that they also change their attitudes and beliefs about themselves. Hence, they become "that kind" of person—and the desired behavior follows naturally. The key for change is an internal attribution. Now, let's change things and ask what happens instead when people use external attributions.

Consider this situation before we look at a research example. If children are made to question their behavior ("Why is this classroom so neat and clean?") and they produce an external attribution ("Because the teacher is watching"), what kind of behavior would we expect? Well, as long as the teacher is watching, the kids will be neat. But as soon as the teacher turns his or her back … a big mess. The kids believe that their behavior is under the control of an external force and not from themselves.

This illustrates the problems that can arise when people use external things (such as rewards and punishments) to influence behaviors. In essence, the reward or punishment can prevent people from making an internal attribution and thus bringing the desired behavior under their control. People may not "generalize" from the reward and acquire the internally motivated habit to produce the desired behavior. Instead, they will expect some external agent (namely you) to cause their actions. Here's a real interesting research study to illustrate. It's with kids, but the same kind of work has been done with adults with the same results.

A group of researchers observed young kids (three to five years old) at play. They noted that most of the kids loved playing with crayons. When these crayons were available, the kids made a beeline for them and would use them with great concentration and apparent pleasure. According to attribution theory, we would claim that these kids used these crayons for internal reasons. There was no external force causing them to play with them. Instead, the kids freely chose the crayons and enjoyed them for intrinsic reasons.

Next, the researchers promised and then gave one randomly selected group of children "Good Player Awards" as a reward for their drawing efforts with the crayons. For one week, these children knew that they would get a "prize" at the end of the week for their drawing behavior. For the remaining children, no such promises were made.

There was a significant change in the crayon use among the kids who were promised external rewards for their drawing. These kids reduced how often they played with the crayons and reduced how much time they spent with the crayons. In contrast, the children who were not promised external rewards maintained their normal frequency and duration of use.

From an attribution perspective, it's easy to explain this outcome. We know that the kids already wanted the crayons for internal reasons and were intrinsically motivated. However, the introduction of an external attribution changed the children and their behavior. When asked, "Why do you play with those crayons?", the kids answered "Because of the award."

However, it should be quickly pointed out here that external attributions are not a uniformly bad thing. The preceding discussion makes it seem that things such as rewards and punishments and other external forces are undesirable influence tactics that never work or that only work when you are around to guard your clients, customers, children, or anyone and dole out the carrots and the sticks to keep them on track. Reinforcement does work; it just may require more effort on your part.

External forces can also be effective if the receivers believe that they "earned" the external factor for internal reasons. Thus, rewards work well when the receiver thinks, "I got the gold sticker because I am a good student who did a good job on this assignment." Or, punishments work well when the child thinks, "I got punished because I did a bad thing." If people believe that the external reward or punishment is essentially an indicator of their internal motivation (the harder you work, the more you earn), then reinforcers are less likely to undermine that internal motivation and control.

Playing the Game with Skill

First, explanations really do drive change. We think, feel, and act quite differently depending on just that one little thought in our head: the "because to the why." We won't litter. We try harder at math and feel better for the attempt. We schedule doctor's exams. We love the volunteer and dislike the hired gun. And on the dark side, our explanations can undermine things we used to love—just from an attribution.

Second, it's simple to persuade an attribution. Just a few well-chosen and well-placed words are sufficient to trigger the desired attribution. There are no big production scenes or fancy props—just you and a few well-timed words.

Third, take two key steps toward attribution action: get people to ask, "Why?" and then offer a positive internal attribution.

It's easy to make people think about why things are happening. All you have to do is make a good show of looking around, looking thoughtful, perhaps a bit puzzled, and then just ask, "Why?" The other people in the situation will most often take you at face value, look around, and start thinking, "Hmm, I wonder why?" Then, you step in with the positive internal attribution.

Almost all the time, you want to provide an explanation to the other person that either addresses her motivation or her ability to act in the way you desire. Consider these statements: you are a neat, clean person. You're a pro who always hits deadlines. You really care about helping others. You always have a plan in every sales situation.

> **Unintended Consequences**
>
> You want the other guy to believe that he is a "good" person doing "good" things. In the attribution game, the glass is never half empty; it is always half full. Pitch to the person's best, and let him rise to it.

You wouldn't say the following: "Yeah, it has to be neat in here or else I'll kill you." "Yeah, they hit deadlines because we fire 'em if they don't." "Yeah, they care about helping others because they're too lazy to do it themselves." "Yeah, they have a plan; they're a bunch of robots doing what I tell 'em to do."

Realize that internal attributions address either the person's ability or motivation. Ability is knowledge, skill, experience, training, talent, a knack, and a gift; it's the motor that drives the vehicle. But, the motor needs fuel to run. Motivation is the fuel, and motivation means desire, drive, energy, ambition, need, enthusiasm, impulse, and the gas to fire the engine. Internal attributions should point to either ability (you really know how to sell) or motivation (you love doing sales, don't you?).

Finally, if you think about it, attribution gives credence to the admonition, "Less is more." The less you do, and the more you let the receiver think, then the more change you can get. You just have to make sure that the little things you do lead to positive internal attributions.

The Least You Need to Know

- Explanations drive action. Internal attributions can make for self-starters, while external attributions make receivers look for your guidance.
- Make people ask, "Why?" then supply the "Because" attribution.
- Offer attributions that are "internal causes" for either ability or motivation.
- Less is more: the less you do, the more you let the receiver think, and the more change you can get.

Chapter 10

Consistency and Dissonance

In This Chapter

- Using consistency in our mental worlds
- Inconsistencies produce dissonance
- Key steps to successful dissonance
- Dissonance motivates strange behaviors
- Dissonance plays demand great skill and planning

This is the Weird Sisters section of the book. (Remember the Weird Sisters from Shakespeare's play *Macbeth?)*

> ACT I, scene i. A desert place. Thunder and lightning. Enter three Witches.
>
> ALL: Fair is foul, and foul is fair: Hover through the fog and filthy air.

Fair is foul with this strangest theory of persuasion: dissonance. Dissonance explains how good people can do bad things and still feel good about themselves. In reading this chapter, you need to open your mind to weirdness. Up to now, everything you've read has been pretty straightforward—and once you see the trick, it's pretty easy to understand. With dissonance, you may find yourself more than a bit confused the first time. Don't panic. Just have a shot of witches' brew and keep reading.

Consistency Is Persuasion Gravity

People crave *consistency*—knowing that when you wake up in the morning, your world will be very much the way you left it before you went to sleep. Each connection, bond, relationship, and attachment will exist as you left it—and you can pick up each thread where you left off and expect to find things are pretty much the same. In all matters large and small, we expect consistency in our worlds—and most importantly, in our heads. Everything should hold together and make sense in our minds. And when things are inconsistent, that's a problem. Consider this story.

> **def•i•ni•tion**
>
> **Consistency** is two thoughts that go together and form the basis of persuasion gravity.

I met my friend, a test pilot, who had just completed an around-the-world flight by balloon. With the pilot was a little girl of about two.

"What's her name?" I asked my friend, whom I hadn't seen in five years and who had married in that time. "Same as her mother," the pilot replied.

"Hello, Susan," I said to the little girl.

How did I know her name if I never saw their wedding announcement?

Take a minute to figure this one out, then look at the end of this section for the answer. Were you right? So obvious. So simple. So stereotyped. Mental prejudice, right?

In a mild way, this thought problem demonstrates our need for consistency and how we react to inconsistencies. Because consistency is so important to us and inconsistency discombobulates us, we've got a great persuasion opportunity. If we can make inconsistencies arise in other people or can influence how other people resolve inconsistencies, we can change the way they will think, feel, or behave in the future.

Now, this approach is not intuitively obvious to most people, which is why dissonance theory is an advanced persuasion play. Sure, everybody knows that people like consistency—but can you figure out how to use persuasion with that knowledge? That eludes most folks. The key element here is approaching dissonance a bit like judo. You'll use all the energy in the other guy to move him around. You don't have to do a lot of arguing or shouting. You just want to get the other person moving under his own steam, then give a little nudge here and a sidestep there and let the opponent roll himself into change. It's tricky making this happen, but once you understand the basics of dissonance theory, it will make sense.

Oh, and by the way … the pilot is a woman, and she named her daughter after herself (like some men do with their sons).

Process of Dissonance Theory

Dissonance theory operates in a three-stage sequence. You've already lived it many times yourself, and it has happened many times to people you know. You just didn't realize it:

1. People expect consistency.
2. Inconsistencies produce dissonance.
3. Dissonance motivates us to restore consistency.

def•i•ni•tion

Dissonance theory explains why we persist with behaviors that cause suffering in ourselves and others and the conditions that must be met for that persistence to occur.

Step 1: People Expect Consistency

This is a law of human nature. We have a strong preference for consistency in our lives. And this consistency must occur in our minds—in that mental map we have of ourselves and our world. Consistency becomes like a form of human gravity. It holds everything down and together. It helps us understand the world and our place in it. Most importantly, consistency creates a sense of harmony or balance with all the thoughts we have in our minds in any given moment.

Step 2: Inconsistencies Create a State of Dissonance

As much as we need consistency, however, there are many occasions when things occur in surprising and unexpected ways. It's your wedding anniversary, you're expecting a special gift from your significant other, and you get … an electric toothbrush. You love your child, but you forget to attend his or her piano recital. You're a good citizen who respects the privacy of others, and your child won't stop making a scene on an airplane. What happens?

The state that arises following inconsistency is called *dissonance*. This mental state is one of mild confusion and interruption. Our feeling state becomes filled with mild anxiety or distress as if we were nervous. Dissonance shows physiologically with an elevated heart rate, increased blood pressure, and sweaty hands. Put all of that together—cognitive confusion, emotional distress, and physiological arousal—and you have an unpleasant state of being. In fact, if there were a pill that gave people dissonance, no one would buy it. Dissonance is uncomfortable—a condition to be avoided if possible. No wonder we are motivated to get rid of it!

def•i•ni•tion

Dissonance is the cognitive, emotional, physiological, and behavioral state that arises in us when things do not go the way we expected them to go.

Step 3: Dissonance Drives Us to Restore Consistency

Given that dissonance is an unpleasant experience, when we have it, we want to get rid of it. We want to get back to the state of consistency—back where things made sense and we didn't have that awful dissonance. How do we accomplish this?

To remove the dissonance, we do mental work that permits us to readjust our shaken-up world and get back to consistency. We change our thoughts. And we do this rapidly—usually without much awareness that we have done it. It's not a conscious, controlled, and directed process ("Gee, I'm feeling weirdly upset here; it must be dissonance, so let's engage a cognitive process of changing our thoughts so that we readjust") but rather an uncontrolled process. Once we've readjusted our thoughts, the state of dissonance goes away and we're back to normal.

We desire consistency like it's fame or fortune, yet we're doomed from the start. Consider the inconsistency of our folk wisdom in these painfully paired proverbs:

- Absence makes the heart grow fonder.
- Out of sight, out of mind.
- Haste makes waste.
- Time waits for no one.
- It's better to be safe than sorry.
- Nothing ventured, nothing gained.
- Actions speak louder than words.
- Too many cooks spoil the broth.
- The squeaky wheel gets the grease.
- He who hesitates is lost.

The Sizzle

Dissonance is a central-route play with high-WATT thinkers who generate their own very intense "conversation." There is no low-WATT dissonance play.

Dissonance in Action

Now, this three-stage process sounds pretty simple when you look at it on paper—and you might be wondering how we're going to get any persuasion from it. People like consistency, inconsistency causes dissonance, and the dissonance drives us to readjust our thoughts. So what?

First, you must understand how to cause inconsistency. Second, you must understand that mental readjustment process. Let's look at several illustrations that look unrelated at first glance.

Less Is More, or Insufficient Justification

We begin with perhaps the most outrageous persuasion study ever done. In 1959, Professors Leon Festinger and James Carlsmith, both at Stanford University at the time of this work, reported an experiment that violated every persuasion principle held holy, eternal, and proven at the time. Their results did not go down well in the profession, and you can still start screaming arguments with normally staid professors over it. Here's what happened.

Festinger and Carlsmith recruited college adult males (no females—for a reason) to participate in a study on manual learning. An experimenter met a participant in the recruitment room, then explained briefly the upcoming study. From this introduction, they went to the experimental room and began. Each participant took a tray with 12 spools in it. He removed the spools, then replaced them in the tray one at a time using only one hand and working at a comfortable speed. He did this for 30 minutes. Then he was given another tray with 48 square pegs in it. He lifted each peg, turned it a quarter turn, and replaced it in the tray. He did this another 30 minutes. All the while, an experimenter in the white lab coat—armed with a clipboard—made notations, uttered "hmm's" and "ahh's," and acted observant.

Think about these tasks: replacing spools and turning pegs. One hour of your life spent *doing these zombie tasks*, all in the name of science. And having some guy monitor you to make sure you're actually doing it. And kids, this was only the setup. Now, things get complicated.

The experimenter began the manipulation. He sat down with each participant, lit a cigarette (really—this was 1959, a great year for cigarettes), and told a story. He said that this study had two groups in it. One group ("the one you were in") just did these tasks without any explanation. The other group ("the one you were not in") was met by *another student who had just completed the manual learning study* and had described it as "... very enjoyable, I had a lot of fun ... interesting ... intriguing ... exciting." The experimenter then explained that the purpose of the study was to compare how people responded to the manual learning task with either no instructions or the description from another participant. It was a test of "expectations."

Then the study divided into three groups. For the control group, the experimenter thanked the participant and sent him to the secretary's office to complete an opinion survey on the task. For the remaining two groups, which we'll call the "$1 group" or the "$20 dollar" group, the script changes.

Here, the experimenter got embarrassed and appeared nervous and apprehensive. He told the participant that there was a problem. The student who was supposed to meet incoming participants in the recruitment room and explain the study had failed to show. The *experimenter was in a jam* because he needed that student to meet a new person who was waiting to start the study. The experimenter then asked the participant to help out and perform this recruiting task. The experimenter offered to *pay for the help.* Some participants were offered $1 (about $6 in today's money) while others were offered $20 (about $125 today!).

After accepting the money (and everyone did), the experimenter took the participant back to the recruiting room where, sure enough, there was another student waiting—a female, in fact. The experimenter left the participant—(a male) and the new student—(a female) alone. The participant then explained the study. As soon as the participant made any kind of positive statement about the study ("enjoyable," "fun," "interesting," "intriguing," and so on), the young woman jumped in with a scripted line: "That's funny! My roommate did this study last week and told me it was boring!" Virtually all the male participants responded by saying, *"Oh, no; it really was interesting"* or words to that effect. And to verify these conversations, the experimenters recorded the conversation with a hidden tape recorder.

The experimenter returned and took the participant to a secretary's office to *complete a survey.* During this brief interaction, the experimenter again referenced how "interesting" the study was and thanked the participant for doing it. While in the secretary's office, the participant completed a brief survey for his opinions about the manual learning task.

This is complicated, so let's recap. Pretend you're the participant. You show up for this research. A guy wearing a lab coat meets you and takes you to a room where you do 60 minutes of simple, repetitive tasks. The guy talks about the experiment, saying that the "other group" got the "fun" expectation. Then you get an offer to help the experimenter for money. You agree and accept the cash. You talk with a person of the opposite sex about the task you just completed. You then fill out a survey about the task. Also realize that all participants were randomly assigned to one condition, the experimenters carefully controlled all the scripts, they had different groups for comparison, and they quantified their results.

Remember, too, there are three groups in this experiment. The control group did just the task and survey; they did not do the recruiting conversation with the young woman (who was a paid confederate, of course, acting from a script). The remaining two groups got paid either $1 or $20 to help recruit a new person into the study. Here's a table that combines the key elements for quick and easy comparison:

	Control	**$20**	**$1**
Meet experimenter	Yes	Yes	Yes
Do one-hour task	Yes	Yes	Yes
"Expectation" story	Yes	Yes	Yes
"Help me" story	No	Yes	Yes
Receive money	No	Yes	Yes
Recruit girl	No	Yes	Yes
Take survey	Yes	Yes	Yes

Let's look at the results now. First, just exactly how do people view the task if we don't mess around with them? The control group tells us how boring or interesting the task was. And they found it boring! They gave a *negative opinion* of the task (imagine that). This gives us a baseline for comparison to the other groups. Now, what about the folks in the other two groups? Festinger and Carlsmith manipulated them quite a bit to try to test the effect of inconsistency. Let's think about this.

From the reinforcement section discussed in Chapter 4, you might expect that when people get paid to do something related to a task, they might like that task better. So, a commonsense prediction here might be that the $20 group liked the task more than the $1 group, who would like it more than the unpaid control group. In the late 1950s, this was the dominant perception—and most persuasion researchers would have bet that more pay led to more positive opinions.

But it didn't.

The $20 group also rated the task with a negative opinion, just like the control group. So, after all that elaborate cover story in the $20 group, we get the same results as the control group—the task was BORING. Now, what about the $1 group?

In surprising contrast, the $1 group rated the task with a positive opinion that was significantly different from both the other groups. For you number crunchers, the correlation effect size of this difference was .37 (a "medium" effect), with a window pane value of 69/31 (which means this is an obvious, easily observable difference).

In other words, people who got paid less reported liking the task more.

What's going on here? Dissonance explains it! All the young men paid to recruit that young woman clearly misrepresented the experiment. They had just completed the task, and they knew it was a boring hour (the control group results confirm this, right?). Yet, during the recruitment phase of the study with the young woman, the participants all made positive comments—and we have the tape recording to prove that. Thus, two groups of men engaged in a boring task, then were unknowingly manipulated into deceiving a young woman about the true nature of that task, and they were paid either $1 or $20 for it.

Here's the dissonance train: I did a boring task. I took money to help someone concerning that task. I "misrepresented" the task to a young woman. Now, what's my opinion of the task? Festinger's answer is that the $20 payment overjustified the action. "Why did I deceive that girl? For the money, of course!"

In contrast, the $1 payment in no way explained the deceptive behavior. Instead, the dissonance caused by that social deception caused those young men to adjust their opinions—truly, honestly, and sincerely—to be more positive, thus removing the dissonance. "Because I have a favorable opinion of the task, I did not deceive that girl." In dissonance parlance, the $1 pay was an insufficient justification for the inconsistent behavior.

The crucial part of the dissonance train is the authentic opinion change in the $1 group. To resolve the apparent inconsistency, the guys were persuaded to change their opinions in a more favorable way just as if they had read a compelling editorial about manual learning tasks. They made a rational, thoughtful, and considered change in their opinion.

Now, in this case the change was obviously self-serving. It was a classic example of biased high-WATT processing where you adjust the facts to fit an existing position ("I don't deceive people; therefore, the task must be fun").

This surprising study launched a thousand new experiments as researchers tried to understand dissonance. Let's consider more weird ones.

Loyalty and Its Discontents or Disconfirmation

Returning to the thought problem with the test pilot that started this chapter, some people have trouble getting this problem because we don't expect women to be test pilots and because we don't expect women to name their daughters after themselves. In other words, we have sex role stereotypes.

Well, imagine that the people who missed this problem were ardent feminists who strongly believed in the equality of the sexes. A research study by Professors Steve Sherman and Larry Gorkin at Indiana University did just this to a group of feminists. The researchers had one group of feminists try to solve a sexist thought problem (which they all failed) while another group of feminists worked on a thought problem unrelated to sex roles.

First of all, we can bet that the people who failed must have experienced some serious dissonance. There they are, advocates of equality—and zap! They fall victim to stereotyped thinking. That's a major inconsistency! But what happens next is the interesting part.

The researchers then had both groups of feminists read a transcript about a sex discrimination case. Their task was to decide who was wrong in the case and make an award. How do you think the feminists responded?

One might reasonably expect that the ones who failed the thought problem should have "logically" moderated their feminist beliefs. Obviously, that failure indicated that they were not as clear thinking and free of bias as their feminist philosophy would demand. They should probably see themselves as less feminist now. Therefore, they should be less likely to see sex discrimination in the transcript and probably give smaller awards in the case.

Here's what happened. The dissonant feminists were much more likely to find that sex discrimination had occurred, and they gave much larger awards compared to a group of feminists who had not failed the thought problem. In other words, the feminist failures became even more feminist.

They fail the problem, and that's an inconsistency—so dissonance is aroused. They must get rid of the dissonance, but how? They engage in a mental process of adding more supportive thoughts ("Hey, I missed that dumb problem, but I'm on it with justice, discrimination, and penalties; I'll show you my true colors now!"). In other words, they add even more fervor to their existing beliefs to counteract the dissonance they felt at failing the thought problem.

This kind of failure followed by bolstering has darker implications. Researchers have developed dissonance explanations, in part, to understand some types of violence and why victimized people stay in dangerous relationships or groups. They see this situation as a perverse kind of loyalty manipulation where the greater the attack, the more they love the attacker or attacking group. For example, consider hazing. According to dissonance theory—under key conditions—the greater the hazing, the stronger the loyalty, as described by Dr. Shelby Hinkle's work on a dissertation at the University of Northern Colorado. Now, think about domestic violence. Again, under key conditions, greater violence can lead to more relational commitment, according to Dr. Karen Rosen's work at Virginia Tech. While the great majority of people hate violence and will avoid it, there are instances in both hazing (those physical and psychological trials that group members inflict on initiates joining a fraternity or sorority or squad or team) and domestic violence where people seem to accept and almost value the abuse and turn it into loyalty.

The Path Not Taken or Decision Making

Consider this study by Professor Jack Brehm, then at Yale University. Adult women were recruited for a marketing study. Individually, each woman was shown a table that displayed several different household goods and appliances (mixers, electronics, cleaners, and so on). After looking over each product, each woman was asked to provide her opinion of each on a 10-point rating scale—with the higher score meaning she thought the product was "better" and lower meaning it was "worse." Just a marketing study, right?

To compensate her for her time and trouble in the marketing study, the woman was then given a free product. She could choose between two products that she had just reviewed and rated. And this is where the experiment really begins. See, the experimenters used the ratings each woman had provided to guide their selection of products to offer as free gifts. For some women, the experimenters looked at her ratings and picked two products that the woman had rated at the higher end of the rating scale. Her choice was between two equally attractive products. For the other women, the experimenters picked two products that had been rated at opposite ends of the scale. Their choice was between two unequal products. Each woman then made her choice.

The Sizzle

Think about decision-making dissonance as it applies in everyday life. What happens when you have to choose between two jobs, two universities, or two dating partners? This research would imply that you would increase your liking for the choice taken and decrease your liking for the choice rejected. Does that square with your experience or with what you've seen in others?

What do we have here? Each woman does this task by herself, so she doesn't know what's going on with anyone else. She rates familiar household items. She is given a choice between two products as compensation for her time and effort. She doesn't know that the two products were presented to her under an experimental plan, and she doesn't know why she got the choice she got. Which condition she receives is randomly selected by the experimenter, but she doesn't know any of that. And then she makes her choice.

Now, the marketing representative asks her to rate the products one final time after she has had a little more time to think about them. So, once again, the woman rates each product—including the one she picked and the one she didn't pick—on that 10-point rating scale.

The interesting question here is: did the ratings change from Rating 1 to Rating 2? Why should they change? They're the same products each time. There's no new information about them. The only variable is the chosen free gift. Could the act of choosing to take or choosing to reject change the ratings?

For women given the choice between two differently rated products (one "better" versus one "worse"), there was no change in the product ratings. There was a slight tendency for the women to rate the product they had picked as "better" the second time, but this was a trend and not statistically significant.

For the women who had been given the choice between two equally attractive products, something funny happened with the ratings. First, looking at all the products *except* for the two offered as compensation, there was no change in the ratings. Second, the ratings for the two products available for gifts changed dramatically. The rating of the product taken increased, and the rating of the product not taken decreased. If she took it, it got better. If she rejected it, it got worse. And yet, we know that her first rating showed she actually liked both products equally. The act of choosing changed her opinion.

Wise Lines

These results provide the first evidence of decision rationalization in children and nonhuman primates. They suggest that the mechanisms underlying cognitive-dissonance reduction in human adults may have originated both developmentally and evolutionarily earlier than previously thought.

—Egan, Santos, and Bloom, *Psychological Science* (2007)

(Professor Egan and colleagues did a "forced-choice" study with very young children and monkeys in the style of the marketing study with household goods. Using colorful, attractive stickers for the kids and M&M candies for the monkeys, they found the same preference shifts. Kids and monkeys disliked the option not taken and liked the one chosen.)

Guilt: Good or Hypocrisy?

Let's see how to use dissonance in a more prosocial fashion. Researchers led by Professor Jeff Stone at the University of California at Santa Cruz in 2003 approached sexually active college students with this appeal: "We're trying to develop an intervention to reduce risky sexual behavior in high school kids. We interviewed a bunch of these kids, and we found that they viewed college students as more credible sources of information compared to older adults, like teachers or parents. We'd like to ask you, as college adults, to share your thoughts about safer sex, then we'll play them for high school kids. Coming from you, your arguments should be more compelling with these kids." Everyone then wrote an outline for a persuasive speech about safer sex for high school kids.

Then the researchers actually began the dissonance experiment. Half the college students were randomly selected to complete a survey that measured attitudes toward safer sex. This is the control group who just thought about safer sex and developed arguments in favor of it. The other half of students got hit with a double dissonance play. First, instead of only writing an outline, these students delivered the speech on camera so that it could be shown like a commercial for high school kids. Second, the researchers asked, "Would you take a moment to help us with another research idea we're working on? We want to understand why people do not engage in safer sex. Please write down all the times you engaged in sexual behavior but *did not* practice safe sex." The college students were given a sheet a paper and allowed to write as long as they wanted about all the instances when they did not practice safe sex. Afterward, they took that survey on safer sex. All participants (treatment and control) in this study were also paid for their efforts, then given a chance to anonymously buy condoms for 10 cents and pick up informational brochures on safer sex. Finally, the researcher contacted all participants six months later and surveyed them on their attitudes and behaviors about safer sex.

What makes this experiment unique is the double dissonance play. The researchers figured that students who had to write down their personal failures at safer sex *after* shooting their mouths off about safer sex for "the kids" would have a ton of dissonance and would resolve it by changing attitudes (the survey) and behaviors (buy condoms, take information, and report sex behavior in a later interview).

And that's exactly what happened. College adults who made the speech, then got the hypocrisy manipulation, resolved the dissonance in a favorable way. Ninety-two percent of them either bought condoms, took information, or both, compared to 44 percent of the control group. At the follow-up interview 6 months later, 92 percent of the dissonance group reported using condoms since the experiment versus 55 percent for the control group.

Wise Lines

I sometimes like to summarize all this by saying that … people come to love things for which they have suffered.

—Leon Festinger, professor and researcher of dissonance studies

Using Dissonance

From our survey of the dissonance field, you should get a strong sense of how difficult it is to make dissonance happen. This isn't an easy persuasion play like the Two Step (see Chapter 8), where you simply string together two straightforward requests. The dissonance play requires careful attention to the setup. Consider what we've just seen:

1. **There must be inconsistency.** Creating inconsistencies is hard work and often requires a fair amount of misrepresentation, deception, and sleight of hand.
2. **You can't let them make external attributions.** As you can reason from these dissonance studies, it was essential for participants to believe that they had personal responsibility for the inconsistency. If anyone had known that an experimenter was messing with them (deliberately constructing a thought problem that would fool them, such as forcing a choice between two equally attractive consumer goods or setting them up to deceive a young woman), the participants would have jumped off the dissonance train and blamed the inconsistency on an external cause. They had to make an internal attribution and stick with it.
3. **It really helps to involve self-concept.** If you look back at our dissonance illustrations, you'll see that they all hook into beliefs or actions that are self-involving. Your self-esteem or basic self concept is put on the line. The feminist failure example clearly hits at core beliefs and values. Even with the simple marketing decision study, while consumer goods are probably not key parts of our self-concept, how we act and decide in front of other people is. Those participants were being watched for their decisions and were being paid for their evaluation of the products.
4. **When the inconsistency is more "negative" than "positive," the manipulation is stronger.** People were made to look bad in these setups. They risked looking foolish, weak, inattentive, or thoughtless. Dissonance plays almost never make someone look good to produce the effect. Instead, the plays are typically aimed at negative consequences.

These four factors make dissonance plays a true expert's domain. If you are going to *perform* dissonance, you must engage in much planning and preparation.

Consider this personal example from my days as a professor. When I first started teaching this dissonance theory in a plain way, many students simply didn't believe it. They found the theory and the research ridiculous, unbelievable, and foolish. So I started doing a dissonance play in my classes.

I'd walk into my persuasion class like usual, carrying books and papers. But this time I had a letter with a fancy envelope. I'd ask one of my students if she'd heard of some administrator named Dickenson. "Yeah, Dr. John Dickenson with Academic Affairs. Anyone know him?" Almost always, somebody did. Then I'd start reading from the letter. "The university is considering a new policy of requiring a senior comprehensive exam prior to graduation … in testing phase … given your expertise in persuasion, we solicit your help … what would make this policy more acceptable to undergraduates … could you provide assistance … yours truly, yada yada."

You could hear a pin drop in the room. A comprehensive exam before you can graduate? I told the class that this was private information and not to share it outside of class. For effect, I'd glance at the open classroom door, then quickly move over and close it. "Here's my idea. Since you guys are students here, you understand the implications of senior exams. I figured you could help me out here. It would really help me, if you'd like to volunteer for this, to please take out a sheet of paper and write down all the strong arguments that make a convincing case for senior exams. You don't have to put your name on it. I'll read them and combine them into one big list."

I'd give the students 5 to 10 minutes, then collect their papers. Then I'd give them an attitude survey on senior exams "to see where everyone stood on the issue." And here's the part they'd all forgotten—during the first week of class, they filled out a bunch of papers for class—which included an attitude survey on senior exams.

After thanking them for their help, I'd start teaching today's lesson on dissonance theory. While I was doing this, my course assistant would add up the attitude scores before the essay on senior exams and afterward. By the time my assistant was done, I was ready to use the information as a teaching lesson. Every time I did this manipulation, there was a huge change in attitude scores from before and after. The scores always became a lot more favorable just as dissonance theory predicts and explains.

As we reviewed the results, the students were typically surprised and impressed. They'd look at their pretest surveys and realize, yep, we really were against it—and now after voluntarily writing arguments in favor of senior exams (an inconsistency, right?), their attitudes had become wildly more favorable.

Notice the kind of detail I had to follow for just this simple play. I had to create a real letter from a fake person about an untrue policy. I had to act out the role of a surprised professor just trying to help an administrator. Then I asked for help from my beloved students. Dissonance is a major production. If you ever read any of the original research, you'll almost always find these elaborate cover stories that function like a scene in a play. Dissonance is like cooking a complex dish.

Sometimes It's Easier to Wait Than to Manipulate

Putting this all together strongly suggests that you can probably find more success with dissonance by waiting for it to occur naturally, rather than making it happen yourself. Consider each of the major areas of dissonance we looked at and how they might naturally occur.

"Disconfirmation" happens constantly in our lives. We start a new project at work with high hopes and great expectations of success, then it blows up and we fail. This is enormously dissonant for many people. We strive for success, and when we instead get failure, we've got a big inconsistency. Most people try to run away from failure (remember Chapter 9 on attribution?). Dissonance theory strongly suggests that you might want to try to keep everyone on the dissonance train to strengthen their commitment and loyalty to the team, job, or project. Thus, some failures in life can actually lead to positive outcomes.

Certainly, this lesson applies to parents and their children. While parents would naturally want to protect and comfort their kids from failure, in some cases it would be wiser to keep the child on the dissonance path and let the reduction process generate more loyalty and commitment.

Of course, there is a downside to disconfirmation. Professor Festinger and another set of colleagues conducted an interesting case study of a religious "doomsday" group that had publicly declared an official date for the end of the world. When the end of the world did not come, many group members became more committed to the group. They redoubled their recruiting and proselytizing efforts despite the disconfirmation. While this case of "Dr. Armstrong" and "Mrs. Keech" seems an obvious scary case of dissonance, it is tricky to know when dissonance is leading to a good outcome (losing an important game can lead to more team loyalty) or a bad outcome (failed prophecy leading to fanaticism). Here, our values become more important than persuasion skills and plays.

Now consider decision making. When people confront equally attractive options and pick one, the dissonance process will cause them to devalue the path not taken. Well, sometimes in life you must revisit decisions and reconsider old options. When that happens, we tend to forget how attractive those old options used to be, and we may overlook their potential. If you're in a leadership position (supervisor, teacher, or parent), you might encounter a lot of resistance in others when you revisit those old options and their dissonance reduction is part of the problem. This suggests that you need to think carefully when setting up decisions. You might, for example, make the first decision a tentative choice to keep "the path not taken" on the table.

Unintended Consequences

Dissonance is how we can think of ourselves as basically good people, yet still do bad things. When we do those bad things, we move to reduce the inevitable dissonance. It allows us to justify ourselves by minimizing, trivializing, or misperceiving our bad actions. It's one of those ways we demonstrate that we are a little bit less than angels.

Dissonance and the Persuasion Rules

Dissonance is directly tied to three of the persuasion rules I discussed in Chapter 3:

- Rule No. 3: People Tend to Resist Change.
- Rule No. 5: If You Can't Succeed, Don't Try.
- Rule No. 8: Remember the Persuasion KISS: Keep It Simple, Sweetie.

Whenever you try to persuade someone, you are trying to change them. Change implies an inconsistency. Inconsistency starts the dissonance train, and everybody knows intuitively where that goes—so they resist persuasion attempts to avoid dissonance. Whenever you start persuasion, realize that you may have to handle potential dissonance issues (biased thinking that serves to explain, justify, and support "bad" outcomes).

You now understand more clearly why failed persuasion is so harmful. Follow the chain again: persuasion requires change, change implies inconsistency, and inconsistency starts dissonance. A failed persuasion attempt probably induces some dissonance, which means your target will find ways to justify and strengthen the very thoughts, feelings, and behaviors you're trying to alter. So not only did you *not* succeed, but you also made things worse.

Finally, dissonance works best when you get it started, then get out of the way. Return to the judo metaphor. Once the dissonance train begins, all of the energy is in the target—and you need to make simple moves. You don't need to point things out, provide more arguments, wave your hands, or do anything. In fact, the more you do once dissonance begins, the greater the risk that you provide an external attribution so your target can find a convenient escape.

Unintended Consequences

Think about habits you'd like to change. Maybe you eat too much or risk too much time and money on gambling. Maybe you shop even though you have a closet full of unworn clothes. When you get in those situations, try listening to yourself for signs of dissonance reduction. You'll hear yourself explaining why you need to eat that box of chocolates, why gambling is not so bad, or why shopping makes you feel so good. All of those conversations is dissonance reduction.

Dissonance and Our Human Nature

We started with a simple observation: people expect consistency. We then asked what happens when inconsistencies arise. What we found was the weird world of dissonance effects that occur under particular and specific circumstances. It isn't merely inconsistency that produces dissonance but rather inconsistencies plus negative consequences, internal attributions, and so on. Thus, dissonance is *not* an inevitable law of human nature but rather a principle that arises under certain conditions. However, when those conditions do arise, the upside-down world of dissonance emerges. Smaller incentives produce greater changes. We alter our evaluations of "the path not taken" and tend to downgrade options that once seemed alluring (but after we choose, now become ugly). Dissonance opens an interesting window on human nature and demonstrates a reasonable mechanism that people employ to make their crazy lives seem more acceptable and understandable.

The Least You Need to Know

- Dissonance is a three-stage process: people expect consistency, inconsistencies produce dissonance, and dissonance motivates us to restore consistency.

- Inconsistency starts the process and should involve the self-concept, produce negative consequences, and demand an internal attribution.

- Dissonance motivates weird behaviors as we try to understand and justify our actions even though it causes us and others to suffer.
- Dissonance is difficult to manipulate and requires detailed planning and a cold eye at execution.

Chapter 11

Inoculation Theory

In This Chapter

- Strengthening—rather than changing—thoughts, feelings, and actions
- Another application of the central-route conversation
- Weak offenses can build strong defenses—really
- Old hands helping newbies through hard times

Beginners approach persuasion in a simple, direct fashion. They want to charge in, change the other guy, and create a complete turn of direction from "against us" to "for us." And all of the persuasion plays we've studied provide exactly that kind of action. But, persuasion is more sophisticated than simply aiming at a change in direction.

Think about a situation where the other guy is already in your camp but is only a shaky friend. We don't want to change him or her in a directional way; rather, we want to strengthen him or her. We want this person to hold more closely to an existing thought, feeling, or action. This is a new and different kind of change, not a change in direction—positive to negative—but a change in strength (strong to weak).

Inoculation theory moves us into this new way of thinking about persuasion. It is also a tricky, subtle tactic that requires considerable skill in planning and execution. Most beginners could never discover inoculation for themselves. It is such a dangerous and counterintuitive tactic, but if you understand it, you step into a zone of excellence most people won't achieve. You truly become an advanced student of the persuasion play.

False Strength: American Traitors

During the Korean War (1950–1952), the American public was introduced to a new idea: brainwashing. This word was invented to explain the unexpected acts of treason that were committed by a few American soldiers who were captured. For the first time in our history, a small but significant number of our captured soldiers willingly cooperated with the enemy. It was a jarring shock to America, and it caused people to try to figure out what had happened.

The first speculation was that the enemy had used a clever combination of torture and punishment to beat our soldiers into submission. The evidence suggested otherwise. The "brainwashing" sessions did not necessarily include torture but rather featured a lengthy debate between the captured soldier and a skillful questioner. And the debate was about America and American beliefs about freedom, democracy, and equality.

Some soldiers had great difficulty defending their political and social beliefs. They believed that democracy was the best form of government, but they could not explain why this was true. And their captors merely attacked these simply held beliefs until the soldiers began to doubt their validity. After that, the road to "treason" was easy. Thus, because their thoughts, feelings, and actions were only weakly held, when they were attacked the soldiers could not defend these positions—making a change in direction easier to take.

The lesson learned translated into important changes for the American military. New soldiers began to receive more extensive political training along with the typical military instruction. No soldier would ever hold naïve beliefs or be unable to defend America verbally or militarily.

The same problem occurred in the Vietnam War. Senator John McCain, a prisoner of war (POW) for five and a half years, wrote a research paper for the National War College when he returned home describing many of the same psychological and physical tactics and offering ideas for helping captured soldiers resist. While he didn't use the term, some of his suggestions are based in *inoculation theory*.

def•i•ni•tion

Inoculation theory explains how to strengthen receivers' existing thoughts, feelings, or behaviors by making weak attacks on the existing positions. Thus, a weak offense builds a strong defense.

When Strengthening Is More Important Than Changing

These concerns translated into one of the most interesting persuasion tools ever developed. The most important question was, "How do you get people to hold a belief more strongly?" It was obvious from the war experience that mere education was not sufficient training to strengthen important beliefs. You can lecture people about the joys of democracy and capitalism, and they can learn the lecture well enough to pass a true-false test on it—but when the real world mounts a serious attack on the information, many learners will crumble. And it is not just in matters of patriotism and defense but also with any kind of thought, feeling, or action.

Think about the beliefs and values you want your children to hold, maintain, and display even in the face of temptation and dispute. Consider the principles and standards you want your colleagues, supervisors, and subordinates to hold as part of your organization. In fact, ruminate over any kind of human relationship and organization, and you can always find thoughts, feelings, and actions that are simply crucial to the survival, health, and productivity of that relationship.

How do you get people to hold on to these key elements—to embrace them more strongly?

Inoculation theory, that's how.

The main point of inoculation theory is that weak attacks make existing thoughts, feelings, and actions stronger. Stated a clever way, the best defense is a weak offense.

To understand this theory, we need to draw on a medical analogy. Remember being a little kid and going to the doctor's office for a shot? Ouch! It hurts, but it's good for you!

Insight from the Doctor's Office

The term "inoculation theory" is drawn from the public health practice of giving shots to prevent serious diseases. Almost every American gets some kind of shot to prevent polio, diphtheria, and a wide range of other viruses. How does this process work?

Interestingly, the shot actually gives the person a weak dose of the virus. This in turn activates the body's immune system. The immune system fights off this weak attack, and (here's the good part) the immune system actually becomes stronger. Thus, the next time the virus attacks, the immune system can handle an even larger assault.

The key word is "weak." If the shot contained too strong a dose, it would overwhelm the immune system, make the person sick, and perhaps even kill the person. The dose must have enough of the virus to activate the immune system but not be so strong that it overpowers.

Inoculation Persuasion Theory

The application to persuasion is apparent. If we want to strengthen existing attitudes, beliefs, and behaviors, inoculation theory suggests that we should present a weak attack on them. Again, the key word here is "weak." If the attack is too strong, it will cause the attitude, belief, or behavior to get weaker or even move to the opposite position. The attack has to be strong enough to challenge the defenses of the receiver without overwhelming them.

Wise Lines

What does not kill me makes me stronger.
—Philosopher Friedrich Nietzsche

Here are the steps of effective inoculation:

1. Warn the receiver of the impending attack.
2. Make a weak attack.
3. Make the receiver actively defend.

Warn of the Attack

The warning plays a key role in the inoculation process. It serves to activate the existing defenses in the receivers. As soon as the warning is made, receivers are threatened. They know an attack is imminent, and they must get ready for it. Threat here does not mean that you induce fear, panic, dread, or anxiety (in other words, some serious negative emotional response). Rather, the threat you want to trigger is more cognitive, such as playing a game of basketball and noting that a new player is on the sidelines and will enter the game soon. That new guy will change the game and is a "threat."

When people are threatened in this way, they immediately begin to generate possible defenses against the coming attack. In fact, people will produce ideas that may never be directly useful or necessary during the coming attack. It's like a group of soldiers who have some time to prepare for the enemy. They may not know exactly what the enemy is going to do, so the soldiers get every weapon and construct every barrier they can. Maybe they won't use everything, but it's there if needed. Threatened receivers perform the same kind of mental preparation and draw upon all available defenses.

It's crucial that receivers overprepare in this way. All that extra work is not wasted, even if it's not used to defend against the coming attack. Just thinking the defensive thought is sufficient.

Make a Convincing but Weak Attack

If you think about it, an "attack" is simply an act of persuasion. An attack is an attempt by some source to change the thoughts, feelings, or behaviors of receivers. Advertisers "attack" our existing attitudes when they try to get us to prefer their product over a competitor's. Parents "attack" their kids' beliefs about proper conduct in public. In fact, most of this book is aimed at making you a more effective "attacker" in your world. So understand that the attack in the inoculation process is nothing special or different.

It's important, however, for the attack to be weak and ineffective. That sounds completely stupid compared with the rest of this book, but think about it. If you produce a strong attack, what will happen? Whatever you wanted to strengthen will get weaker and maybe even move in the opposite direction. It would be as if Louis Pasteur used too strong a shot in his smallpox vaccine and it killed everybody. (Great theory; terrible application.)

The attack must be strong enough to force the receivers to defend. It must not be so strong as to overcome the defense, however. Thus, you must strike a dynamic tension between two opposite forces. First, you have to look serious and credible. Second, you must produce weak arguments. You want the receiver to take your words seriously and actively react to them, but then again you have to throw a punch that misses or lands softly. This is a tricky dynamic to master and requires planning and practice.

Encourage Active Defense

Many years of careful research have shown that the more actively the receiver defends against the attack, the stronger the existing thought, feeling, or action will become. An active defense occurs when the receiver does more than merely think but also performs actions. It's therefore important to get the receivers to verbally and behaviorally express all those defensive thoughts.

It's also crucial that the receiver does the defending with as little outside assistance as possible. Again, a fighting analogy is useful. People will not learn how to physically defend themselves during an assault if someone else intervenes. The inoculation process operates the same way. The receivers must do their own fighting with their own resources and learn not to rely on others.

The Sizzle

In some cases, it may be required that you provide argumentative assistance. Some receivers may struggle even in the face of a weak attack, and you must provide help. You might want to provide supportive information *before* the attack so that an inexperienced receiver has some ammunition when you launch your weak attack.

See the High-WATT Light

Inoculation works because it causes the receivers to engage in central-route processing about the thought, feeling, or action. The weak attack threatens the receivers and forces them to think more carefully, deeply, and with more effort. In essence, inoculation is a kind of judo move where the receivers are rolled into thinking about the object. The more they think, the stronger the thought, feeling, or action becomes. And the receivers do all the work. All you do is provide the weak attack that gets the entire process started. Thus, inoculation aims at throwing people into one of those long, central-route conversations that generates a lot of ideas, claims, arguments, and chains of reasoning. Once again, less is more.

The entire point of inoculation is to get people to think for themselves. When people actively generate their own ideas and thoughts, then have to vigorously defend them—they will develop considerably stronger attitudes, beliefs, and behaviors. Thus, inoculation is a central-route process where forewarning and attacking produces high-WATT thinking and a focus on self-generated arguments. It literally provokes a highly biased, deeply elaborated response.

And it is most effective if the target doesn't realize it is a deliberate weak attack. Thus, inoculation requires a fair amount of finesse on the part of the source. You not only have to be smart enough to make a weak attack but also have to be self-effacing enough to look like a loser.

Unintended Consequences

When receivers stay low WATT, inoculation will fail. You can never perform this tactic as a persuasion cue with peripheral thinkers.

Inoculation in Action

Before we look at academic research on inoculation, we'll consider examples of practical application. A few years ago when the telephone industry was broken up into smaller, more competitive businesses, one of the problems the new companies faced was holding on to existing customers. Several employed inoculation ad campaigns in the mass media. The ads featured a customer getting a phone call from "another phone company" making a pitch to steal the customer away. The ad even quoted the pitch, then showed the customer actively fighting off the pitch with a series of arguments against it. Thus, the ad contained all the elements: the threat of a call from the "other company," quoted examples of the "weak attack" by the "other company," then clear, strong defense replies from the customer.

You also see this kind of strategy with energy companies. The price of oil skyrockets for some reason (greedy oil companies, greedy speculators, greedy oil nations, or someone being greedy), and energy companies make a lot of money (which annoys people). Or if it's not the price, it's an oil spill. Or drilling through pristine waters, beaches, and parks. Or pollution. Or greenhouse gases. When this happens, there's an angry response. Journalists opine. Advocates orate. Congress investigates. And what do the oil companies do?

When they're smart, they inoculate before the windfall, the spill, or the permit to drill becomes angry public knowledge. Even before the controversy explodes, the oil guys know it's coming before anyone else because that's their business—and they start running ads in the mass media, reminding everyone of the crucial importance of energy in our lives.

Finally, in perhaps the most interesting practical illustration of inoculation, consider the case of former U.S. President Bill Clinton. You might recall his infamous "woman" problem. What you may not remember is that this problem popped up during the presidential primaries held during the winter of 1991–1992. A former amorous partner, Gennifer Flowers, scheduled a press conference to declare her adulterous relationship with Clinton. The Clinton campaign got wind of this planned press conference, and on the Sunday night before that following

Monday afternoon event, Bill and Hillary Clinton appeared on an episode of the popular TV news magazine show, *60 Minutes.* In that episode, the reporter directly asked about the "woman" problem, and the Clintons—especially Mrs. Clinton—responded in a way that acknowledged past marital problems but that these problems were way in the past … and that they were together in marriage as husband and wife.

This is an excellent, practical application of inoculation. Before the "real" attack from Gennifer Flowers could occur, Clinton managed to produce a weak attack on voter attitudes about fidelity, marital privacy, and politics. The appearance on *60 Minutes* was their first national appearance in the media, so many viewers were getting their first look at the Clintons. And that first look included a weak presentation of the "woman" problem and how the Clintons handled it.

When Gennifer Flowers came along the next day, not only was her press conference "old news"—but it was also inoculated news. People had already been attacked on their attitudes about Clinton's character and alleged defects, and they had already defended their attitudes on that issue. When Ms. Flowers came along, many people could easily defend their attitudes and beliefs about Bill Clinton and just as easily discount Ms. Flowers' claims as a tawdry and transparent attempt to gain her 15 minutes of fame.

Even past these interesting and compelling practical examples, there is much research literature on inoculation that is more reassuring about the impact of this theory. Since William McGuire first presented inoculation theory as a viable persuasion concept in the 1960s, there have been many academic research studies. Let's look at a couple on health and politics.

It Works with Smokers

Everybody knows that smoking is harmful to your health. Our society is engaged in a massive campaign to get people to quit. But quitting is difficult, and some people are not able to do it. So our society is taking a different line. We are trying to find ways to keep people from starting this harmful and addictive habit. And who are we targeting?

Adolescents, of course. These young kids are the ones who will be most likely to start and will probably find it most difficult to quit. So how can we keep these kids from smoking?

Already, you should see that this problem is a perfect application for inoculation. Most kids already know that smoking is harmful and that they should not start. Thus, they already have existing attitudes, beliefs, and behaviors that are "correct"; in other words, their initial position is already leaning in the direction we desire. The problem is, these attitudes, beliefs, and behaviors are not strong enough to keep all kids from starting to smoke. Therefore, we must inoculate them. Research by Michael Pfau and colleagues suggests this approach works.

Middle school students were simply shown one inoculation video during regular class time in their health classes. Six months later, the attitudes of these students were assessed with self-report scales. With students of low self-esteem, the inoculation video served to strengthen and maintain attitudes against smoking—all on the basis of one inoculation. It also led to less reported smoking.

The Sizzle

Researchers have demonstrated that inoculation also works with other health issues. It has been tested with drugs and alcohol with similar positive outcomes. Interestingly, early research on inoculation by William McGuire used the topic of dental hygiene.

Political Inoculation

Michael Pfau and his colleagues have done some of the best inoculation research over the last 25 years. Pfau conducted a field experiment during an actual election to test the theory and found results that it works. Using direct mail, Pfau employed combinations of inoculation and control messages with both Republican and Democratic voters in the 1988 presidential campaign (George H. W. Bush versus Michael Dukakis). The research was done on just a few hundred voters and was balanced across parties, so there was no partisan impact.

Pfau found that when he properly inoculated a voter from either party, following attack messages had significantly less impact compared to a voter who had not been inoculated. The beauty of Pfau's work is that he used strong experimental methods with random selection and assignment of voters to carefully tested and controlled conditions. Thus, he not only demonstrated that inoculation works in a complex field such as politics, but he also explained why it works.

Fine Points

Recall the three steps of inoculation: warning, weak attack, and active defense. In doing each step, keep in mind three important points:

1. The warning must serve as a threat that an attack is coming. This activates high-WATT, central-route thinking. Next, let there be some delay between the warning and the actual attack. This will permit more thinking and defense building before the weak attack arrives. This is a timing skill. The pause here must be long enough to get the receiver thinking and defending but not long enough so that he or she gets bored. You want the person to be high WATT when the weak attack arrives.
2. The attack must challenge but not overwhelm the receivers. This is a tricky and subtle point. Especially in situations where you are a higher-status source "attacking" the lower-status receiver, it can be very easy for you to overwhelm your targets. Instead of causing them to strengthen the attitude, belief, or behavior, you might cause them to question and doubt it. Use the receiver's behavior as a cue. If the receivers are not defending themselves and instead appear to be nervous or upset, your attack is too strong and will not work.
3. Encourage active defending after the weak attack. Get each receiver to say or do something that shows the defense is working. The research indicates that when receivers have to generate their own defenses, inoculation works better. When you have to provide a lot of assistance, the inoculation approach weakens (but it is still better than doing nothing). Remember, the receivers only get strong when they work for themselves. If you give assistance, then

they will stop thinking and simply respond with the ideas you provide. This is another tricky, subtle element to this persuasion play, which is why it's considered an advanced technique.

The Sizzle

Anyone who has a competitor should think about inoculation as a standard tactic. Consider how hard you work to get a customer, a client, or a volunteer (or whatever name you assign to people from whom you make your living). If these people can take their "business" anywhere else, you need to strengthen their commitment to you.

Good Times, Bad Times

Inoculation is one of the ways you can prepare against bad times, but you have to do it during good times—which is another reason why this is an advanced persuasion play. When things are going well, it's hard to think about the inevitable bad times. To a certain extent, inoculation is an "old-hand" tactic for folks who have lived through several rounds of good times, then bad times, then good times, and so on. Take the stock market over the last 20 years. In that time, there have been several bad periods—the 1987 crash, the millennium technology bubble, the war crash of 2003, and lately the mortgage and credit bust. After each crash, younger and less-experienced investors tended to run screaming for the exits and suffered large losses. A little inoculation in the early stages of the crash might have made these investors more resistant, patient, and thoughtful when the bad times hit.

You can generate your own situational applications past the stock market. Think about counseling young people before marriage, professors working with graduate students, and older supervisors mentoring young workers. If you've been around the block a couple times and you're around people who are just starting, inoculation is an ideal persuasion tactic. You don't want to change them; rather, you want them to strengthen the thoughts, feelings, and actions that drew them into your world.

Finally, at first glance, inoculation theory seems crazy. "Let me get this straight. I attack people who support me to make them support me even more? And I have to make this attack look incompetent so they defeat me? Yeah, poke the bear and look stupid while doing it!" Yet that is exactly what inoculation is about.

Remember two key persuasion rules from Chapter 3: Rule No. 2, It's About the Other Guy, and Rule No. 7, All Bad Persuasion Is Sincere. These rules go to the heart of effective inoculation. You aim strictly and exclusively at the other guy, and you allow yourself to look less credible to achieve your goal. Effective inoculation plays are the mark of a confident, experienced, and advanced communicator.

The Least You Need to Know

- The best defense is a weak offense.
- The sequence of inoculation is 1) compelling threat, 2) weak attack, and 3) active defense.
- You must appear credible but act weak to perform inoculation.
- Get in front of bad news to minimize its effect.

Finally, at first glance, insinuation theory seems crazy. "Let me get this straight. I attack people who supposedly I want to make think smart or even more? And I have to make this attack look incompetent so they defeat me? Yeah, pose the bait and look stupid while doing it." Yes, that is exactly what insinuation is about.

Remember two key persuasion rules from Chapter 2: Rule No. 2, It's About the Other Guy, and Rule No. 3, All Real Persuasion Is Sincere. These rules go to the heart of effective insinuation. You aim sincerely and exclusively at the other guy, and you allow yourself to look less credible to advance your goal. Effective insinuation plays are the mark of a confident, experienced, and advanced communicator.

The Least You Need to Know

- The best defense is a weak offense.
- The sequence of insinuation is 1) compelling threat, 2) weak attack, and 3) decisive defense.
- You must appear credible but act *weak* to perform insinuation.
- Get in front of bad news to minimize its effect.

Chapter 12

What You Don't See Is What You Get

In This Chapter

- Studying the world of unconscious influence
- Using technology to deploy subliminals
- Noting different outcomes for thinking and feeling versus behaving
- Finding limitations in effects

People are always looking for a sure thing: a car that gets 50 miles to the gallon, costs less than $10,000, and always has a parking place. Wouldn't it be great if there was a machine that shot hidden persuasive messages at people as they walked down the street, down a supermarket aisle, or inside a voting booth? Wow—think how simple persuasion would be then. Think of all the money you could make. But … is it really possible?

The Queen of Tomorrow Controls the World!

Once upon a time, there was a woman who discovered the principles of *subliminal* persuasion. She could display messages that on the surface were quite innocent, but below the surface dwelt subliminal exhortations that motivated receivers to vote, buy, prefer, smile, frown, or do whatever she wanted at the time.

def•i•ni•tion

A **subliminal** message is a real, observable message that operates below receiver awareness and consciousness, but still changes thoughts, feelings, or behaviors.

She formed a small technology company that put all kinds of cool functions in a wireless set worn as eyeglasses. She also invented those super-cool iEye visors you see everyone wearing; they're especially popular in the U.S. Navy. Then she embedded her subliminal messages within the wireless functions that displayed on the iEye, such as the "heads-up" cockpit screen for fighter pilots (whether in a real F-22 or the Xbox version). So every time somebody called up a map, an e-mail, or the latest Amazon Kindle book, stuck within the text was a subliminal message. And if you have the iEye with the iAkoostik ear buds option, you also get subliminals with every MP3 you hear. The Queen of Tomorrow also developed a subliminal system with olfactics, but it hasn't been well received in the marketplace (perhaps because of the name: iSmell).

Soon, her company was bigger than General Electric, Exxon/Mobil, and Microsoft combined—and every elected official was her best friend forever. The guys in the band U2 do all of her benefit concerts without being asked. And Al Gore has a really happening slide show he's touring now. Maybe another Nobel Prize is in the offing. Former president George W. Bush has her down at the ranch in Crawford, Texas, where she and Dick Cheney go hunting. And our beloved current president has built a hideaway bungalow for the Queen of Tomorrow just off the White House, near the Rose Garden.

When she realized the power she had, she also realized something else: if I found out about it and put it in my book, she'd be ruined. But because I don't own a pair of iEyes, she can't control me.

What did she do?

Is Subliminal Persuasion Real?

Enough with the fairy tales. What's the science of subliminal persuasion? Most researchers define subliminal persuasion as messages that operate below the level of conscious awareness but nonetheless influence the way a person thinks, feels, or behaves. Thus, for subliminal persuasion to occur, there must be three elements: a message, unconsciousness, and influence.

A Message That Does Exist ...

Science requires each of these assumptions to be as obvious as possible, because science is about as subtle as a hammer on your thumb. Thus, here's the first element: the subliminal message has to be apparent, concrete, existent, and *there*. The message is not inferential or interpreted, as when someone looks at the clouds in the sky and sees dragons fighting with Cupid over a box of Twinkies—and then poof, it's now a six-pack of beer riding a horse in a basketball arena. The message exists without an assist from Dr. Freud.

Unintended Consequences

What about those Freudian subliminals that find a hidden meaning in ice cubes, clouds, cigars, and wavy hair versus a buzz cut? We won't consider this line of thinking, because frankly, it's crazy. It's hard enough to create understanding with obvious words and images, much less expecting everyone to look at a picture of bare trees and worry about never getting pregnant (bare trees bearing no fruit, right?). Some folks see it, but most don't. It's unreliable, fleeting, and in most cases just plain silly. It does make for interesting TV shows and websites, however.

But Is Below the Conscious Awareness of the Receiver ...

Next, this concrete message has to move below the receiver's level of conscious awareness. The entire conscious-unconscious distinction is one of those issues that can easily evolve into a bar bet with people yelling at each other over whether "unconscious" really truly exists. Let's put it this way. If I put you in front of a subliminal message and it influences you, and then a little later I show you that message again, stick it right in your face and say, "Hey, you see this message?" if you don't remember seeing the message, we'll call it unconscious awareness. If a message is below your awareness, it means I showed it to you but you didn't see it—but it did influence you. And later when I show you the message, you don't recognize it.

And Influences the Receiver

Finally, this observable (if you knew how to look for it at the time) yet unobserved (below conscious awareness) message changes you. You think, feel, or act differently after exposure to the subliminal.

At this point, you might feel exasperated with science. To be scientific, we've defined subliminal persuasion as something that is transparently absurd. If you're feeling like this, don't worry. There's a simple trick that makes the enterprise plausible: you must use a technological device to transmit the message.

What Do Popcorn, Shoplifting, Self-Esteem, and Weight Loss Have in Common?

One of the earliest recorded claims for subliminal persuasion occurred in the late 1950s. An advertising man, James Vicary, claimed that he had embedded subliminal messages such as "Eat Popcorn" and "Buy Coke" in movies being shown in outdoor theaters. Vicary claimed that he spliced just a few frames of the subliminal message into the movie so that there was a very brief exposure to the message. Thus, everyone "saw" the message, but it zipped by so fast it had to be below their conscious awareness. Vicary claimed that sales of popcorn and colas increased after showing these subliminals.

This story feels like an urban legend, but Mr. Vicary is real—and he did make these claims. (If you want to learn more about it, search online using the key words "Vicary, subliminal, and popcorn.") Note three details about Vicary's claims:

- See how we solve the apparent problem of "now you see it, now you don't" through the use of technology. It's possible to show a message very rapidly and in a context with a lot of other information so that the message does exist, yet most people would not know it happened and would not recognize the message later if you showed it to them clearly.
- Observe that this claim occurs in the context of making money. We'll see this frequently. Many claims of subliminal effects arise from people trying to make a buck.
- Note the absence of any scientific testing here. One guy says he did something and it increased sales. That's it. There's nothing about the conditions of the tests, the people involved, or the methods.

Given my cautions here, you'd think that Mr. Vicary would be just a quirky footnote—but his claims caused a phenomenal uproar in the United States. Many people understood the dark implications of this claim. Hey, if this guy can make us buy more popcorn without us knowing it, then he can be king of the world and make us vote in a way we don't intend or prefer. People met. People voted. Laws changed. Subliminal persuasion is banned as an illegal communication activity. So this is the end of subliminal persuasion, right?

Where do I begin … how about with Lorelei Communications doing business on the World Wide Web? The company offers a "Shrinkage Control" system that delivers anti-shoplifting messages for use in department and other retail stores. These messages are mixed in with the music typically played in these settings. On its website, the company claims a 37 percent reduction in shoplifting losses. We move along to self-help. Want to lose weight, quit smoking, or boost your self-esteem?

Visit www.freepatentsonline.com/4777529.html. Pick your problem, send them money, and they'll send you audio tapes. As with Mr. Vicary and Lorelei Communications, the purveyors of these self-help tapes claim to improve whatever it is that ails you.

The Sizzle

Go to your favorite search engine and do your own investigation. Note all the exclamation points, percentages, and money claims. It's the new thing, baby! Improve your IQ by 68 percent! Earn millions while you sleep!

Scientific Analysis of These Studies

These claims reek with falseness. Mr. Vicary claims to sell more popcorn and cola when everyone knows what's really going on at the drive-in theater in the huge backseat of your father's Oldsmobile. Lorelei Communications claims that you can stop shoplifting with the simple addition of faint voices saying, "Don't steal that CD" to the background music in a department store.

Let's be serious. There is no science offered in these claims. Somebody did something, and something else good supposedly followed. There were no comparisons to prior sales, there were no control groups, there was no randomization, and there was no careful quantification except for magic percentages.

And then, consider how these folks claim to deliver a subliminal message. Splice in 10 milliseconds of film with "Eat Popcorn" in the middle of some movie that's headed right for DVD in the next week. Sure, get someone who sounds like your mom to hiss into a microphone, "Don't shoplift," then layer that into a hit from Milli Vanilli. One of the best researchers in testing these money-making subliminal schemes is Professor Anthony Pratkanis at the University of Washington. You can easily find his work on the Internet if you want more details, but for now, I'll just share his conclusions. He notes, "During the past few years, I have been collecting published articles on subliminal processes—research that goes back over a hundred years (Suslowa, 1863) and includes more than 100 articles from the mass media and more than 200 academic papers on the topic (Pratkanis and Greenwald, 1988). In none of these papers is there clear evidence in support of the proposition that subliminal messages influence behavior."

"Influence behavior" is the key point. No one has been able to produce scientific evidence of getting serious, practical, profitable behavior change from subliminals. But what about changes in thinking or feeling? Professor Pratkanis only declared behavior change as null and void.

Break Them on the Rock of Science

While it appears that the excited claims of business marketers do not produce the desired behavior change, it is still possible that subliminal messages might affect thoughts and feelings. Through technology, we can deliver subliminals. It *is* possible to shoot these speedy messages to people.

What happens to possible effects on thoughts and feelings with subliminal persuasion when you do some serious research on them? Let's take a look.

Whisky and Sex in the Lab

Let's consider a good example by Professor William Kilbourne and his colleagues at Sam Houston State University. They took ads then running in a national print campaign promoting a premium brand of Scotch whisky, Chivas Regal. They then created two versions of one ad. In the control condition (no subliminal messages or images—at least as far as they could see), the ad displayed a classy photo of the bottle of whisky all alone on the page. In the treatment condition (with a deliberately designed subliminal image) the researchers smoothly blended in a small silhouette of a nude female rear end on the slope of the bottle cast within a glinting reflection of light on the glass. They pretested the subliminal ad by having people look over the ad without warning about subliminals. After viewing, the people were asked about the ad. No one reported seeing this silhouette. However, when it was pointed out, everyone could see it and agreed that it was a nude image.

While there were several different ads used in this experiment, we'll only focus on the Chivas ads. A large group of volunteer undergraduates were randomly assigned to see a series of ads that contained either the control version of the ad or the subliminal treatment version. To measure everyone's responses to the ad, the researchers collected several different items. They asked each subject to rate the quality of the ad and their attitude toward the product. The researchers also obtained a measure of physiological arousal through monitoring Galvanic Skin Response (GSR). GSR measures anxiety, stress, or general activation through electrical resistance. Because the subliminal ad contained a sexual image, the researchers hypothesized that participants would become aroused. The researchers also hypothesized that the sexual image, especially in the context of alcohol, would cause participants to prefer the ad with the subliminal and to have a more favorable attitude toward Chivas Regal.

We've got a pretty good test here. A large sample of young adults who might be familiar with sex and alcohol, random assignment to controlled conditions, and multiple measures of the outcome variable. Throw those subliminal claims on the stone of science, and what do you get?

Everyone liked the subliminal ad more—noticeably more.

People randomly assigned to the treatment condition rated the ad itself as being "better" than the control version, showed a more favorable attitude toward the product, and—get this—also demonstrated higher GSR scores indicating more arousal when viewing the subliminal ad. And best of all (I left this out in the method setup), the researchers also asked everyone in both conditions if they noticed anything unusual about the ad. No one suspected any subliminals, and just like the folks in the pretest, when the researchers pointed out that glint on the bottle, everyone immediately saw the nude silhouette.

The Sizzle

Kilbourne also used a subliminal ad for cigarettes that tastefully displayed an aroused male. Women reacted with the subliminal response, but men didn't. Draw your own conclusions.

The Bodice Ripper and the Pope

In this study, Professor Mark Baldwin and colleagues at the University of Winnipeg recruited volunteers who were female, practicing Catholics. All of the women first read a passage from a romance novel describing consenting sex between a man and a woman in a romantic setting. After reading this passage, the women were randomly assigned to a viewing task in one of three conditions. The viewing task involved them looking at a screen where they were exposed to extremely brief bursts (4 milliseconds or .004 seconds) of 5 images. In the "negative" subliminal condition, some of the women saw images of a frowning Pope John Paul. In the "neutral" subliminal condition, some women saw images of an unfamiliar face with no expression. Finally, in the control condition, the remaining women were given bursts of light. After this exposure, all the women were asked to complete measures that assessed their self-evaluation—whether they felt good about themselves or felt guilty, ashamed, or embarrassed.

Once again, we have a good scientific study here. People are randomly exposed to only one condition. The viewing exposures are extremely brief. Four milliseconds means these images were on screen for 4/1000 of a second. That's Superman fast. That's faster than an airbag at 50/1000 of a second.

The researchers hypothesized that after good Catholic girls had read a sexy, romantic passage and then saw subliminals of a frowning Pope John Paul, the women might feel a negative self-evaluation while the other women exposed to either an unfamiliar face or a mere burst of light would not experience a momentary sense of embarrassment or guilt.

As with the Kilbourne study, Baldwin and colleagues found evidence to support the subliminal effect. The Catholic women exposed to the frowning pope had significantly lower self-ratings than the other two conditions, which were almost identical to each other. For you gearhead statistics mongers out there, the effect sizes were moderate with an effect size of .50 (or, expressed another way, a binomial effect size of 35/65). These numbers mean the effect was obvious to the naked eye (that's not subliminal, just funny). If you had talked with each woman after each test, you would probably have been able to tell who had seen the frowning pope. The researchers also asked each woman to report what image had been flashed before their eyes. All of them reported seeing a "burst" as the screen went from dark to the image display, but no one could report any details.

Mommy and I Are One

Professor Lloyd Silverman of New York University and his colleagues spent many years using subliminal messages to test psychodynamic theory. Briefly, psychodynamic theory is based in the work of Sigmund Freud, who looked for the causes of our adult social and psychological problems in our childhood past. You might recall the famous line, "The child is father to the man." In particular it was believed that we carried many unresolved childhood conflicts in our unconscious memory and this affected our behavior. Now, the discovery of pharmacological treatments for problems like depression and anxiety revolutionized this area of work, but there are still useful applications of the so-called "talking cure" (where you talk about your problems and gain insight into them). Given the importance of the unconscious in psychodynamic theory, Silverman and his colleagues explored the application of subliminal messages.

Silverman's work was aimed at people with extreme mental illness such as schizophrenia, but he also worked with people who had less-severe problems classified as "neuroses" rather than "psychoses." And some of his work also employed "normal" folks like you and me (although our friends and colleagues might dispute that "normal" classification for us). With Silverman's work, the crucial point is not just the subliminal presentation of the message, but also the content of the message. The most famous message employed is:

> Mommy and I are One.

Take a moment and let that percolate:

> Mommy and I are One.

Just on a conscious level—forget the subliminal—reading that sentence can be a highly activating process for most of us. Mommy and I are

One. No fear. No anxiety. No tension. Calm. Peaceful. Harmonious. Mommy and I are One.

Silverman's ideas generated abundant research using this paradigm. Commonly, the participant (either a healthy person or someone with a serious mental illness) is exposed to either the subliminal treatment message (Mommy and I are One) or a subliminal control message (People are Walking). Usually, there are several trials involving five or more exposures. These sessions may occur only once, several times a week, or during several months. After the exposure, the participant either self-reports or is rated by someone else for outcomes such as mood state, emotional memories, or severe psychological distress (such as depression or obsessive/compulsive behavior). The bet is that exposure to the positive message of Mommy and I are One will produce more favorable mental health outcomes.

A summary of 28 studies involving more than 2,800 participants supported that bet. Folks of all types exposed to Mommy and I are One either reported or were rated as having more positive mood states, more positive emotional memories, and fewer severe psychological symptoms. The effect size expressed as a Pearson correlation of r was .20 or expressed as a binomial effect size of $^{40}/_{60}$, which means the average person couldn't tell the group differences with the naked eye. You'd have to do statistical testing to prove it. Even with a small effect, however, Mommy and I are One worked.

I Don't Recognize It, but I Sure Like It

The final test of subliminal messages occurs in the work of Professor Robert Zajonc, then at the University of Michigan. Zajonc developed the "mere exposure" paradigm that tests a simple proposition: the more you see something, the more you like it. He busts this proposition down to its barest bones. He'll take some meaningless symbol—something you've never seen before and couldn't pick from a lineup if it robbed you in broad daylight. What kind of symbols are we talking about? Zajonc would take ideographs from Chinese. He would then have American subjects use a *tachistiscope* to look at literally hundreds of trials of these "meaningless" symbols. For almost all of these trials, each meaningless symbol would be presented only once. Zajonc would, however, systematically manipulate the number of presentations for one randomly selected symbol and have participants see it 5 times, 10 times, or more—all randomly varied with the sequence of the other hundred unique presentations.

def•i•ni•tion

Researchers employ a **tachistiscope** for subliminal testing. It looks like a World War II radar screen. It's a bit like putting on a swimming mask in that there is a rubber shield running around the screen. You press your face into the rubber tube to block your peripheral vision and to screen out environmental light.

Here's an illustration. A participant would look in the tachistiscope and see a blank screen. Every few seconds, the scope would present a four-millisecond exposure of one symbol, then the screen would go blank—then the process would repeat with another subliminal burst of a symbol.

In this session, there would be 20 bursts of symbols with 17 being unique—but with one symbol repeated 3 times. Keep in mind these unfamiliar symbols are zooming into view in four-millisecond bursts. You may see a burst of light, but you certainly can't see the actual symbols.

The key point here is that people are getting subliminal exposures to many unique symbols, but within this long string, Zajonc is systematically showing one symbol many times. Thus, some participants would be randomly assigned to see one symbol repeated 10 times while another group would get 5 repetitions—and the control group would get only the long, unique string of symbols. Got it?

Zajonc would then give a recognition test and an attitude test to each participant. Here, the participant would be shown a symbol at regular speed (in other words, putting the symbol on the screen and leaving it there in the center of visual attention, telling the person to look at it). The participant would then be asked whether it was in that long series of subliminal symbols and how well the symbol was "liked." To make things even more complicated, during this testing phase Zajonc would sneak in a couple new symbols that had not been shown during the subliminal exposure to look for "false positives" (the way police do with a properly conducted witness lineup).

This sounds more than a bit absurd and wildly complex. The methodology is a classic experimental design with the kind of controls one would use for testing a hydrogen bomb. And what is it all about? Just a bunch of symbols and squiggles that mean nothing to viewers. Do people still like something they've "seen" but don't recognize?

That is exactly what Zajonc found. If he repeated a nonsense symbol five times, people liked it more than the control group. If he repeated a nonsense symbol 10 times, they liked it more than the fiver group. If he repeated it 15 times, they liked it more than the 10-ers or the fivers. And—here's the kicker—although they liked it more, they still didn't recognize it at a greater rate! In other words, even when you don't know it, the more you see it … the more you like it.

Another researcher, Professor Robert Bornstein at Gettysburg College, conducted a summary of results from more than 200 of these "mere exposure" studies involving hundreds of different people. The main finding from the many tests Bornstein reported is that the more people were exposed to "nothing," the more they "liked" it. The largest effect Bornstein found was a Pearson correlation of r of .50 or a binomial effect size of $^{25}/_{75}$, which is a huge difference in social science. It means you could have easily seen which group of people was exposed more often to the same nonsense symbol, because that group would have expressed more liking for symbols they couldn't even recognize.

You Mean It's Real?

We started this chapter with a look at many infamous popular claims of subliminal power. We noted the scientific failure of all of them to achieve behavior change. Yet when we take a scientific approach to subliminal messages, we find pretty good evidence to support their existence and impact on thoughts and feelings. What gives?

Images or words displayed at incredibly fast speeds produce a consistent effect across a wide range of applications. Nudie subliminals produce physiological arousal and more positive evaluations and ratings. Frowning popes elicit mild feelings of embarrassment for sexually aroused Catholic women. The phrase "Mommy and I are One" makes us feel better about ourselves. And experiments about nothing generate more positive feelings. It appears that our minds are an active environment of meaning-making, learning, and memory in processes that continue even when we are not trying to control them. This is a marvelously interesting aspect of human nature.

Put on Your Tin-Foil Hat and Goggles

As I think about all this evidence (plus a lot more not presented here), it's clear to me that subliminal persuasion does occur. However, that Queen of Tomorrow thought problem that started this chapter seems foolish in the extreme. The science we reviewed does show the subliminal effect, but consider what those effects were: physiological arousal, more positive attitudes about Chivas Regal and its print ads, and a happier mood and stronger feelings of self-worth when we see the phrase "Mommy and I are One." We read a sexy book, then get a jolt from the pope and feel a little embarrassed or guilty. Wow. The more "nothing" we see, the more we like it.

The Sizzle

Watch the John Carpenter cult film *They Live.* Starring wrestler "Rowdy" Roddy Piper, the film features helpful aliens who employ a sophisticated subliminal technology to save earthlings from themselves. Look for the special sunglasses that Rowdy Roddy discovers.

Nothing with scientific control comes anywhere close to our Queen of Tomorrow, who manipulated our actions. Subliminal effects do occur, but they operate at a very low level of cognitive and affective change. Nothing we have seen demonstrates any strong, compelling, or obvious behavior change.

Why would there be this disconnect between the obvious cognitive and affective changes we've documented and the desired behavior change one might fear? Think about everything you've read here. First, delivering a subliminal message isn't easy. If the message environment approaches anything like the normal world, where people are freely moving through life, it's virtually impossible to hit them with a subliminal. This technical reason alone explains why so many of those hokey websites offering a marketing advantage, self-help, or whatever could never deliver on their promises. The environments in which their devices are meant to operate are simply too noisy and don't control the processing field.

Second, even after you get the message, you're still not in much of a position to act on it. Consider behavior problems such as smoking or overeating. Even if the audios do have even a moderate effect on attitudes, the users don't listen to those audios while they are in the kitchen or lingering over a cigarette. In other words, there is a disconnect between the internal state and the external behavior.

Third, the processes that cause subliminals to work don't have much impact on behavior. There is still a lot of work to be done to understand the basic systems of subliminal responding, but it appears that a lot of subliminal reactions are along the lines of "alerting" or "activating." This is a very primitive reaction to the world, similar to a preconscious cognitive/affective radar. It also seems that this radar is not strongly related to the kind of large social behaviors that are most interesting and important in the real world.

Putting all this together suggests that subliminals do exist, and they can alter the way people think and feel—but not the way they behave in a practical, profitable sense of the term. This could easily change in the near future. Given the incredible advances in computer technology, it might be possible to have a real iEye visor that controls the visual field. Imagine a grocery store that has special sensors to detect this visor, and as we walked down an aisle, the sensor would transmit a subliminal image (such as that nude silhouette on the image of a bottle of pop) just before we got to the pop display. That might motivate an interesting volitional behavior in a very TACTful way.

Consider other possibilities. Imagine people who volunteer to work in high-discipline situations such as the military, private security, or sports teams. As part of the training program, leaders could employ subliminal technology to condition emotional responses as part of producing more loyalty, commitment, and unity. Remember the "Mommy and

I are One" studies? Substitute the organization name for "Mommy," and away you go. You would have to hide the subliminal training and disguise it as part of a normal activity. For example, you could use a camouflaged tachistiscope to deliver visual training—say, how to use a new piece of equipment—and as part of that training, you could add the subliminals. While I'm not aware of any published scientific studies on this, I suspect you could do this to produce negative emotional responses, too. Trainers could use subliminals to produce anxiety ("I Lost Mommy"), then show subliminal images of opponents.

Another Look at the Queen of Tomorrow

And finally, return with me now to the Queen of Tomorrow, who first discovered subliminal persuasion. Did she keep the secret, or did I save the world from this devious invention? Because you are reading this exposé of subliminal secrets, it must mean that the Queen of Tomorrow has failed. But you know, it's possible she made me write this chapter to make it sound like subliminals were really quite impossible and ultimately harmless. Maybe the Queen of Tomorrow is out there right now running Madison Avenue, the White House, Congress (don't ask about the Supreme Court), and of course, the tobacco companies. How would you know?

The Least You Need to Know

- Subliminal messages exist and operate below conscious awareness.
- Scientific studies demonstrate subliminal persuasion can be effective.
- Subliminals do not yet create serious, practical, or profitable behavior changes.
- Subliminals do have proven, short-term effects on feelings and thoughts.
- While practical subliminal influence is weak, new technology could improve its impact.

Part 4

Payoffs

You can't keep score without a score card, and persuasion is no different. How do you stack up against the competition? How do you know whether you're leading the league? Are you sure you're doing it right? You can prove it to yourself (and to anyone) that you have mastered the moves. And speaking of moves, you can play the way the smart guys do: plan from templates. And now, at the end, you'll see the bigger picture. Look into the gear, the rules, and the plays to see the larger lesson about persuasion and life.

Chapter 13

Prove It!

In This Chapter

- Understanding the scientific foundation for persuasion
- Thinking carefully with chance, comparison, control, and counting
- Using the windowpane to see changes
- Applying scientific principles to your own efforts
- Assessing persuasion claims

The only thing worse than failure is misunderstood success. When you fail, at least you know you've got a problem. When you succeed but misunderstand why, you have a false sense of security. If you think you've got the Hot Move, the New Thing, or the Special Sauce, there's a strong human tendency to believe you're the smartest guy in the room. (And in case you've forgotten how easy it is to manipulate attributions such as this, please go back to Chapter 9.) People want to be successful and can easily fool themselves into thinking they've hit a triple when they were born on third base. The peril of misunderstood success arises when things suddenly start to fall apart and you don't know why. It used to work, and now it doesn't. Panic sets in.

This chapter shows you how to understand why and how things work or don't work when you do them. It provides a set of guidelines and principles you can use in almost any situation to wisely assess what you really know and when you're just fooling yourself. Before you commit time, money, or effort, you should prove it.

Testing Your Persuasion Skills

If you spend any time reading popular presentations on persuasion, one of the most obvious attributes you will see are claims of effectiveness. Typically, the claims are expressed as percentages and exclamation points: increase sales by 47 percent! Cut shoplifting losses by 82 percent! Enhance customer satisfaction by 33 percent!

While everyone learns to take numbers and exclamation points with a grain of salt, you still come away thinking positive thoughts. "Well, maybe it won't be 82 percent, but it will certainly help!"

Most folks working in the real world tend to have an optimistic view of their efforts (who strives toward failure?), and as a result, they tend to overlook possible rival explanations for outcomes. Say you buy one of those self-help books on the power of persuasion and implement the powerful persuasion play described on page 56. And sure enough, something good happens. It must work, right?

If you're old enough, you might remember the Nike shoe campaign with Michael Jordan and Spike Lee. The ads featured shots of Jordan flying through the air with a basketball, displaying his amazing physical talents. Through it all, Spike Lee—playing the character Mars Blackmon—kept hollering, "It's the shoes! It's the shoes!" Today, Nike would shoot this ad with LeBron James instead of Michael—and in another 20 years, it will probably be some kid named Wang Tao. But you get the picture. Now, really, is that kind of athletic performance due to the shoes?

In your head, you know that there's something special about Michael, LeBron, or Wang Tao that you don't have—and that's the difference. But in your heart, you might feel that just maybe if you got those shoes … the same thing can happen with persuasion advice.

Realize I am *not* saying that there is no skill or science in persuasion. This book demonstrates that there are many solid, useful, and provable principles that do work in the real world. It's just not as easy as some would make it seem.

What we need to do is prove it.

> **Wise Lines**
>
> It is the mark of an educated person to look for precision in each class of things as far as the nature of the subject admits.
>
> —Aristotle, *Nicomachean Ethics, Book I*

How Do You Know It Really Happened?

I've had the opportunity to advise, consult, and work in a wide variety of organizations that in some way use persuasion to be successful. The first thing that struck me was how incredibly certain many folks were of some communication tactic, campaign, or intervention. They would describe to me the "Special Sauce"—a marketing cliché that has become a kind of shorthand for the New Thing—they were using to get more customers, make larger sales, or obtain more compliance—and my first thought was, "You've got to be kidding. If you're really doing that, you'll get killed." Rather than blurt out that blunt disconfirmation, I'd restrain myself and ask, "How do you know it works? What are your metrics?"

Someone would then describe how "sales over 12 months" improved, "customer traffic volume momentum" increased, or complaint calls to 800 numbers dropped. I would then note that because a metric went up or down at roughly the same time they were using the Special Sauce, that doesn't mean it was due to the Special Sauce. Average daily temperatures might have also gone up at the same time. Would anyone argue the Special Sauce caused that?

At that point, somebody would make a joke about global warming and then shift the topic to something else.

Part of this disconnect can be explained in the difference between a scientific approach versus the Darwinian approach most people use. As a scientist, it's possible to generate new ideas, test them scientifically, and then implement them successfully. Thus, you can design a test *before* the outcome to determine what's really going on.

A Darwinian approach instead comes up with the next big idea, then flings it into the marketplace and lets survival of the fittest rules apply. If you survive, it must be due to the Special Sauce you're using, right? Thus, the "test" occurs *after* the outcome and looks back to find justification for the current success or failure. Phil Rosenzweig wrote an excellent book, *The Halo Effect* (see Appendix A), that looks at this problem in detail—outlining the many ways that businesses in particular incorrectly explain current success after the fact by looking backward in what Rosenzweig calls "delusions." If you're in business or any larger corporate-type structure (educational, volunteer, or religious), I highly recommend this book for its smart look at how we fool ourselves with this backward-looking, Darwinian approach.

My own problem with a Darwinian approach is that most people and their organizations haven't been around for the millions of years that a Darwinian argument requires. Thus, if you think your Special Sauce works because you're still around, you're using a metaphor to understand your success and not reality. That's like eating the menu at a restaurant.

Darwinian persuaders look at their survival and argue back to past behavior, concluding, "It's the shoes, baby, it's the shoes." While it is possible for the shoes to do some magic, isn't it also possible that there's something else going on? Maybe there's some skulking third variable we're overlooking, such as the superb physical talent and grinding work ethic of an outstanding athlete when we claim, "It's the shoes!" A Darwinian approach cannot easily tease out these possibilities. A scientific approach, however, can.

Two Big Scientific Questions

When you want to know whether something "works," you are asking two questions:

1. Did the shoes really cause the performance, or might there be rival explanations? This is sometimes called *internal validity.*
2. If it appears the shoes did cause the performance in this case, will it generalize to other conditions? This is sometimes called *external validity.*

Especially when we are looking at human behavior in the real world, that first question—what really caused the outcome—is incredibly complicated. Human action is seldom caused by just one obvious factor, and unless you look for and test other rival explanations, it's easy to miss the truth. And if things are going well—you're profitable, you've got happy employees, or you have plenty of contributions and volunteers—you tend to get lazy and look for obvious causes and effects. Only when trouble comes is it crucial to know the truth, and often by then it's too late. A scientific approach helps you understand what really works and why, which makes you more efficient and effective.

def•i•ni•tion

Internal validity looks at the true relationship between a presumed cause and effect. **External validity** looks at how that relationship generalizes to other situations. (Why "effectiveness" is internal and "generalizability" is external, I cannot say. Scientists are awful at naming things.)

The second question asks whether some true effect will generalize to other situations. You may develop a persuasion strategy, test it on a small group of people, and determine it works. But then when you release it more widely your results become erratic. If you've had any widespread experience in business (especially sales), you can see this generalizability problem. The same problem occurs on a smaller scale. With your first child, you could merely offer a gentle scolding to terminate a bad behavior. But when you try that with your second child, he merely laughs joyously and continues squeezing ketchup onto the carpet. Sometimes the play works, and sometimes it doesn't; that's the generalizability problem of external validity.

Both questions are important, and one without the other leaves you hanging. If the shoes do work, but only for LeBron or Michael—in other words, the effect doesn't generalize past these two guys—then who wants the shoes besides two of the greatest athletes of all time? By contrast, if the shoes don't work, who cares if they don't work anywhere, anytime, anyplace, for anyone? Scientists care a lot because such failures are good for theory development, future research, and applications for new government grants, but for the rest of us, failure is just failure.

How do we find the effect, rule out rival causes, and determine generalizability?

The Four Essentials of Truth

Science typically employs four forces to answer these questions: randomization, comparison, control, and quantification. These are the four tests you can apply with any persuasion play (or any other human activity that is supposed to make something happen). Scientists have very rigorous rules for using them and almost all of the ideas in this book are based in studies that have these standards. While it's nice if you've got a white lab coat, a controlled environment, and a squad of graduate students chained to the oars, you don't have to act this way. You just need to think this way.

Roll the Dice

Randomization is the selection of objects such that each object has an equal chance of being selected and that the selection of one object has no effect on the selection of another. If you have a classic two-group experiment with a treatment group (the shoes) and a control group (a competitor's shoes), when you randomize, everyone has the same chance of getting in the treatment group or the control group. Randomizing is the best way to "equalize" the test so that each group is roughly equivalent or similar to each other *before* the test.

Nonrandom tests are fishy. If the boss's niece is in charge of testing the new "shoes," you might be tempted to look at your study volunteers and say, "Hey, all you tall athletic people come over here, and you old, fat, and sick people go over there." Then you give the athletes your "shoes" and the infirm get the competitor shoes. Guess which group does better? Sure, the boss's niece is proud and happy and has a glowing report about your job fitness, but is it the shoes or something else? Randomization helps solve intentional and unintentional bias.

Randomization sounds like a fairly simple-minded approach, and one wonders how it could have any practical impact. Consider, for example, some of the raging questions in society today about climate change or crime.

Some people ardently believe that human activity has changed global climate, perhaps irrevocably, while others acknowledge that the weather has changed, but think human activity has nothing to do with it. And worse still, the science seems to support both positions, plus many stops in between. One huge stumbling block drops in our path, because we cannot randomize anything in our studies of climate. That is, we cannot randomly select samples of planets just like Earth, randomly assign different patterns of human activity, and then sit back, measure what happens, and draw good inferences. Everything in climate studies is based on a sample size of 1 and simply observes what naturally occurs rather than using the powers of randomization. No one would argue that climate study is not scientific, but because we can't use randomization effectively, the scientific method of study is weaker and leads to contradictory information.

Consider now, crime. If you look at crime statistics, especially murder, over the past 50 years, you see a clear rise from the 1950s into the 1960s that continued through the 1980s, leveled off, then fell quite rapidly through the 1990s with the decrease still occurring in the new millennium. Why? If you read the expert literature on this, you get many answers. Some argue that the crime rate followed the demographic bulge of the Baby Boomers. When they were young, they were good little kids, then they went through that adolescent rage period followed by the inevitable domestication process (graduation, steady job, marriage, mortgage, kids) and the even more inevitable ageing process (don't even ask me about life after 50). Others will point to the rise and fall of the American drug culture and the wars over that profitable underground economy. Some will look at police policy, particularly the "broken windows" theory that suggests if you crack down on petty crime (like breaking windows), you'll head off bigger crimes before they can start. Who's right? It's hard to say, again, in part, because we cannot use randomization effectively. The good experiment would be to randomly assign people to communities and communities to different treatments like drug availability or police policies, let this cook for 50 years, then see what we've got. And even though we can generate tons of great data on crime and demographics, drugs, police policy, and so on, we cannot do an experiment with randomization.

Every persuasion play from this book is based on research that employed randomization. I included no persuasion play unless I could find several studies that used randomization with either random selection of participants from a well-defined population or random assignment of participants to conditions and sometimes both types of randomization.

Whenever you read persuasion books, look for statements about randomization. This is especially useful in more results-oriented books that offer some fabulous technique that always works, and here's the story, folks … read the story and make sure you see something that indicates random selection of participants or random assignment to conditions. If you don't see that, be skeptical.

Realize, finally, that in many large-scale settings—large businesses, education, and large charitable organizations—you can use randomization to test your persuasion plays. Even in a small organization, if you apply randomization over longer time periods, you can acquire the same advantage. However, in interpersonal situations, like with family, randomization would probably be a dumb thing to do. It would probably make you look crazy!

Make Fair Comparisons

Two hikers in the woods see a bear off in the distance. The bear first scents the air, then recognizes the hikers and takes off in a dead run for the men. One of the hikers sits down, tears off his hiking boots and laces on a pair of sneakers. His buddy says, "Why are you doing that? You can't outrun a bear." The guy replies, "Don't have to outrun the bear, just have to outrun you." Always make the correct comparison, and you're on the path to truth or survival!

A great jazz number from the 1960s with Les McCann on piano and Eddie Harris on sax offers an ironic tune for our background music. The lyrics describe people "trying to make it real," to which Les McCann sings sardonically, "Compared to what?" (Go ahead, search for a music video of "Compared to What?" and listen to it as you read this section. Adult advisory, though.)

So, you say that the power persuasion play increased sales by 43 percent?

Compared to what? Sales from a year ago? Sales since Friday? Sales from some other number you pulled out of your hip pocket? The concern here is the outcome comparison.

And your power persuasion play, compared to what alternative? Dumb silence? A wink and a smile? The concern here is alternative explanation comparison.

There's always a temptation to test your shoes against some silly alternative or some silly outcome. Let's have our treatment group get the newest version of the shoes while the control group will ... run barefoot ... wear sandals ... wear original 1955 Chuck Taylor high tops ... or worse still, no control group and no alternative comparison.

And there's a tendency to cherry-pick the outcomes for only the good news as we measure our impact. Without naming any names, there have been many companies that have invested a lot of time, money, and personnel on some very bad projects that were made to look better because they cherry-picked the outcomes. Hey, did you know that we actually increased the number of Christmas cards our clients send to us by 47 percent after we started using the new "Special Sauce"? Hey, since we've added our new "Special Sauce," sales of napkins have increased 34 percent. Hubba-hubba.

Phil Rosenzweig demonstrated the danger of weak comparisons with his careful analysis of all those "great" companies described in books like *In Search of Excellence* and *Good to Great* (see Appendix A). Rosenzweig followed those "great" companies in the years after the books and discovered that their "great" performance usually dropped dramatically, so bad in fact that if you were using the same method to find a "great" company to study, you would no longer include it on your list. What gives? How does a company go from "great" to "not so great" in just a year or two? Rosenzweig's argument is that researchers "delude" themselves when testing for "great" companies and make weak comparisons in their testing. They pick companies that look "great" for only a short time period, ignore other factors that contributed to that success, or collect data that fits the hypothesis they already hold. *The Halo Effect* is an excellent business demonstration of the critical importance of comparison.

> **Wise Lines**
>
> Success rarely lasts as long as we'd like—for the most part long term success is a delusion based on selection after the fact.
>
> —Phil Rosenzweig, *The Halo Effect*

Good science always looks for the toughest comparisons to test your Special Sauce. Get hard-headed. Compare your "shoes" to the best competition you can find. Measure the outcomes that are truly critical to your success whether it is measured with sales or souls. Typically the best way to find a tough comparison is to ask someone who competes with you to devise the "other" group. Competitors love our weaknesses and will diligently seek the alternatives and outcomes that make us look bad.

The whole point of science is to find what works and why to the best standard our puny minds can devise. The point is not to reassure yourself or the boss or anyone else that things are just fine and there's no need to think about what we're doing, just keep driving toward that light at the end of the tunnel. It has been my experience that doing science typically makes you feel uneasy, uncertain, and uncanny even when all the news is good. Science almost always gives you bad news, surprising news, unexpected news. If you are sitting around a table looking at any kind of evaluation study of something your team is doing and everyone is happy and smiling, you're probably missing something important. And the easiest way to delude yourself is to make bad comparisons.

Be a Control Freak

If you order two hamburgers at McDonald's and one tastes great and the other doesn't, you've found a control problem. Any time there's variation in a process, you've got a potential control problem. Control is a really big deal in science. Part of control is expressed in the famous "Six Sigma" business theory from a few years back, which focused on removing errors and mistakes in production to get as close to zero as possible.

Is every pair of shoes you test the same quality and fit? For every test is the court smooth and clean? Is the backboard always at the same height and angle? Any element in the test that can vary must be controlled or you've got a problem. Thus, good research applies the Special Sauce the same way every time with every person with every application. When conditions vary without control, then problems arise.

Unintended Consequences

Want a winning bet? Easy: always bet against the "hot hand." Many basketball fans believe in the "hot hand." Sometimes players go on a shooting streak game where they make way too many shots in a row. They've got the "hot hand." Except if you do a scientific analysis of a lot of basketball players over a lot of games, you can't find any evidence to support this claim. Instead, the "hot hand" is just a random run of favorable outcomes. (Don't believe me? Search online for "hot hand" and Gilovich.) If you do believe me, I've just shown you how to win bets during basketball games. Get a "hot hand" believer to bet a buck every time an announcer calls out, "hot hand!" The bet is that after every announcement, the player will make the next shot. If the player does, you pay a buck. If the player misses, you get a buck. If you do this over all occurrences of the "hot hand" you should win much more often than you lose.

A great illustration of the control problem arises in the "lifestyle" factors in mortality and morbidity. Right now, we're trying to understand the role that lifestyle behaviors like diet and exercise play in our health. There's some pretty good evidence that people who eat a "better" diet or get "more" exercise will live longer and be healthier. But when you look more carefully at the evidence, you see a lot of studies with virtually no control or very poor control over these factors. The biggest hassle here is getting an accurate and reliable measurement of something like "diet" or "exercise." Typically, we use self-reports from people and ask them to describe or estimate what they eat or how they exercise. Even if people know the truth and can report the truth accurately, we still have no control over what "treatment" group they are in. This is called *selection bias* and it simply means that when you don't control the Special Sauce, other forces are operating. We might see that people who report "more" of any "exercise" live longer, but since we didn't assign the activity or the amount, we're stuck in a chicken-or-egg dilemma. Do healthy people exercise more and live longer or do people who exercise more live longer and healthier? When we can't control the application of the Special Sauce, we've always got that problem.

Another good illustration of the control problem shows in the current raging arguments over global warming. We've already looked at the randomization problem with understanding global warming and human causes in it. You can't randomly assign planets to climates or even randomly assign different human activities to different climates and planets. We've only got this one case, Earth, so randomization is logically difficult. Well, not only do we have the randomization problem, we've got a control problem. The hypothesized human activities that cause global warming have occurred without any scientific manipulation. Lots of people operating in loose groups have done a lot of different things over the past 100 years. None of that activity was "controlled" in anything remotely approaching a "scientific" sense of the term.

Okay, so does this mean that there is no science with diet and exercise or global warming? Of course not. That's not the point. It's just that the science isn't great, but rather has a lot of holes in it because we lack control over the Special Sauce. This lack of control doesn't mean that eating more fruits and vegetables has no value or that getting more exercise has no value or that human activity has no impact on global climate. It just means we need to be a lot more tentative in our conclusions.

Quick review here: Control addresses how the Special Sauce gets made, assigned, and used. When the researcher controls who gets the Special Sauce, how much, and how often (typically using randomization), then we've got good control in our experiment and we can feel pretty confident about drawing conclusions from the data. However, as we lose control over the application of the Special Sauce, we need to become more thoughtful, more wary, and more provisional. It doesn't matter whether the Special Sauce is a new persuasion tactic, a new diet plan, or just a new sauce. When you have control of the test, the data are better.

Count On It

If you think you change something, then you can quantify it. If you believe you can do something that makes the world better or even worse, you should be able to quantify that thing, that Special Sauce, that move, that New Thing on a simple counting scale. I'd argue that if you can't count it, you really can't change it.

Consider the opposite of this claim. You want to defend instead this proposition: I've got a Special Sauce that I know beyond reasonable doubt produces a desired change in other people at my command; but I can't quantify any of this. I can't even divide the "change" into two groups of "Did Change" and Did Not Change," much less have shades in between.

That's crazy. If you can do something that changes other people, you should be able to count it, even if only with that "Did or Did Not" category system.

If you can count something, that means you can explain it to someone else and they can count it and get the same number you get or at least close to it. If you can't count it, that means you're probably operating in a universe of private meaning where, hey man, it's something that's just got to be true, but I can't explain it to you. That's fine on the street or in a bar, but if you've got time, money, and people riding on the proposition, you need to learn to quantify.

Now, usually when numbers appear on the battlefield some people throw their hands up in the air in surrender as if the enemy has brought up the heavy artillery and rather than face annihilation by quantification, just wave the white flag right now. If you don't like numbers, you can still use quantification to understand persuasion or global warming or anything that makes claims about change in reality. I'm not kidding. Even if you can't count past 10 without taking off your shoes, you can still use quantification to assess the science of claims. Here's how.

Unintended Consequences

The Great New York City Blackout of 1965 left America's largest city without power throughout most of the night of November 9th. Nine months later, a *New York Times* reporter interviewed several local obstetricians and from their anecdotal observations, the reporter concluded that there was a sudden, brief increase in the city's birth rate, no doubt due to that Blackout. The story became urban legend and over 40 years later, some folks still believe it. However, careful counting by a public health statistician demonstrated clearly that there was no increase compared to the preceding five years and that the reporter had clearly made limited data fit a clever hypothesis.

First, we've got to get in the WayBack Machine and time travel back to a smarter and simpler time. We're going to use an approach first described by Professor Robert Rosenthal in the 1970s. He called his method the *Binomial Effect Size Display* (BESD), demonstrating once again the facile skill scientists possess when it comes to naming things. (Can you imagine the words we'd be using today if Adam had been a scientist rather than just a guy?) I call it the Windowpane Display, which is at least transparent. Think about a window. Imagine that it's divided into four equal panes. Easy to visualize, right?

Now, let's put some labels on our window.

We're doing an experiment and we've got two groups. The treatment group will get the Special Sauce while the control group will get something else, the Standard Sauce. For example, the Standard Sauce would typically be the routine, the usual practice, the standard operating procedure, the way we do things around here; while the Special Sauce would be the extra, the new idea from the head shed, the latest inspiration from the boss's niece, or your new persuasion play. You want to compare two ideas, plans, plays, services, products, whatever, under the same conditions. We'll randomly assign our participants to only one condition. To make the math tidy, we'll do this experiment with 200 people, so we put 100 in each group. Now, after we give each person their Sauce, we then observe them to see whether they changed the way we thought they should. We'll make the answer to this question easy with only two possibilities: yes, they changed or no, they didn't change.

Here's a graphic of the windowpane.

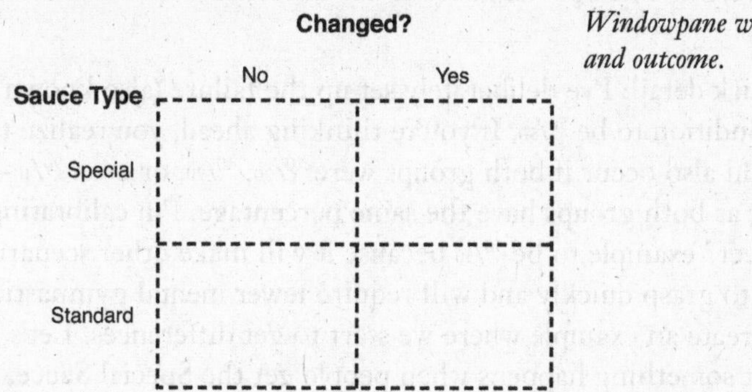

Windowpane with treatment and outcome.

We're testing the Special Sauce against the Standard Sauce. We have 100 people randomly assigned to each group. We then see how the people change either into Yes or No. Now, let's fill in each of the four little windowpanes to demonstrate different scenarios. We'll start, as we often do in science, with failure. Assume that the experiment blows up and that our Special Sauce produces nothing better or worse than the Standard Sauce. We'll call this the no effect condition, because the treatment had no impact, influence, no effect. It looks like the following.

Changed?

Sauce Type	No	Yes
Special	50	50
Standard	50	50

No effect.

We see here that we've got 50 people in each little windowpane. Let's read each row. We started with 100 people in the treatment condition who got the Special Sauce, and when we observed them, we found that 50 of the 100 changed and 50 of the 100 didn't change. We also started with 100 people in the control condition who got the Standard Sauce, and when we observed them, we found 50 of the 100 changed and 50 didn't. No effect. The Special Sauce is not different from the Standard Sauce.

Here's a quick detail: I've deliberately set up the failure (also known as the null) condition to be 50/50. If you're thinking ahead, you realize that failure would also occur if both groups were 10/90, 30/70, or even 90/10—just so long as both groups have the same percentage. I'm calibrating the "no effect" example to be 50/50 because it will make other scenarios a lot easier to grasp quickly and will require fewer mental gymnastics. Now let's create an example where we start to get differences. Let's assume that something happens when people get the Special Sauce, and it looks like the following.

Small effect.

Sauce Type	Changed? No	Changed? Yes
Special	45	55
Standard	55	45

We now see on the rows and the columns a 45/55 effect—a 10-point difference. In social science parlance, this 10-point difference is called a "small" effect as popularized by Jacob Cohen in his work on power analysis and effect sizes. Make sure that you "see" the impact of the treatment. Notice in this example that more people who get the Special Sauce showed the desired change (read the row) compared to people who got the Standard Sauce (read their row).

A difference of 10 percent doesn't sound like much, but consider the practical effect. If you compare the batting averages between "poor" Major League Baseball (MLB) players and "great" MLB players, the statistical difference works out to a "small" effect size. Here's a forced example that scales the comparison for 1,000 at bats. (Yes, I know that nobody gets 1,000 at bats in a season, but you don't want to do the math for seasonal data, and it doesn't matter.)

	Hit	No Hit
Well below average hitter	220	780
Well above average hitter	320	680

If you read down each column, you should spot that .100 (10 percent) difference between hitting skill level. If you compute the proper cross-tab statistic, a phi, the value is .113, which is another way of saying "small effect." Thus, while a .320 average is an All-Star difference compared to a .220 average, statistically this is small.

Wise Lines

You know what's the difference between a .250 hitter and a .300 hitter? About 24 extra hits a season. Six-month season, 24 weeks, that's 1 extra hit a week. You get one extra gork, one more dying quail, one more ground ball with eyes a week, and you're playing in Yankee Stadium.

—Kevin Costner as "Crash" Davis, a minor league catcher in the movie *Bull Durham*

Now, let's increase the effect size. Here's the windowpane for a moderate (also sometimes called "medium") effect.

Moderate effect.

Sauce Type	Changed? No	Changed? Yes
Special	35	65
Standard	65	35

Now our row values are 35 and 65. A moderate effect is a 30-point difference, which sounds somewhat impressive. Think about this moderate effect another way. Notice that 65 is almost twice as large as 35.

Expressed another way, a moderate effect means that you're getting almost twice as much change in the treatment group compared to the control group. A moderate effect is getting to be pretty obvious. Think how obvious a "large" effect must be. It looks like the following.

Large effect.

Sauce Type	Changed? No	Changed? Yes
Special	25	75
Standard	75	25

The row values here are 25 and 75, a 50-point difference. Now the rate of difference is three times, with the treatment producing a 300 percent increase over the control. That's big. Take a quick scan now and review the four windowpanes: no effect, small effect, moderate effect, and large effect. See the numbers change.

The point of this demonstration is to show that you can think with numbers in a practical and efficient way without having a statistician in the room. Anyone can handle the windowpane approach with numbers. Just have a clear definition of changed (yes or no) and a clear definition of the group (treatment or control). Then just count and look for percentage differences. A 10 percent difference is small, 30 percent is moderate, and 50 percent is large. And realize that while "small" may be hard to detect, it can definitely make a big practical effect (you often don't have to outrun the bear, just one other guy).

Smart Planning

Whenever you try to assess a persuasion play, you need to consider the four forces of randomization, control, comparison, and counting. Is any of the evidence you have based on the four forces? In this book, every persuasion play has a great deal of testing using the four forces in both scientific and practical settings. While you may not have the technical expertise or the simple motivation to read the extensive scientific literature on persuasion, you should be able to note in my descriptions of various persuasion plays terms such as "random," "comparison," "effect size," or "controlled." I didn't add those terms as weasel-word marketing ploys, but as descriptive attributes of the study. The researchers did randomly select or assign participants, they carefully controlled different message conditions, they thoughtfully compared outcomes that were scientifically or practically important, and they counted their results. Under those circumstances, I feel comfortable offering these ideas as the best persuasion knowledge we've got.

I want you to think in a similar way with your own persuasion knowledge. When you read or listen to other expert sources, do you hear words such as random, comparison, control, and counting? Do you hear all of those words or just one? If you can ask follow-up questions about these terms, how does the source react? Nervously? Angrily? Change the topic? Or does he or she whip out more bar charts?

And you need to use these scientific principles to assess your own persuasion skill. If you think you're pretty good at it, where's the evidence? Any randomization or control or comparison or counting? Or are you simply taking that Darwinian approach where if you've still got the job, you must be pretty good at it? Use these principles to understand your own skill.

I do not for a moment believe that a scientific approach is the *only* way to understand life and our behavior. Scientists doing science often do very dumb or harmful things. Consider the case of Long Term Capital Management, an investment company led in part by Nobel prize–winning economists. After a four-year start with glorious success, the company maneuvered itself into a catastrophic loss of $4.6 billion in just a few months during 1998 that required the intervention of the federal government to prevent a panic in worldwide

Wise Lines

Science is a lot like Winston Churchill's observation about democracy: "It is the worst form of government, except for all others that have been tried." Science, too, is the worst form of knowing, except for all others.

financial markets. And remember, this was 1998—not 2008, when a really smart investment house, Bear Stearns, collapsed in the credit crisis. And how about the 1989 reported discovery of "cold fusion" by a number of scientific teams across the world? Several physicists staked their reputations on a form of energy transformation that would have revolutionized science and the practical world. Except no one else could replicate their work, and in fact could demonstrate why it was wrong. Science is not perfect.

The Least You Need to Know

- You must know what caused it (internal validity), and if it will generalize (external validity).
- The four forces are randomization, comparison, control, and quantification.
- Randomization is the best way to "equalize" groups before study.
- Comparison considers reasonable alternatives.
- Control makes testing fair.
- If you can't count it, you don't understand it.

Chapter 14

Persuasion Scripts

In This Chapter

- What's a persuasion script, and why do you need one?
- Effective scripts in action
- Weak persuasion scripts
- Is it a script or something else?
- Team persuasion tactics
- Why persuasion scripts work

The largest problem people have with doing effective persuasion is organization. Persuasion in real time is more complex than you realize, and if you simply try to do it on the fly, you will probably fail. (Remember the persuasion rules from Chapter 3? Rule No. 6 is Effective Persuasion Takes Planning, and Rule No. 7 is All Bad Persuasion Is Sincere.)

In this chapter, I provide you with a simple planning scheme called a "persuasion script." It means exactly what it says, and if you use scripts, you will become a very effective change agent.

Persuasion Scripts Outlined

A persuasion plan includes the goal (a TACTful statement of who does what, when, and where) and the persuasion play used to accomplish this goal. To make a working plan that combines a goal with a play, you need a *persuasion script.* If you've ever had a fast-food job at the counter or done telephone sales, you know about scripts. If you have contact with people that is stereotyped, predictable, and stable, then you can profitably use scripts.

def•i•ni•tion

A **persuasion script** is a routine sequence of dialog and action that includes a persuasion play and a change goal involving the thoughts, feelings, or actions of a targeted receiver.

Let's consider an objection to scripts even before we detail them. Many people hate scripts, find them insulting and demeaning, and believe that scripts are not nearly as effective as the performance people could deliver if left to their own devices. If you are a script hater, you need to do more reading and thinking about it. Most people are lousy in situations that call for a script—precisely because those situations are so routine, predictable, and stereotyped. You get bored out of your gourd always doing the same thing, so you start to wing it (or worse still, just get through it). And sad to say, most people are not nearly as good at persuasion and communication as they think they are. If you give them a script, you get a much better average performance. Big business is into scripts precisely because the entire point of big business is to create a fundamental routine that everyone can do profitably. All this "I've got to be me" is nice if you're an entertainer or a rebellious youth, but it doesn't make the dime day in and day out.

If you want to excel, find all of the tasks in your work life that are routine—then build good scripts and *do them every time.* Save your unique talent for places where it's really needed. Why waste your time being unique when a routine will accomplish the same goal?

The Standard Script

Here's a standard script for routine contact with customers, clients, students, employees, and volunteers (in other words, people with whom you do business who are not family, friends, or colleagues). Let's first look at the functions:

- An **introduction** provides the basic "name, rank, and serial number" of the persuasion agent. A smile should accompany this information.
- A **welcome** details the source. This is the name of the company, your logo, and your mission.
- An **orientation** gives the receiver a map of "where you are standing" so the receiver understands the situation from the source's point of view. This is the products or services available here.
- A **persuasion setup** lays the groundwork for a quickly following persuasion tactic. It may be a question posed by the source to get the receiver thinking along a certain line. It may be information provided that gives something of value to the receiver without this actually costing the source anything (such as those "free" appetizers you get at fancy restaurants before they give you the menu). It may be a whiz-bang tactic right out of this book. It's your choice, and you can vary it from day to day.
- A **product or service offer** is the source's primary reason for the contact. It's the main point, the *raison d'être* for the source to talk to the receiver. It tells the receiver that the source can do something and that the receiver can act on it now.
- A **persuasion tactic** is a deliberate source move to change the receiver here and now. The receiver came in for one thing, but now the source is trying to move him or her to another thing. The tactic should not interfere with anything related to the actions from the service offer at the prior step. You must deliver the service the receiver expected or you will not get another contact with him or her. Don't goof this up with a clever persuasion move.

- A **transition** moves the receiver from this source to another source. You've made a good impression on the receiver, you delivered the service, and you executed the persuasion tactic. Now, send the receiver to the next organization source who will repeat the script but will provide a new service and perhaps a new persuasion tactic.

Consider this situation. We're running a physician's office in one of those mini mall–type places. We want our clients to discover information about a new service we're offering because we don't want to appear to be selling it. We've created an information kiosk that is plastered with brochures, pamphlets, stickers, magnets, and other doodads explaining this new service. We've packaged the information as both a cue and an argument, so it won't matter what WATTage the receiver has. We want the receivers to find this information, and during their time in the clinic, somebody will make a pitch to them if they bring it up. Here's the script for the receptionist:

> **Introduction:** Hi. How are you doing today? My name is Steve, and I'm the receptionist.
>
> **Welcome:** The Mountaineer Health Clinic wants to be there for you and provide the best care at the best price in our state.
>
> **Orientation:** I'll get your name and appointment information and make sure you get to the people you need to see.
>
> **Persuasion setup:** By the way, I hope you like our new waiting area. We asked our clients what we could do to improve it, and they suggested we make more space for children and also make the room a little brighter. We recently remodeled it, and we hope that you find it more comfortable.
>
> **Product or service offer:** May I take your name and the name of the physician you're here to see today? Okay, do you have any questions about the appointment or insurance or anything else I might be able to help you with?

Wise Lines

If it ain't on the page, it ain't on the stage.

—An old show business saying that illustrates you don't get in front of customers without a script

Persuasion tactic: Please take a seat anywhere. You might like to look at our information kiosk in the new waiting room. It has a lot of helpful free information.

Transition: A nurse will come into the waiting room and call your name when they are ready for you. The nurse's name is Mary.

This script makes the client aware of many things. We listen to our customers and try to give them things they like (remodeled for more space and a kid-friendly area). We point them to the kiosk and tell them everything is free. Even if this is their first visit, they will probably cue off the "brighter," "space for children," and "more comfortable" language and respond with a positive effect. And because everyone waits longer in a waiting room than they expect, odds are real good they'll check out that kiosk, take our sales pitch for the new service in the format (brochure, magnet, and so on) they like best, and read it. And later in the appointment, somebody else in the organization will hit them on that new service.

You think that might work?

Let's work the standard script in another setting. How about in a tire store?

Hi. How are you doing today? My name is Steve, and I'm a sales agent.

The Mountaineer Tire Store puts tires where you go and aims to make your driving safe.

If you can tell me your driving requirements, either I can help you right away or get the expert you need to see.

By the way, I hope you noticed our new garage. We've expanded the number of bays and hired three more experienced mechanics.

What kind of vehicle do you drive, and what kind of driving do you do?

I've got three options for you. I'll show those to you, but you also might want to think about doing a tire balance and rotation, too. With our expanded garage, we can get this done faster so you don't have to wait as long.

I'm going to send you to Bob on this one. He knows more about high-performance tires than anyone else, and he can give you the rundown on the best options.

How can you afford *not* to use scripts? How can there possibly be any serious cost, barrier, or risk with a well-designed, properly executed script? Do you really think that the spontaneous, off-the-cuff, just-wing-it performance will beat a good script day in and day out?

This is an absolute no-brainer.

When you have routine, stereotyped, and predictable contacts with clients, you've simply got to design, train, and implement scripts. Scripts are easy, fun, and popular.

Easy? Come on. You've got the basic outline for a generic script right here. If you're still surviving in your business, you're smart enough to customize them to your own situation. Fun? Of course it's fun. Think about plotting, planning, and scheming with your crew to develop these things and use them. It will be a good laugh doing this, because everyone sees the advantage, it's easy to implement, and no one's job is going to get downsized. Building and doing scripts gets everyone involved.

Popular? You don't think your competition's doing this? Hey, look around. Join the twenty-first century. Lots of people are doing this. They're called winners.

Persuasion scripts are the way to go. They focus everyone on the main point of the work and their jobs. It gets everyone in the same boat and rowing in the same direction. Scripts provide great work markers (if you're in the script, keep doing it; if you're not in the script, wake up). They give you a flexible structure for delivering a consistent message. You can vary the persuasion games by day or week. You can train your people to work cooperatively in a team persuasion approach so that you have interlocking scripts. Then, people can train in each script and move dynamically from part to part with the work flow. In other words, one person doesn't always have to be

The Sizzle

Persuasion scripts plus the routine and predictable interactions in your work will lead to better luck (and success).

the receptionist or the performance tire expert; rather, everyone can rotate through these roles.

Contrasting Good and Bad Scripts at Restaurants

Let's explore more applications of persuasion scripts. Consider persuasion and food. My wife Melanie and I like good food. One of the great delights of my life and marriage is the continuing conversation we have over white linen or chipped Formica as we wolf down haute cuisine anywhere or at Al's beefs in Chicago. What's this got to do with persuasion scripts? Quite a bit, actually.

One night, I accompanied Melanie on a business dinner. Her department was interviewing candidates for a professor position, and she took the current candidate out to dinner. She also dragged me along as the chauffeur and tag-along go-fer.

We ate at a new place in town. Inevitably, when I'm in a restaurant, I evaluate the place because I really like food and good eats. One place that Melanie and I both enjoy is Emeril's in New Orleans. Not only is the food great, the room beautiful, and the service outstanding, but the entire dining experience is clearly designed, planned, and choreographed to produce delight in the customer. Part of that planning is based on persuasion scripts.

One time many years ago, Melanie and I made reservations at Emeril's (at the Food Bar). We made the reservations for the first seating—5:30 P.M., I think. And because we're always hungry, we arrived early. Somebody let us in although the place was not officially open. As we stood in the bar area just outside the main dining room and Food Bar, we could see and hear the staff finishing up a meeting. The leader ran a spirited, energetic presentation that described the evening's specials with a focus on key terms to be used when offering the dish. The key terms were not simply a list of ingredients with jazzy modifiers but rather were aimed at making the listener happy and interested. The key terms included "what's new and different" and "why you would like this" ideas. Through it all, the leader maintained high energy and encouraged a similar feeling in the staff. The leader then concluded the meeting with what must be the Emeril's cheer. For the remainder of the evening, I was struck by the repetition of key terms and energy from that meeting with the various servers and staff people who worked the room. I could overhear snippets from the servers as they described various dishes with those "new and different" and "why you'll like it" suggestions. I could see the controlled bustle of every staff person, whether out front serving or in the kitchen preparing. And every time we've gone back to Emeril's in New Orleans, we've had that same kind of experience even though we haven't caught the staff rah-rah meeting that precedes service.

My claim is that the staff meeting is based in part on a persuasion script orientation. I'm sure that the staff completes a training session at a place such as Emeril's, where the basics of the ingredients, preparation, and service are drilled. But Emeril Lagasse goes a step further and also focuses on the customer's response to the experience and builds in ways of enhancing pleasure and satisfaction. That's where the script comes in. The staff meeting that precedes the evening provides some structure and a lot of content for everyone's script that night. I suspect that if there have been problems with past specials (too spicy, too rich, too small, too large, or too whatever), the new script includes tactics to address those problems in a positive manner.

Now, back to my experience at the new place in town with my wife's job candidate. There's no reason why everyone in the restaurant business cannot deliver an experience similar to Emeril's. Sure, Emeril has a particular and unique genius that is his alone—but that genius is not the key point here. His genius plus persuasion scripts (and other elements that go past our interest here) make for his success. Why can't all servers be well trained in the basics of the business and also have persuasion scripts that enhance customer pleasure and satisfaction?

Wise Lines

I just get up every day and try to do a little better than the day before, and that is to run a great restaurant with great food, great wine, and great service. That's my philosophy.

—Chef and restaurateur Emeril Lagasse

Our server that night in the new, local place clearly knew the business of serving at a good restaurant. But she was only perfunctory, providing bare-bones attention to the most basic elements of service (what do you want, here it is, is it okay, anything else, and here's the check). As I scanned the room and listened to other staffers, the same kind of bare-bones behavior was evident. We haven't been back.

Persuasion scripts allow you to design communication that should produce desired outcomes in clients. With scripts, you can change the way they think, feel, and act. And with scripts, you get all the advantages that planning, control, and structure bring. You can train to criterion. You can measure. You can provide great, accurate feedback with a minimum need for punishment. You can see what works and what doesn't; have a sense of why the success or failure occurred; and make specific, targeted changes. That's the beauty of planning, control, and structure.

Bad Scripts: Rather Be Right or Presidential?

We compared a great script at Emeril's to a nonscript at another place. Let's now look at weak scripts. These folks are trying to do the script thing but are not quite hitting the mark. I'll draw two examples from past political campaigns.

Howard Dean, 2004

You'll recall that Howard Dean, former governor of Vermont, ran for the Democratic nomination for president in 2004. He came out of nowhere, launched a meteoric campaign, then burned out when the first primaries voted. Let's look at a Dean script for campaign workers.

Here's an extended quote from a story about Howard Dean's primary run in 2004. The author is Ryan Lizza. Lizza writes that the script calls for the volunteer to deliver a tough version of the Dean stump speech: "Governor Dean is running for president to stand up to George Bush and take back our country. His opponents are going after him with negative attacks designed to confuse people. All they can do is attack, because while Governor Dean was standing up to George Bush, they were surrendering to him in Washington. They surrendered when they gave George Bush a blank check in Iraq and when they passed his No

Child Left Behind Act. And, while Governor Dean was ensuring health care for every child in Vermont, his opponents were spinning their wheels in Washington."

If this still doesn't persuade the Iowan on the other end of the line, the script offers a section titled "Tips" to strengthen the message. "People are sick of hearing about the caucus," it notes. "Empathize. Share your frustration. Tell them your story. Tell them why you dropped everything and are sleeping on a floor in Iowa to make Howard Dean president." Of course, empathy doesn't always work. Sometimes you need to be a little tougher. That's when you move on to the script under the heading, "If they get pissed and try to cut you off or hang up." The way to deal with a pissed-off Iowan is to push back. "Assertively tell your story," the persuasion script counsels.

Let's pull out the key elements of this script. First, the script calls for direct argumentation, or what I'll call a debate script. It provides specific issues, a stand on those issues, reasons to support the issue, attacks on other stands, and reasons to support those attacks. This is an obvious demonstration of a central-route persuasion approach where you first get a high-WATT thinker, then provide strong arguments. Second, the script calls for emotional awareness of the receiver advising to look for either burnout (sick and tired of the primaries and all the shouting) or anger (dislike of your candidate, and here's why) and then provide more arguments for handling a high-WATT thinker who is either weary or annoyed.

These debate scripts appear to be the most common approach for folks wanting any structure to their persuasion efforts. I'll commend them for at least having enough foresight to realize that planning beats spontaneity when it comes to persuasion. (Or, as Rule No. 6 states, Effective Persuasion Takes Planning.) A prepared persuader is much more effective.

However, the planning here is so earnest, sincere, and authentic as to render it useless in most instances and counterproductive in others. It's a great example of Rule No. 7: All Bad Persuasion Is Sincere. This script is designed to elicit a prepared defensive response from almost all receivers even before the arguments are presented. The script immediately warns the receiver that he or she is entering into a debate and that he or she is going to get arguments. Such warnings have the unfortunate effect of producing biased high-WATT thinkers rather than objective high-WATT thinkers.

In other words, the debate script puts people in a frame of mind where they think they have to defend themselves, rather than listen with an "open mind" or what in theory parlance I'd call "objective processing." Thus, by unintentional design, this debate script reduces its chances for success from the beginning.

Worse still is the effect of a debate script when it fails. Whenever high-WATT processors are confronted with contrary arguments, actively consider those arguments, and then reject them, their position has become stronger. Now, if the Deaniacs wanted voters to be even stronger in their dislike of Howard Dean, the script makes sense. Start a fight with voters, make them think real hard, make them actively fight you off, and what do you get? A stronger enemy, not a weaker enemy. (Recall Rule No. 5: If You Can't Succeed, Don't Try.)

The Sizzle

Howard Dean's persuasion performance has changed greatly since his 2004 presidential bid. As chairman of the Democratic National Committee, he's now more structured, complex, and subtle in his communication.

This debate script explains in part the spectacular failure of Howard Dean in the primaries of 2004. You'll recall that he was a monumental favorite with all the flash of the shooting star rising in the heavens, only to crash after the first votes were cast in the first primary: Iowa. What happened? Certainly there are many factors in a vote, but this script approach illustrates in a small way the larger strategy Dean employed—and clearly, it did not work.

A persuasion script in contrast to a debate script is open to a wide variety of psychological elements that drive voting decisions. Attributions of causality and responsibility; perceptions of unfair restrictions; negative consequences from planned actions; cue-based associations of liking, credibility, comparison, scarcity, reciprocity, and public commitments; and even simple rewards all can determine how people vote.

A persuasion script is open to all of these elements and can move flexibly, depending on the characteristics of the voter in the here and now.

A debate script is the mark of an advocate and is much more concerned with looking right than with getting the desired outcome.

Paul Wellstone, 2004

This example is from the Paul and Sheila Wellstone Foundation, which is aimed at providing training and development for progressive politics. You may recall that Mr. Wellstone was the senator from Minnesota who was killed in a 2002 plane crash. Here's a snippet of their persuasion script:

> "Hi. My name is (give first name), and I'm here tonight in regard to the upcoming presidential election. Do you have a quick minute?"
>
> (Pause for a reply, and if the person says they are busy, tell them you have only two questions.)
>
> "Does it concern you that President Bush's tax cuts went primarily to Americans earning more than $150,000 a year, yet they created record budget deficits that will take decades for our children to pay back?"
>
> (Wait for an answer. If "yes," go to Option A. If "no," go to Option B.)
>
> Option A: "It bothers me, too, especially since those deficits have also forced states to cut eligibility requirements for health insurance and raise co-payments and cut funding for schools—all of which benefit average middle-class families. Do you think this is right?"
>
> (Wait for an answer and acknowledge it, engaging in a brief conversation, but do not get into a debate.)
>
> "Okay, one last question: if the election were held today, who would you most likely vote for: John Kerry, George Bush, or Ralph Nader?" (Let them volunteer "undecided.")
>
> "Thank you very much for your time today."

Option B: "Okay, thanks. Does it concern you that these deficits have forced states to cut eligibility requirements for health insurance and raise co-payments and cut funding for schools—all of which benefit average middle-class families?"

(Wait for an answer and acknowledge it, engaging in a brief conversation, but do not get into a debate.)

"Okay, one last question: if the election were held today, who would you most likely vote for: John Kerry, George Bush, or Ralph Nader?" (Let them volunteer "undecided.")

"Thank you very much for your time today."

We can immediately note the obvious similarity to the Howard Dean script. This is clearly a debate script aimed at direct argumentation with issues, stands, evidence, and reasoning. No doubt this can be persuasive and lead to changing the way someone thinks, feels, or behaves, but I suspect that such scripts are more likely to fail (and in some cases more likely to produce boomerang outcomes that serve to make things worse).

Realize that such an approach immediately triggers a high-WATT processor—someone who is actively involved but responding defensively, knowing that someone is going to argue with them and against them. The Wellstone script here immediately forewarns receivers that they are in a debate even before the specific issues, positions, and arguments are made. This is certainly a sincere and authentic approach, but not likely to be effective.

The script in no way instructs or plans for the source to get any kind of "audience analysis" before launching into the debate. (Remember Rule No. 2: It's About the Other Guy.) Note that the script doesn't advise to look at the house, the neighborhood, or the people on the street to get a sense of what kinds of people live here and how they might already be thinking, feeling, or behaving. There is certainly nothing in the script that guides the source in sizing up the person who answers the door. What's his or her mood? Is the person attentive or distracted? How is he or she dressed? How quickly does the person respond to your questions? Nothing in the script assesses the immediate mental state of the receiver at the door. (Remember Rule No. 4: All Persuasion Is Local.) Just bang away with the arguments, and "if they say X, then you say Y."

It's also worth noting that both debate scripts have been connected with Paul Wellstone and Howard Dean, two men associated with high-intensity, in-your-face communication styles. The fact that both are or were progressive Democrats is less relevant. It's not the content of the politics; it's the style of the persuader that's the point.

People using these debate scripts are more likely to find kindred spirits rather than actually change anyone's thoughts, feelings, or behaviors in a positive direction. Certainly, there's nothing wrong with attracting those who are attracted to you—but you have to realize in this case that attraction is not the same thing as persuasion. And when you use debate scripts that attract those attracted to you and then label it as an exercise in persuasion, you are misleading yourself about what you are doing, the impact it is having, and why things are occurring the way they are. In other words, under the surface of your current success courses a deeper tide running toward failure. Attraction is not persuasion.

Unintended Consequences

Why do people do what you want them to do? Sometimes it occurs because you attracted them into doing what they were already going to do. That's not persuasion. Persuasion requires change. You need to understand the difference so that you know what works for you and why.

Do Persuasion Scripts, Not Persuasion-Like Scripts

"Persuasion scripts," as a term, is not unique to me. I did an Internet search on the key term in 2008 (if you try to replicate it, use the quoted search "persuasion scripts" and "-austen" or else you'll get many hits for the nineteenth-century classic *Persuasion*, a novel by Jane Austen). I found several existing webpages that employ the specific label. That's how I found the Howard Dean and Paul Wellstone scripts. In my reading of several other websites, my sense of persuasion scripts swerves away from these other uses in a way that makes my idea different, independent, unique—and perhaps peculiar.

Here's an example of how you can find the same label, "persuasion scripts," but find a different product. Once again, we're in the realm of politics where organizations are using their "persuasion scripts" to affect elections. This one is from an advocacy association, the International Association of Fire Fighters (IAFF).

The persuasion scripts are telephone-based scripts that only have the caller ask the respondent questions about whether the respondent is going to vote for or against a candidate or issue. It is essentially a polling script. The script looks fine to me and would be effective in field use for collecting poll information.

My quibble is with the label. Where's the "persuasion" in voter position? How are you trying to change, influence, sway, motivate, manipulate, swerve, bend, or alter anybody with a polling script?

Okay, so this is not really a "persuasion" script. It is a polling script, and we call them "persuasion scripts" because somebody typed that label on the first Word document file. What's the big deal?

You mislead yourself when you mislabel. If you call a "polling script" a "persuasion script," then sometime later when somebody asks, "Hey, are we doing anything to influence or persuade voters?", then you have an answer. "Yeah, sure. We've got persuasion scripts, so we're okay on that one."

Except … you are polling, you are not persuading. And you've not only lost the opportunity to change the world, but you've also fooled yourself into thinking you've already got that covered when you don't.

Please realize that I am not criticizing the content of these scripts. The folks at IAFF are a fine bunch of people dealing with a dangerous occupation. My concern here is that there's more to the word "persuasion" than these scripts use, and if you open the word to its wider meaning, there is a large world of potential good for you.

Teamwork and Persuasion Scripts

I once ran a persuasion seminar in a corporate communication program. During our discussion of CLARCCS cues (see Chapter 7), one participant, John, shared an interesting observation he'd made on a shopping trip that, at the time, didn't seem quite that meaningful. But upon learning about cues and unthoughtful persuasion, he realized he'd witnessed a very powerful persuasion tactic.

John was shopping for a new computer at one of those large office equipment chain stores. During checkout, the sales clerk left John alone—and while John was waiting, he noticed a small printed sign taped to the cash register that had several typed lines of instructions. Being curious and left alone, John read the page. In essence, the sign described a team approach to persuading customers.

When a customer entered the store, Employee 1 would make a friendly greeting—and unless there was an immediate request, Employee 1 would walk away. Shortly thereafter, Employee 2 was directed to contact the customer and point out current sales—and again, unless there was an immediate request, Employee 2 would then walk away. Employee 3 would then enter the scene with a "How may I help you?" approach. Employee 3 would then work with the customer to connect him or her to the needed product or service, then direct the customer to Employee 4, who would complete the transaction at the register.

This pattern of employee behavior looks like normal business behavior. The novel, interesting, and useful persuasion tactic, however, comes from the deliberate sequencing of steps through different employees. By assigning different specific communication tasks to each role in this play, the business makes it more likely that each customer will "get" all the information the business wants out there. Furthermore, by distributing each message across multiple sources, it becomes less likely that the customer will feel like a persuasion target and more like someone shopping in a store with a lot of helpful agents.

This team persuasion tactic is a brilliant application of the principles of persuasion within the spirit of persuasion scripts. It provides a formal and ongoing structure for the business to deliver persuasion (that typed sign on the register). It hides the persuasion attempt across multiple sources. It has to be great for team morale, because each person on the team will play different parts in the scene. You can imagine the signaling they invent and use, just like a baseball coach on third base giving signs. And I've got to believe that team persuasion goes right to the bottom line with increased sales and customer satisfaction with the greatest benefit of all: no one even knows it's happening. It's an excellent application of persuasion rules.

Practical Benefits of Scripts (and Planning)

Persuasion plays work. They change people. If you can tie that change to some goal you desire, then you can get to your goal faster, more cheaply, and more easily. You can make more money; attract more volunteers; generate more commitment, loyalty, and support; motivate, energize, and invigorate. In other words, you get what you want. Persuasion scripts improve your ability and skill at persuasion. They put you ahead of the actual communication encounter and let you select in advance the ways and means of your persuasion so that you're at your best.

How much "more" change can you expect with these persuasion plays, especially within well-planned scripts? On the basis of published studies from others or from my own, I'd estimate that well-done persuasion plays should produce a 10 to 30 percent increase over the current baseline. My only caveat here concerns whether you're already doing persuasion plays. Obviously, if you know about these ideas and have already implemented them, there's not much new here, right? If you're doing your standard practice and that standard does not include an explicit use of persuasion, then that 10 to 30 percent improvement should occur.

Unintended Consequences

Scripts must be both routine and opportunistic. You must be able to recognize when the script is not working with a particular receiver or when something better might apply. Rigid persistence in a script also draws attention to itself. You're always trying to change the other guy, not just act out a script.

Realize that the benefits of skilled persuasion plays are not automatic as if you just wave your hands, shout "Shazam!", and success falls on your head. You have to have the "right" TACTful behavior. You have to know your receivers. You have to select the right persuasion play. You have to do the play correctly all the time. And if you are trying to get a group of people (team persuasion) to do persuasion plays, they *all* have to do this correctly. Persuasion is a quality control process, and you can bring that kind of scrutiny to it where you carefully identify all the steps in the persuasion process, monitor them, and remove errors.

The Least You Need to Know

- A persuasion script is a routine sequence of dialog and action aimed at achieving a goal.
- Consider scripts for all interactions that are routine, stereotyped, and predictable.
- Use the persuasion rules to guide the persuasion plays you script.
- Develop team-based scripts that vary persuasion plays and roles for each person.

Chapter 15

Graduation Day

In This Chapter

- Organizing your persuasion plays in the "persuasion toolbox"
- The practical application of persuasion
- Persuasion and human nature
- What path is in your future?

At the end, we consider our lessons learned and find a grand perspective. We've mastered a large body of ideas and terminology in the last 14 chapters, and we need a simple scheme to organize them all. Consider the "persuasion toolbox" as that scheme. Then think about the lessons we've learned about practical persuasion—actually using it. Finally, realize that persuasion tells us a lot about human nature.

Cue the Band!

Here we are in the stadium wearing those silly hats and gowns and praying that everyone else is wearing clothes under their gowns. Filled with nostalgia, we can't help letting our minds fill with memories ... definitions, models, the Communication Cascade, the persuasion rules, those cute beginning plays and then those daunting advanced plays (especially that weird dissonance), and now ... what? What does it all mean?

The Persuasion Toolbox

While the persuasion plays are nicely explained within each chapter, how do you relate them together? I mean, how do you organize ideas as different as dissonance, attribution, the Two Step, and obedience?

The best approach is the persuasion toolbox, a three-category system for classifying all persuasion plays. With it, we can organize all the ideas in this book into useful categories that help us see critical similarities and differences among and between the plays. The persuasion toolbox has three "trays":

1. **WATTage:** the receiver's mental state or willingness and ability to think, switchable between a high and a low setting so that the WATTage setting determines the route.
2. **Central route:** a means of change that requires that long, involved conversation in our heads as we think about the persuasion; it also has a divider for *objective* (following information to a conclusion) or *biased* (making information fit a conclusion).
3. **Peripheral route:** that quick, snappy, often accurate, mental shortcut requiring little conversation in our minds. In our dim mental state, we look for bright, shiny cues to lead the way.

We can put each of our persuasion plays into one of these three main trays.

Start with WATTage

This is the crucial persuasion variable. The receiver's mental state determines what happens next in every persuasion play. For example, if the receiver never gets high WATT, dissonance will not happen. If the receiver never gets low WATT, the Two Step will not work. I'll leave you with one of those annoying professor tricks: you scan back through the book and consider each play from the WATTage angle. What happens with the play when the receiver is high WATT or low WATT? With all the persuasion plays, WATTage is the first driving force.

Realize that WATTage is both something we can monitor in other people—and, most importantly, manipulate in other people. The fact that we can actually move the WATTage switch through our own independent and volitional skill is one reason why persuasion is so powerful. You can cause things to happen. As a sharp point of contrast, the "tipping point" idea operates an after-the-fact description of some change process that has already occurred. Simply understanding the "tipping point" does not give you any ability, action, or skill to make it happen. You can observe it, comment on it, and explain it … after it happens. WATTage is something you can change deliberately and before the fact.

With inoculation, you create high WATTage through that threat of attack against an existing belief. With Thoughtful Persuasion, you generate high WATTage by demonstrating how involving and important it is to the other person. With more effort, in dissonance, you create high WATTage through inconsistencies that produce negative outcomes tied to self-concept—all surrounded by internal attributions.

For the various persuasion cues, you can create low WATTage through distraction, deception, repetition, boredom, confusion, tiredness, emotional arousal—in other words, all those things that happen in normal life that cause us to respond as humans rather than as the classical "rational actor."

The persuasion light bulb determines what follows next in a persuasion play. High WATTs will travel the central route. Low WATTs will amble down the peripheral route.

The Sizzle

WATTage can be manipulated or monitored. You can make it happen (manipulate) on your schedule, or you can simply watch others and assess (monitor) it. After either, you then deliver arguments. Either is fine as long as it is set to the right position (high or low) for your play.

On the Central Route

Now, consider the central route with either objective or biased processing. Generally speaking, the persuasion plays in Thoughtful Persuasion, dissonance, and inoculation are prime central-route plays. Often, the persuasion plays of attribution work best on the central route, and attribution also plays a key role in the central-route impact of dissonance (remember that if people go external, they fall off the dissonance train).

Remember all these plays start with a high-WATT receiver. Just think about how "hot" all of these plays cook. They require an actively involved person who is really generating a lot of conversation. In Thoughtful Persuasion, the central-route processor seeks arguments—key pieces of information, facts, statistics, evidence, reasoning, or logic—then actively considers that information in a deeply elaborated mental discussion. In dissonance, that inconsistency triggers a hot dissonance-reduction process as people deal with the inconsistency of "good person, bad outcome." And in inoculation, we deliberately flaunt a threat and motivate people to actively defend a belief or attitude. Each of these plays also delivers a desirable outcome: when they work, your job is done. Central-route plays deliver long-lasting, internal change that requires less future effort from you.

We see biased processing in both dissonance and inoculation. In each case, the conversation serves to support an existing belief, idea, or conclusion, and all the argument and message processing is distorted to fit that existing position. While "accuracy" or "truthfulness" is important, the bigger emphasis is on sheer processing: get them to generate that hot and active self-defense, and we'll work on the details later. But for now, you want a hot defender.

Each central-route process operates in a slightly different fashion. Thoughtful Persuasion follows the more classic, beginner idea of persuasion: Everything is high WATT: a hot source confronts a hot receiver with hot arguments that produces a long conversation in the receiver's mind, leading to the change. Dissonance starts with an important inconsistency that triggers that hot dissonance-reduction action, which includes a conversation about adjusting the "good person" and "bad outcome" balance. Inoculation starts like Thoughtful Persuasion with a hot source and a hot receiver, but instead of providing arguments, the source instead lets the threat lead the receiver into his or her own long, internal conversation. See the nuance and variation in each, but realize all share the common threads of high-WATT responding.

Ambling Down the Peripheral Route

Finally, think about the peripheral route. Generally speaking, the persuasion plays of conditioning and modeling, obedience and authority, UnThoughtful cues, the Two Step, and subliminal persuasion are peripheral-route plays. In each case, we are dealing with a person who is not at the top of his or her cognitive game and is doing the best imitation of the "rational actor" that he or she can deliver. The most obvious marker of the peripheral play is a short-term effect. When we are caught in a peripheral process, the play affects us only in that immediate situation. It rarely generalizes to similar situations. It almost always requires some external source watching us and delivering cues. In the short term, we are persuaded—and sometimes we can make permanent mistakes in an instant. But usually, the cue effect rapidly dissipates, and we're back to "normal" and under our own control soon.

If you are the persuasion source, the peripheral-route plays are attractive because they are quick and effective—but they do come at the price of constant vigilance and action on your part. You always have to act like an authority, always deliver the reward, or always Two-Step them.

Realize, too, the enormous variation between all the cues of the peripheral route. Liking, whether through physical attractiveness or social charm, produces positive feelings in the receiver, which leads to cue-based change. Comparison, by contrast, simply provides interesting and apparently important models doing something we're not—leading to a mild cognitive response that looks intelligent compared to the liking cue. And, while I provided seven different cues (CLARCCS and the Two Step), know that there are many more. And while each is different in some way from the others, they all share the common link of low-WATT processing. Receivers engage shallow, easy, and quick cognitive work to arrive at a change.

The persuasion toolbox is a great way to organize this wide range of seemingly disconnected and unrelated persuasion knowledge. Every play we've looked at can be understood with the three simple ideas of WATTage, central route, and peripheral route.

> **Unintended Consequences**
>
> Always match the right persuasion play to the right mental state. High-WATT processors are marching for the central route, and if you try to cue them, you'll fail and look like an idiot. Persuasion always requires a combination of elements.

Practical Persuasion

Throughout this book, I've aimed at the practical application of persuasion principles in the real world in real time with real people. Although we've looked at cold data from the four forces of science, each persuasion play is presented as a communication skill anyone can learn to perform.

Active or Reactive?

You can perform almost all of the plays in either an "active" or "reactive" form. In the active form, you plan then execute the play on your schedule. You literally and truly make the change in others happen when you want it. In the reactive form, you have to wait for the circumstances to turn in your favor before you can make one or two persuasive actions. Take Thoughtful Persuasion as an example.

With an active form, you target your receiver (Rule No. 2: It's About the Other Guy), determine the TACT (Rule No. 4: All Persuasion Is Local), figure out what moves the WATTage switch, then turn the switch to high WATT and deliver arguments that will produce the long conversation in the receiver's mind. You make it all happen through the skillful use of your persuasion knowledge in the active form.

Now, consider Thoughtful Persuasion in its reactive form. Let's assume you're trying to persuade several different people. You may not be able to determine in advance exactly what you can say to each person to dial up the persuasion light bulb. Instead of manipulating the switch, you monitor each person—making a real-time assessment of the receiver's

WATTage until you observe him or her in a high-WATT state. Then you deliver your arguments—producing that classic central-route change.

This active versus reactive thinking can also be applied with cues on the peripheral route. For example, in the active form, you plan and deliver each element in a Two Step. You've got them in a script, and you just deliver the same persuasion performance with each receiver. In the reactive form, you might seize upon a chance—and when you observe that your receiver has already taken the first step in the Two Step through the action of someone else, you might then deliver the crucial second request for your own purposes.

If you think about this distinction, you realize that it's also a marker of your persuasion skill as a communicator. If you are strong, then more of your persuasion plays employ the active form. You make it all happen under your control. If you are weaker, then more of your persuasion plays are reactive (where you simply observe your receivers and wait for the right moment to apply your skills). Now, just because you do not have excellent command of your persuasion skill and cannot easily and frequently make the skill work does not mean that you are a lousy persuader. Even in the reactive form, you can still get to the same change as you would in the active form; it just takes longer and requires more patience and observation on your part.

A Tool for Self-Defense

While I've tried to make this book a manual of action for producing persuasion, you can also read it as a self-defense manual. If you know how to do it with others, you know how to see it when others aim it at you.

The single largest self-defense lesson from this book is WATTage. When you are in your low-WATT mode, you are extremely vulnerable to those quick-hitting cues on the peripheral route. And as long as you stay low WATT, those cues are effective.

Everyone knows their own low-WATT state. You know how you feel, how you think, and when it is most likely to occur. And after reading this book, you are a lot more sensitive to this knowledge and are much more likely to recognize it in yourself. Armed with new and enhanced self-knowledge, you should become much more aware (and more quickly aware) of those instances when you're ambling down the peripheral path. You should now recognize these cases and realize that you're essentially caught in a social error. You are acting less than a fully rational, logical, and controlled person should. Big deal. You made a momentary wrong turn in the walk of life.

Now, just get out of it. Stop it. Don't go down the peripheral route. Just smile and say something like, "These pretzels are sure making me thirsty," "I'm happy to be here; I hope I can help the team," or "I never did mind the little things"—then move away.

Or, if you are of a certain turn of mind and disposition of character, you might try to reverse the situation on the source who's after you. The reciprocity cue springs easily to mind here. "When the source does something for you, you should do something for the source."

Well, if you allow yourself to wander down the peripheral route and give the source what he or she wanted, you've started the reciprocity cue with that person. You've given him or her something. Now you can aim at getting something in return (something larger, of course).

Or how about dissonance? A sales clerk has just used a CLARCSS cue on you to get you to make a purchase, and you say, "You wouldn't be trying to take advantage of me and get me to buy something I don't really need or want, would you?"

Boom. They have an inconsistency, because no one wants to believe that they deceive, manipulate, or trick their customers; they freely did this with you so they have to make an internal attribution; they've got a negative consequence of being exposed as a cheat; and it definitely affects the person's self-concept. Talk about getting hit with the dissonance train. To change the balance of "good person" to "bad outcome," he or she could easily offer you better deals on other products or services to demonstrate that he or she isn't the kind of person who manipulates customers.

Reading this book should make you a much tougher persuasion target. It gives you more control and flexibility in your choices.

The Importance of Planning

But for the simplest cues (liking, particularly), the remaining persuasion plays all require planning. When you reread various plays, you'll be struck over the detail in making the play successful. While there may be a lucky few born to persuasion greatness, for the rest of us common folks, persuasion skill demands planning. Remember Rule No. 6: Effective Persuasion Takes Planning.

Planning contains two elements: the TACT and the play script. You must specify the Target, Action, Context, and Time (who does what, where, and when), and then you must determine your dialog and action to produce dissonance, Thoughtful Persuasion, or a CLARCCS cue. Planning is both that simple and that difficult. Kids never forget Rule No. 7: All Bad Persuasion Is Sincere. Stated another way, in persuasion you are always your own worst enemy. You always want the easy way, the quick way, or the simple way to great success. It's human nature, but it injures your persuasion skills. The first mark of your seriousness is whether you plan.

Human Nature and Persuasion

While this book is most directly aimed at providing practical information, it also presents a window into human nature. If you ever wonder why the world is the way it is and why people do what they do, just think about persuasion. Through a wide variety of tactics, mere words can alter our thoughts, feelings, and actions in just one instant. And the diversity of these tactics amazes: simple cues, complex arguments, fake attacks to strengthen, and clever inconsistencies for hot dissonance. We think of ourselves as capable, deliberate, striving, wise, and accomplished—and then we run on automatic pilot as we fall for a friendly smile, a Two Step, or an authority figure. There's more going on in human nature, and persuasion proves it.

Let's pull a couple of great examples from one of the oldest authenticated texts in human civilization: the Old Testament. Whether you are pious, skeptical, nihilistic, or any shade between, almost everyone accepts the scientific analysis that these old books about the human experience were written by people thousands of years ago. What do they say about persuasion and human nature?

The Sizzle

Persuasion was one of the first subjects of formal study of human nature and psychology. Plato in the *Phaedrus* and *Gorgias* dialogs discusses persuasion, as does Aristotle in his *Rhetoric*. The first universities founded in medieval times included persuasion (as rhetoric) in the "trivium," or the three foundational studies of grammar, logic, and persuasion.

Start with King Ahab.

Ahab, an evil King of the ancient Israelites, sinned greatly and unforgivably against God. Through his carnal love for his disbelieving wife, Jezebel, Ahab turned against God and begun to worship the false idols of his woman. Furthermore, Ahab's sins caused other Israelites to sin similarly against God. God decided to punish Ahab in a way that will also demonstrate to others that they should keep their faith and respect the covenant with God.

God gathers His angels about Him and solicits their recommendations. At least two unnamed spirits speak and their ideas are not accepted. Then, one, most probably Satan, suggests a plan that he thinks will work. The evil angel will cause Ahab's prophets to speak falsely to Ahab about a war and Ahab's chances of success in it. Satan will become a "lying spirit" who will speak through the mouths of the prophets, thus deceiving Ahab and encouraging him to rash action that will cause his death and the death of many other sinners.

Here's how the King James Bible describes this:

> And the LORD said, "Who shall persuade Ahab, that he may go up and fall at Ramothgilead?" And one said in this manner, and another said in that manner. And there came forth a spirit, and stood before the LORD and said, "I will persuade him." And the LORD said unto him, "Wherewith?" And he said, "I will go forth, and I will be a lying spirit in the mouth of all his prophets." And God said, "Thou shalt persuade him, and prevail also. Go forth, and do so." 1 Kings 22:20-22.

"I will be a lying spirit in the mouths of his prophets." Satan has a lot of great lines, doesn't he? (For a fabulous fictional representation of Satan, John Milton's epic masterpiece, "*Paradise Lost*," is unexcelled in showing his exuberance of evil.)

Please note two important persuasion angles in this example:

- Observe that God does not persuade, but rather permits Satan to use persuasion on humans. Even if you are not a believer, it is interesting to imagine a god concept that is all knowing and eternal. How could something as uncertain, conditional, and incomplete as persuasion be of any use to anything that already knows everything? This suggests an important limitation to the concept of persuasion and to human nature. It is unworthy of God or god, but most useful to humans.
- Note how Satan decides to use persuasion. He becomes a lying spirit that lies in the mouths of prophets who then tell the lies. Thus, Satan cloaks himself in the cloth of credibility, perhaps the oldest persuasion play in human history.

Again, regardless of whether you are a believer, the concept of a "prophet" suggests an operatic scale of competence and character, the two prime elements of credibility. Whether the prophet is possessed of Satan or merely just a human prophet with human limitations and frailties, Satan certainly chooses well and human-wisely when he lies in the mouths of the most credible sources in the Old Testament, a king's prophets. If you know anything about biblical texts, you realize that the books of the Old Testament are among the most ancient, verified manuscripts existing in human possession. Regardless of religious beliefs, we still accept them as part of the historical record and realize that these words were written by people thousands of years ago. Thus, in one of the earliest books, one topic mentioned is persuasion. How that story is presented speaks volumes about our current point of view on persuasion. So even in this extremely old text, we learn almost everything we need to know about a definition of persuasion. It uses communication. It works well with credible sources. And it can be used to change others with mere words.

The term "persuasion" is used several times in both the Old Testament and the New Testament. Interestingly, the term is never used in reference to the speech of God but is primarily used when describing human interaction. There's that one case with Satan and the lying spirit. However, Satan is an angel—and angels, like humans, were created by God and by definition are less powerful than He. This is helpful in understanding the limitations of persuasion. God does not persuade because He is omniscient and omnipotent. With that kind of power, God does not need a limited tool such as persuasion. Only those of us who are not omniscient and omnipotent need another kind of tool to move others: persuasion. And only those who are not omniscient and omnipotent could be moved by something as limited as persuasion.

Consider, too, persuasion in *Genesis*, there at the beginning. Again from King James:

> Now the serpent was more cunning than any beast of the field which the LORD God had made. And he said to the woman, "Has God indeed said, 'You shall not eat of every tree of the garden'?"
>
> And the woman said to the serpent, "We may eat the fruit of the trees of the garden; but of the fruit of the tree which is in the midst of the garden, God has said, 'You shall not eat it, nor shall you touch it, lest you die.'"
>
> Then the serpent said to the woman, "You will not surely die. For God knows that in the day you eat of it your eyes will be opened, and you will be like God, knowing good and evil."
>
> So when the woman saw that the tree was good for food, that it was pleasant to the eyes, and a tree desirable to make one wise, she took of its fruit and ate. She also gave to her husband with her, and he ate …
>
> … and the LORD said, "Who told you that you were naked? Have you eaten from the tree of which I commanded you that you should not eat?"
>
> Then the man said, "The woman whom You gave to be with me, she gave me of the tree, and I ate."

> And the LORD God said to the woman, "What is this you have done?" The woman said, "The serpent deceived me, and I ate."
> *Genesis 3:1–6, 11–13.*

This passage illustrates numerous persuasion concepts. First, note that Satan takes the central route with Eve. He uses a dissonance-like tactic to stimulate higher-WATT processing with his taunting observation that God said you can't do this.

Second, he provides arguments that compel Eve to break a law of God. As described here, there is no doubt that this exchange is a harrowing example of central-route persuasion. Eve is clearly "thinking" about the serpent's arguments, and she elaborates on those arguments: the fruit of the tree is good for food, the fruit of the tree is pleasant to behold, eating this fruit will make me wise, and finally, I'll be like God. She gives voice to that conversation in our heads and lets us know that she is really thinking about Satan's arguments. There are no cues for this woman.

Third, realize in contrast that Adam ate the fruit based on cues from UnThoughtful Persuasion. He falls for "If others are doing it, you should, too" and "If you like the source, do what she requests" from CLARCCS cues. He clearly was low WATT and took his fall down the peripheral route.

The fourth persuasion variable comes from Adam's sorry performance. When questioned by God about his actions, what does Adam come up with? "My wife made me do it." Thus, we see the first record of external attribution deployed to escape the consequences of bad behavior. And this is not just a guy thing: Eve blames her attitude change and behavioral choices on the serpent. Here, we have the first recorded attribution of "The devil made me do it."

Fifth and finally, when Eve used external attribution, where did she get it? She apparently modeled it from Adam's example. There they both stood, naked and now ashamed. God questions Adam, and Adam blames Eve. Eve watches this, and observing Adam's apparent success with this action, she imitates it herself: the serpent made me do it!

Genesis provides a demonstration of the major processes of persuasion in one compact example. We can clearly see the persuasion toolbox and the operation of the three main variables. And you should begin to realize that persuasion is a fundamental element of our eternal and evolved human nature. Our ability to give and receive persuasive words marks us as human from the beginnings of our recorded history.

Your Future with Persuasion

Hey—the music has stopped and you've got a sheepskin in your hand. You're now entitled to all the rights, honors, and privileges thereunto pertaining to this course of persuasion study.

A door opens, and through it a light shines.

You're on the path.

The Least You Need to Know

- You can organize the persuasion plays with the toolbox trays of WATTage, central route, and peripheral route.
- Persuasion is a communication skill anyone can learn to apply to practical situations.
- Persuasion is a fundamental part of human nature.

Appendix A

Further Reading

The world abounds with persuasion information. Your toughest task is determining which information is both useful and trustworthy. In this appendix, I include sources for the studies described in this book. If you want to read more about it, you can pursue sources I at least find practical and reliable. Many sources are from the original scientific literature, which may be beyond some people's interest, motivation, or access. If you never read these reports, please realize they do exist and form the basis for a scientific foundation for persuasion. Finally, as you read any persuasion source, go high WATT and take the central route. Or as my great-grandfather Wil Hains taught me: always cut the cards.

For more information about any of the topics in this book, visit my website: www.HealthyInfluence.com.

Books

Bandura, A. *Social Learning Through Imitation.* In M. Jones (Ed.) *Nebraska Symposium on Motivation*. Lincoln, NE: University of Nebraska Press, 1962.

———. *Social Learning Theory*. Englewood Cliffs, NJ: Prentice-Hall, 1977.

Bem, D. *Self-Perception Theory*. In L. Berkowitz (Ed.) *Advances in Experimental Social Psychology (Vol. 6)*. New York: Academic Press, 1972.

Campbell, D., and J. Stanley. *Experimental and Quasi-Experimental Designs for Research*. Boston: Houghton & Mifflin, 1963.

Chaiken, S. *The Heuristic Systematic Model of Persuasion*. In M. Zanna, J. Olson, & C. Herman (Eds.) *Social Influence: The Ontario Symposium*, Volume 5. Hillsdale, NJ: Erlbaum, 1987.

Chaiken, S., A. Liberman, and A. Eagly. *Heuristic and Systematic Information Processing Within and Beyond the Persuasion Context*. In J. Uleman & J. Bargh (Eds.) *Unintended Thought*. New York: Guilford, 1989.

Cialdini, R. *Influence: Science and Practice (2nd Ed.)*. Glenview, IL: Scott, Foresman & Company, 1980.

Cohen, J. *Power Analysis for the Behavioral Sciences (Revised Edition)*. Orlando, FL: Academic Press, 1977.

Collins, J. *Good to Great*. New York: HarperCollins, 2001.

Cooper, J., and R. Fazio. *A New Look at Dissonance*. In L. Berkowitz (Ed.) *Advances in Experimental Social Psychology*, Vol. 17. New York: Academic Press, 1984.

Cotton, J. *Cognitive Dissonance in Selective Exposure*. In D. Zillmann & J. Bryant (Eds.) *Selective Exposure to Communication*. Hillsdale, NJ: Erlbaum, 1985.

Donnelly, Robert. *The Complete Idiot's Guide to Statistics*. Indianapolis: Alpha Books, 2004.

Festinger, L. *A Theory of Cognitive Dissonance*. Stanford, CA: Stanford University Press, 1957.

Festinger, L., H. Riecken, and S. Schachter. *When Prophecy Fails.* Minneapolis: University of Minnesota Press, 1956.

Gladwell, M. *Tipping Point.* New York: Back Bay/Little, Brown and Company, 2000.

———. *Blink.* New York: Little, Brown and Company, 2005.

Havens, R. *Hypnotherapy Scripts.* New York: Brunner Mazel Press, 1989.

Heider, F. *The Psychology of Interpersonal Relations.* New York: Wiley, 1958.

Hovland, C. I., I. L. Janis, and H. H. Kelley. *Communications and Persuasion: Psychological Studies in Opinion Change.* New Haven, CT: Yale University Press, 1953.

Jones, E. E., and K. E. Davis. *From Acts to Dispositions: The Attribution Process in Social Psychology.* In L. Berkowitz (Ed.) *Advances in Experimental Social Psychology (Volume 2).* New York: Academic Press, 1965.

Kahneman, D., P. Slovic, and A. Tversky. *Judgment Under Uncertainty: Heuristics and Biases.* New York: Cambridge University Press, 1982.

Kelley, H. H. *Attribution Theory in Social Psychology.* In D. Levine (Ed.) *Nebraska Symposium on Motivation (Volume 15).* Lincoln, NE: University of Nebraska Press, 1967.

Kerlinger, F., and H. Lee. *Foundations of Behavioral Research (3rd Ed.).* New York: Holt, Rinehart, Winston, 1999.

Koffka, K. *Principles of Gestalt Psychology.* London, England: Kegan Paul, Trench, Trubner and Co., Ltd., 1935.

Kohler, W. *Gestalt Psychology.* New York: Liveright, 1947.

———. *The Mentality of Apes.* New York: Harcourt Brace, 1925.

McGuire, W. *Inducing Resistance to Persuasion: Some Contemporary Approaches.* In L. Berkowitz (Ed.) *Advances in Experimental Social Psychology (Vol. 1).* New York: Academic Press, 1964.

———. *Theoretical Foundations of Campaigns.* In Ronald Rice and William Paisley (Eds.) *Public Communication Campaigns.* Thousand Oaks, CA: Sage, 1981.

Milgram. S. *Obedience to Authority.* New York: Harper and Row, 1974.

O'Keefe, D. *Persuasion: Theory and Research. (2nd Ed.).* Thousand Oaks, CA: Sage Press, 2002.

Pavlov, I. I. *Conditioned Reflexes* (translated by G. V. Anrep). London, England: Oxford University Press, 1927.

Petty, R., and J. Cacioppo. *Attitudes and Persuasion: Classic and Contemporary Approaches.* Boulder: West View Press, 1996.

———. *Communication and Persuasion: The Central and Peripheral Routes to Attitude Change.* New York: Springer-Verlag, 1986.

Peters, T., and Waterman, R. *In Search of Excellence.* New York: Warner Books/HarperCollins, 2004.

Rosenzweig, P. *The Halo Effect.* Tampa, FL: Free Press, 2007.

Shimp, T. *Advertising, Promotion, and Other Aspects of Integrated Marketing Communications (6th Ed.).* Florence, KY: South Western College Publishing, 2002.

Skinner, B. *Science and Human Behavior.* New York: MacMillan, 1953.

———. *The Technology of Teaching.* New York: Appleton-Crofts, 1968.

Steiner, C. *Scripts People Live: Transactional Analysis of Life Scripts.* New York: Grove Press, 1994.

Thaler, R. and C. Sunstein. *Nudge*. New Haven, CT: Yale University Press, 2008.

Weinberger, J. *Validating and Demystifying Subliminal Psychodynamic Activation*. In R. F. Bornstein and T. S. Pittman (Eds.) *Perception Without Awareness*. New York: Guilford, 1992.

Journal Articles

Baldwin, M. W., S. E. Carell, and D. F. Lopez. 1990. Priming Relationship Schemas: My Advisor and the Pope Are Watching Me from the Back of My Mind. *Journal of Experimental Social Psychology* 26: 435–454.

Booth-Butterfield, S., and B. Reger. 2004. The Message Changes Belief and the Rest Is Theory: The "1% Or Less" Milk Campaign and Reasoned Action. *Preventive Medicine* 39: 581–588.

Bornstein, R. F. *Exposure and Affect: Overview and Meta-Analysis of Research*. 1968–1987. *Psychological Bulletin* 106: 265–289.

Brehm, J. 1956. Postdecision Changes in the Desirability of Alternatives. *The Journal of Abnormal and Social Psychology* 52: 384–389.

Cacioppo, J., R. Petty, and C. Kao. 1984. The Efficient Assessment of Need for Cognition. *Journal of Personality Assessment* 48: 306–307.

Cantril, J., and D. Seibold. 1986. The Perceptual Contrast Explanation of Sequential Request Strategy Effectiveness. *Human Communication Research* 13: 253–267.

Cialdini, R., et al. 1975. Reciprocal Concessions Procedure for Inducing Compliance: The Door-in-the-Face Technique. *Journal of Personality and Social Psychology* 31: 206–215.

Dillard, J. 1991. The Current Status of Research on Sequential-Request Compliance Techniques. *Personality and Social Psychology Bulletin* 17: 282–288.

Dillard, J., J. Hunter, and M. Burgoon. 1984. Sequential Request Persuasive Strategies: Meta-Analysis of Foot-in-the-Door and Door-in-the-Face. *Human Communication Research* 10: 461–488.

Dolin, D., and S. Booth-Butterfield. 1995. Cancer Prevention and the Foot-in-the-Door Technique. *Health Communication* 7: 55–66.

Down, A. C., and P. Lyons. 1991. Natural Observations of the Links Between Attractiveness and Initial Legal Judgments. *Personality and Social Psychology Bulletin* 17: 541–547.

Festinger, L., and J. M. Carlsmith. 1959. Cognitive Consequences of Forced Compliance. *Journal of Abnormal and Social Psychology* 58, 203–211.

Freedman, J., and S. Fraser. 1966. Compliance Without Pressure: The Foot-in-the-Door Technique. *Journal of Personality and Social Psychology* 4, 195–202.

Hinsz, V., and J. Tomhave. 1991. Smile and (Half) the World Smiles with You, Frown and You Frown Alone. *Personality and Social Psychology Bulletin* 17: 586–592.

Kilbourne, W. E., S. Painton, and D. Ridley. 1985. The Effect of Sexual Embedding on Responses to Magazine Advertisements. *Journal of Advertising* 14: 48–56.

Lepper, M., D. Greene, and R. Nisbett. 1973. Undermining Children's Intrinsic Interest with Extrinsic Reward: A Test of the "Overjustification" Hypothesis. *Journal of Personality and Social Psychology* 28: 129–137.

Milgram. S. 1963. Behavioral Study of Obedience. *The Journal of Abnormal and Social Psychology* 67:, 371–378.

Miller, R., P. Brickman, and D. Bolen. 1975. Attribution Versus Persuasion as a Means of Modifying Behavior. *Journal of Personality and Social Psychology* 31: 430–441, 1975.

Pfau, M., and M. Burgoon. 1986. Inoculation in Political Campaign Communication. *Human Communication Research* 15: 99–111.

Pfau, M., et al. 1990. Efficacy of Inoculation Strategies in Promoting Resistance to Political Attack Messages: Application to Direct Mail. *Communication Monographs* 57: 25–43.

Pfau, M., S. Van Bockern, and J. Kang. 1992. The Effectiveness of Peer and Adult Inoculation Videos in Promoting Resistance to Smoking in Adolescents. *Communication Monographs* 59: 213–230.

Rothman, A. J., et al. 1993. Attributions of Responsibility and Persuasion: Increasing Mammography Utilization Among Women Over 40 with an Internally Oriented Message. *Health Psychology* 12: 39–47.

Sherman, S., and L. Gorkin. 1980. Attitude Bolstering When Behavior Is Inconsistent with Central Attitudes. *Journal of Experimental Social Psychology* 16: 388–403.

Stone, J., et al. 1994. Inducing Hypocrisy as a Means of Encouraging Young Adults to Use Condoms. *Personality and Social Psychology Bulletin* 20: 116–128.

Taylor, T., and S. Booth-Butterfield. 1993. Getting a Foot in the Door with Drinking and Driving: A Field Study of Healthy Influence. *Communication Research Reports* 10: 95–101.

Welbourne, J., and S. Booth-Butterfield. 2005. Using the Theory of Planned Behavior and a Stage Model of Persuasion to Evaluate a Safety Message for Firefighters. *Health Communication* 18: 141–155.

Wild, T. Cameron, Michael E. Enzle, and Wendy L. Hawkins. 1992. Effects of Perceived Extrinsic Versus Intrinsic Teacher Motivation on Student Reactions to Skill Acquisition. *Personality and Social Psychology Bulletin* 18: 245–251.

Zajonc, Robert B. 1980. Feeling and Thinking: Preferences Need No Inferences. *American Psychologist* 35, 151–175.

Appendix B

Glossary

argument Crucial information of central importance about an object, issue, or person. An argument can be words or images.

attitude A person's evaluative response (speech, thoughts, actions, and feelings). Attitudes express whether a person likes or dislikes something. Attitudes are not emotions, feelings, or moods but rather "hot" thoughts and memories.

attribution An explanation that assigns causality. Attributions are either internal (the cause is within the person) or external (the cause is outside the person in the situation).

attribution, person Also called the fundamental attribution error. Assigning causality to the actor rather than the situation, because while we usually think others act under their own choice and control, we rarely think the same about ourselves, especially when the outcome is negative.

attribution, situation Assigning causality to situational factors rather than to internal qualities of the actors in the situation. Often the attribution of choice when bad things happen to us.

authority, cue The perceived competence and character of a person used to guide change for a low-WATT processor on the peripheral route rather than a careful consideration of relevant arguments.

behavior A concrete, observable response a person shows in a situation.

belief A statement about the truth of a proposition that does not necessarily depend on the truth of reality.

beliefs, behavior Attributes of a behavior that a person believes on a "good-bad" scale.

beliefs, control Attributes of a behavior that a person believes on an "easy-difficult" scale.

beliefs, normative Attributes of a behavior that a person believes other important people accept on an "approve-disapprove" scale.

central route A means of change that occurs when a person carefully and with much effort thinks about arguments to determine new beliefs and attitudes. It requires "higher" WATTage, strong arguments, and production of cognitive responses (elaborations). *Compare to* the peripheral route. *See also* processing, WATTage.

channel The means of message transmission for communication. It corresponds to the five senses of sight, sound, taste, touch, and smell.

CLARCCS An acronym to aid memory of six common and powerful persuasion cues: Comparison, Liking, Authority, Reciprocity, Commitment/Consistency, and Scarcity. Each element functions as a cue that influences a low-WATT receiver on the peripheral route.

classical conditioning Begins with an existing stimulus-response relationship (unconditioned), and through repeated pairing of a new stimulus over time, the organism will show the old response to the new stimulus (conditioned relationship). Classical conditioning is also sometimes called respondent conditioning. *Compare to* operant conditioning.

coding The relationship between symbol and meaning. Encoding moves from meaning to message while decoding moves from message to meaning. Sources encode while receivers decode.

commitment/consistency, cue When you take a stand, you must remain consistent with it. While the general theme of this cue is admirable, it can lead people to engage in foolish consistencies that may cause harm in other ways.

communication The process of stimulating meaning in the minds of others through the use of verbal or nonverbal messages.

Communication Cascade The three-stage sequence of reception, processing, and response that messages must take receivers through before ultimate behavior change can occur. *See also* processing, reception, and response.

communication, model A diagram of the moving parts of communication that includes source, message, channel, receiver, coding, feedback, noise, and goals.

comparison, cue If others are doing it, you should do it, too. A cue that can have useful properties in many instances, but when applied in a low-WATT condition can lead to harmful or foolish actions.

comparison, four forces of science A careful, tough, and controlled test of an idea against a similar, but different idea. Comparison in science always contrasts a finding against some other standard.

conditioned stimulus/response A learned connection between a new trigger (stimulus) and an old reaction (response). A key relationship in classical or respondent conditioning. *Compare to* unconditioned stimulus/response.

consistency Two thoughts that go together and form the basis of persuasion gravity. Human cognition requires that we hold ideas that "go together" or "stick together" as if bound by a psychological kind of gravity. Inconsistencies often motivate us to compensate.

contrast, principle of Information is more likely to be noticed and received when it "stands out" in the processing field. A key communication strategy to generate higher levels of message reception in the Communication Cascade.

control, four forces of science Ensuring that all elements of an experiment operate fully and equally at all times for all participants. Poor control introduces bias and can mislead our understanding of what works and why.

cue A tactic that creates change without requiring elaborative processing; any persuasion tactic that does not need an argument or argument processing. Also called heuristics, choice architecture, blink, rules of thumb, click, whirr.

dissonance The cognitive, emotional, physiological, and behavioral state that arises when things don't go the way we expected.

dissonance theory A complex and highly developed and tested statement that describes the key components of dissonance, how it arises, how people reduce it, and the persuasion implications of this change. Dissonance theory was first proposed by Leon Festinger in 1957 and many of his original assertions are still found to be accurate.

elaboration A unique thought or cognitive response a person generates when thinking about change. One piece in that long conversation we have in our heads when we take the central route with strong arguments.

elaboration activity The process of generating cognitive responses; that ongoing conversation in your head as you think about a persuasive message.

elaboration likelihood Willingness and Ability To Think (WATT) and generate elaborations that range from "higher" to "lower."

elaboration likelihood model (ELM) Rich Petty and John Cacioppo's theory of persuasive communication that explains how messages produce change through either central- or peripheral-route change. *Compare to heuristic systematic model* (HSM).

elaboration moderator A personality or situational characteristic that affects elaboration likelihood. *See also* the persuasion light bulb.

eliciting beliefs Research process of discovering which Theory of Planned Behavior beliefs drive the targeted behavior. It's typically a two-step procedure where first you determine the "universe" of all possible beliefs, then second compare "doers" and "nondoers" beliefs to discover which beliefs are most discriminating.

external validity Looks at how a relationship generalizes to other situations. *Compare to* internal validity.

feedback The receiver's response to a source message.

goals The change, the point, and the desired outcome; usually achieved through the proper application of persuasion plays.

heuristic systematic model (HSM) A persuasion theory developed by Shelly Chaiken that focuses more specifically upon thinking and cognitive activity and is frequently used as a special case of the elaboration likelihood model. *Compare to* elaboration likelihood model (ELM).

inoculation The deliberate delivery of a weak attack aimed at generating an active and strong defense from receivers to produce stronger existing beliefs or positions. Rather than changing the direction of beliefs as with most persuasion plays, inoculation seeks to strengthen beliefs. It is based on a direct analogy to medical inoculation where patients are given a weak dose of a disease that stimulates and strengthens immune system responding.

intention Planned and thoughtful likelihood of future action. Scientific studies demonstrate that intention is an extremely strong predictor of voluntary behavior, especially under the TACT Principle. Intention is not a feeling, emotion, or action; rather, it's a type of cognition. People have conscious awareness of their intentions and can remember them.

internal validity Looks at the true relationship between a presumed cause and effect. *Compare to* external validity.

justification The way we explain ourselves rationally, but also a dissonance-reduction process. Determining whether your "justification" is rational or dissonant is typically determined by values.

liking, cue When you like a source, you will do what is requested. Low-WATT processors often permit the positive feelings they experience with a friendly or attractive source to influence their actions.

message A coded meaning, such as English, Braille, Morse Code, or Fortran.

message testing A research process aimed at creating and validating messages that can change key beliefs. It's typically a two-step procedure where you first determine a wide variety of different arguments that seem plausible, then test the various arguments on samples of your target receivers to determine the "best" arguments.

modeling Change through observing another person's behavior and gaining desired consequences as a result. Often a low-WATT and almost unconscious influence play.

need for cognition (NFC) A stable personality preference for the persuasion light bulb. People with high NFC tend to respond high WATT most of the time while folks with low NFC tend to respond low WATT. However, strong situation forces (relevance or distraction) can alter NFC.

noise Anything that interferes with communication.

norms Descriptive (what is done) or prescriptive (what should be done) standards of action. A norm can be held by an individual or a group, and it may be actual or perceived. A norm is not a feeling, emotion, or action but rather a type of cognition.

obedience Receiver compliance with source authority.

operant conditioning The theory that consequences drive behavior. Also described as a process of When-Do-Get that shows the three key elements in the chain of events that must occur for this type of change to occur. *Compare with* classical or respondent conditioning, and note that operant conditioning always requires a consequence (a reinforcer) while respondent conditioning does not. Also known as reinforcement theory.

outcomes, of persuasion Magnitude (amount of immediate change), persistence (how long a change lasts before it decays), resistance (how much of a change will survive future counter-arguments), and prediction (what future actions the change will produce).

peripheral route Means of change that occur when a person reacts to cues to change. It requires low WATTage and strong cues. *Compare to* central route.

persuasion Using words to change the way people think, feel, and behave.

persuasion light bulb Another name for an elaboration moderator or something that changes the WATTage (high or low) of a receiver during a persuasion message.

persuasion plays Specific persuasion actions that reliably produce change.

persuasion script A routine sequence of dialog and action that includes a persuasion play and a change goal involving the thoughts, feelings, or actions of a targeted receiver.

persuasion toolbox A three-category system for classifying all persuasion plays; it's composed of WATTage, the central route, and the peripheral route.

placement, principle The theory that a message is more likely to be received when it is placed in locations where the receiver goes. For example, messages advertising beer are well placed in sports programming and poorly placed on PBS.

power The ability to deliver rewards and punishments to another person to change his or her behavior.

processing The act of attending to, comprehending, elaborating on, and storing persuasive information and cognitive responses; the second stage in the Communication Cascade.

processing, biased High-WATT thinking on the central route that makes arguments fit existing beliefs; the source of rational prejudice, foolishness, and occasionally wisdom.

processing, cue based Low-WATT thinking on the peripheral route. It's usually a safe strategy for receivers but is incredibly vulnerable to attack by a well-trained persuasion source.

processing, objective High-WATT thinking on the central route that focuses on arguments. Objective processing follows arguments to conclusions while biased processing bends arguments to fit pre-existing conclusions.

randomization, four forces of science Where all objects have an equal chance of being selected and the selection of one object in no way affects the selection of another object.

reactance A perceived unfair restriction on one's freedom; a dissonance-like motivation.

receiver The target of communication; the person we want to change.

reception Making a message available to receivers; getting the message. It's the first stage in the Communication Cascade. Reception is driven by the principles of placement, repetition, and contrast.

reciprocity, cue When a source gives you something of value, you should give something of value in return. This form of mere politeness is turned into a cue when a low-WATT receiver does not realize that the source gives less than the receiver leading to a deliberately unfair exchange.

reinforcement theory *See* operant conditioning.

repetition, principle The theory that a message is more likely to be received when it is repeatedly (time and space) placed in locations where the receiver goes. Repetition is enhanced when elements of the message are varied to make the message look "new" (although it says the same thing).

respondent conditioning *See* classical conditioning.

response The change in behavior, norm, or control beliefs that a message generates in a receiver. It's the third stage in the Communication Cascade. In behavior theories, a response is something that is elicited by a stimulus.

routes, of persuasion One of two distinct and separate paths receivers take when dealing with persuasive messages. Central-route thinkers start high WATT, seek out strong arguments, and think carefully and effortfully about those arguments before changing. Peripheral-route thinkers begin low WATT, respond to available and simple cues, and think at a shallow, surface level of analysis before changing.

rules, of persuasion Ten general guidelines for effective development, execution, and assessment of persuasion.

scarcity, cue When it is rare, it is good. A powerful fact of economic wisdom can be turned into a cue when a low-WATT thinker is fooled into believing something is scare and therefore valuable, when the object is not truly scarce.

source The initiator of communication.

standard model A persuasion engine that drives behavior change. The model takes the general stages of the Communication Cascade and details them with specific concepts and operations for planning, implementing, and assessing persuasion.

stimulus Something that elicits a response.

subliminal A message that operates below the receiver's conscious awareness.

tachistiscope A device that researchers employ for subliminal testing. It looks like a World War II radar screen. It's a bit like putting on a swimming mask in that there is a rubber shield running around the screen. You press your face into the rubber tube to block your peripheral vision and to screen out environmental light.

TACT An acronym for Target, Action, Context, Time, the TACT principle specifies in detail the target behavior change and is the crucial first step in planning persuasion.

team persuasion An organized script that assigns different plays to different players to achieve the same goal.

theory of planned behavior Icek Aizen's model of human behavior (based on the theory of reasoned action), which says that volitional behavior is driven by intention and that intention is, in part, driven by behavior, norm, and control beliefs. *See also* theory of reasoned action.

theory of reasoned action Martin Fishbein and Icek Aizen's model of human behavior, which says that volitional behavior is driven by intention—and that intention is, in part, driven by behavior and norm beliefs.

Thoughtful Persuasion The central-route process of a high-WATT thinker seeking strong arguments, engaging in a careful consideration of those arguments before changing. *Compare to* UnThoughtful Persuasion.

Two Step A sequential request message strategy that makes the receiver say either "yes" or "no" to a first request to increase compliance to a second request (the real goal).

unconditioned stimulus/response A pre-existing trigger-reaction (stimulus-response) relationship like the eye blink reflex to a puff of air or the foot snap when the patella of the knee is tapped. This pre-existing connection is the basis for classical conditioning as a new trigger (like a bell) is applied simultaneously with the old trigger until the new trigger elicits the old reaction. First described by Ivan Pavlov. *Compare to* conditioned stimulus/response.

UnThoughtful Persuasion The peripheral-route process of a low-WATT processor who prefers easier cues to harder arguments, responds quickly and often thoughtlessly to the cue and changes. *Compare to* Thoughtful Persuasion.

values Enduring ideals held with strong feelings.

WATTage Willingness and Ability To Think. The mental state of the receiver—usually categorized as "higher" (that produces central-route processing of arguments) or "lower" (that produces peripheral-route processing of cues). WATTage can change rapidly (in a few seconds), but people tend to persist in one mode during a particular persuasion play.

Index

A

B

C

D

E

F

G

H

I

J

K

L

M

N–O

P

Q-R

S

T

U-V

W-X-Y-Z